Mercatus Studies in Political and Social Economy

Political economy is a robust field of study that examines the economic and political institutions that shape our interactions with one another. Likewise, social economy focuses on the social interactions, networks, and communities that embody our daily lives. Together, these fields of study seek to understand the historical and contemporary world around us by examining market, political, and social institutions. Through these sectors of life, people come together to exchange goods and services, solve collective problems, and build communities to live better together.

Scholarship in this tradition is alive and thriving today. By using the lens of political and social economy, books in this series will examine complex social problems, the institutions that attempt to solve these problems, and the consequences of action within such institutions. Further, this approach lends itself to a variety of methods, including fieldwork, case studies, and experimental economics. Such analysis allows for deeper understanding of social phenomena, detailing the context, incentives, and interactions that shape our lives. This series provides a much-needed space for interdisciplinary research on contemporary topics on political and social economy. In much of academia today, scholars are encouraged to work independently and within the strict boundaries of their disciplines. However, the pursuit of understanding our society requires social scientists to collaborate across disciplines, using multiple methods. This series provides such an opportunity for scholars interested in breaking down the boundaries of disciplines in order to better understand the world around us.

All proposals submitted to the series undergo documented single-blind peer review by subject-matter experts (SME). In addition, all manuscripts are reviewed by SME prior to acceptance through a documented single-blind process.

Mikayla Novak
Editor

Liberal Emancipation

Explorations in Political and Social Economy

palgrave
macmillan

Editor
Mikayla Novak
Arlington, VA, USA

ISSN 2946-5656 ISSN 2946-5664 (electronic)
Mercatus Studies in Political and Social Economy
ISBN 978-3-031-94405-5 ISBN 978-3-031-94406-2 (eBook)
https://doi.org/10.1007/978-3-031-94406-2

Cover illustration: 35007 via Getty Images

This Palgrave Macmillan imprint is published by the registered company Springer Nature Switzerland AG
The registered company address is: Gewerbestrasse 11, 6330 Cham, Switzerland

Acknowledgments

The production of this book represents a cooperative effort by numerous individuals, and it is appropriate to acknowledge the key individuals who have been involved in making this study on the theme of liberal emancipation a reality.

I wish to thank the team at Springer Nature for agreeing to publish this book, as part of the Mercatus Studies in Political and Social Economy series. In particular, Bronwyn Geyer and Geetha Chockalingam were instrumental in arranging the contractual partnership culminating in the publication of this book. I thank them, and their colleagues, for their efforts.

This book is not possible without the sterling efforts of the contributors who elected to take on the conceptually and empirically demanding project of studying emancipation processes through a classical liberal lens. I thank each and all of the contributors for the time they invested in preparing their chapters, and in helping me with the logistic implications of putting this book together.

A number of the chapters appearing in this book (by Rosolino Candela, Erwin Dekker, and Otto Lehto) were presented at the Mercatus 2023 Markets & Society Conference. I thank Rosolino, Erwin, and Otto for presenting early versions of their work at the conference, and for the keen interest in the subject of liberal emancipation by the attendees.

I also would like to thank my Mercatus Center colleagues Kristen Collins and Arielle John for agreeing to provide feedback to me on the introductory and concluding chapters, respectively. Their insights were very much appreciated, and the feedback was embraced in ways that strengthened the book as a whole.

Several intellectual figures are implicated in the development of my own thinking concerning emancipation as an analytical, empirical, and normative priority of classical liberal thinking. Three modern-day figures whom I've come to know, in person or virtually, have meaningfully contributed to my understanding of emancipation and what it implies for liberalism: Peter Boettke; Steven Horwitz (1964–2021); and Deirdre McCloskey. I thank them sincerely for their endeavors in advancing contemporary theories of liberal emancipation.

Last, but not least, I thank my spouse Deanna Trainham for her unwavering encouragement and support, as well as our beloved feline friend Sylvestine (decd. September 2024) whom we'll always remember fondly.

November 2024 Mikayla Novak

Contents

1 **Introduction: The Meaning of Liberal Emancipation—An Outline** 1
Mikayla Novak

2 **Property Rights and the Liberating Effect of Generalized Increasing Returns: A Reassessment of the New History of Capitalism and the Economics of Slavery** 33
Rosolino Candela

3 **Buchanan's Theory of Emancipation: Artifactual Man in Perspective** 57
Alain Marciano and John Meadowcroft

4 **Power to the Powerless: Evolutionary Freedom as Emancipation** 79
Otto Lehto

5 **Liberal Emancipation as a System of Social Learning** 103
Emily Chamlee-Wright and Mikayla Novak

6 **Ostromian Self-governance: Emancipation or Simply Changing the Locus of Servitude?** 133
Roberta Herzberg

7 **How the Other Half Lives: The Emancipatory Contributions of the Chicago School of Sociology** 157
Erwin Dekker

8 **The Classical Liberal Response to Critical Race Theory: Material Gains, Expressivity, and Divisions of Power** 183
Fabio Rojas

9 **Emancipation and "The Woman Question"** 203
Jayme Lemke

10 **A Radical Liberal Approach to LGBTQ Emancipation** 229
Nathan P. Goodman

11 **Conclusion** 259
Mikayla Novak

Index 269

List of Contributors

Rosolino Candela Mercatus Center at George Mason University, Fairfax, VA, USA

Emily Chamlee-Wright Institute for Humane Studies at George Mason University, Arlington, VA, USA

Erwin Dekker Mercatus Center at George Mason University, Fairfax, VA, USA

Nathan P. Goodman Mercatus Center at George Mason University, Fairfax, VA, USA

Roberta Herzberg Mercatus Center at George Mason University, Fairfax, VA, USA

Otto Lehto School of Law, New York University, New York, USA

Jayme Lemke Mercatus Center at George Mason University, Fairfax, VA, USA

Alain Marciano Department of Economics and Statistics, University of Turin, Turin, Italy;
Karl Mittermaier Centre for Philosophy of Economics, University of Johannesburg, Johannesburg, South Africa;
Mercatus Center at George Mason University, Virginia, USA

John Meadowcroft King's College London, London, UK

Mikayla Novak Mercatus Center at George Mason University, Fairfax, VA, USA

Fabio Rojas Virginia L. Roberts Professor of Sociology, Indiana University, Bloomington, IN, USA

CHAPTER 1

Introduction: The Meaning of Liberal Emancipation—An Outline

Mikayla Novak

This book explores the conceptual and empirical bases of emancipative change. The elements and implications of emancipation have long attracted the interest of social scientists, and emancipatory events throughout human history have been the subject of political and public narratives and sensemaking efforts, if not valorization. The emancipatory prospects of freeing individuals and entire groups from various forms of constraints, whether they be formal restrictions or informal kinds of oppression, has gripped the imagination of reformists throughout history. Emancipation is an important source and consequence of change in the world, and contemporary interest in the subject reflects the incompleteness of emancipative projects in many regions of the globe.

The objective of *Liberal Emancipation: Explorations in Political and Social Economy* is to better understand the nature and consequences of emancipation, in terms of theory as well as practice. To this end, the

M. Novak (✉)
Mercatus Center, George Mason University, Fairfax, VA, USA
e-mail: mnovak@mercatus.gmu.edu

M. Novak (ed.), *Liberal Emancipation*, Mercatus Studies in Political and Social Economy, https://doi.org/10.1007/978-3-031-94406-2_1

contributions that comprise this volume seek to answer a range of fundamental questions. What is emancipation? What makes certain patterns of economic, political, and social change emancipative in its effects? In what ways has emancipation been realized in historical and contemporary senses? Perhaps most fundamentally, how do emancipative processes affect people?

As is implied by these high-level questions, the contributions in this book refuse to exclusively immerse themselves in emancipation as a concept, as important as this may be. There is an empirical dimension to emancipation which raises the prospect of informing social scientists about important phenomena and events that shape our world, and these empirical concerns warrant careful intellectual consideration. As the chapters which follow will indicate, the authors who have contributed to this book have taken care to blend conceptual and empirical insights when describing what emancipation is, and how it has affected (and promises to continue to affect) our lives.

In his recent collection of essays in political economy and philosophy, *The Struggle for a Better World*, Peter Boettke insists that emancipative ideas and practices rest within the core of (classical) liberalism.[1] Boettke states that "[t]he liberal project … was born as an *emancipation project* – freeing individuals from subjugation by the Crown, from the dogma of the Altar, from the violence and oppression of the Sword, from the bondage of Slavery, from the miserable poverty of the Plough and from the special privileges granted to the Mercantile Interests" (Boettke, 2021: 3). He elsewhere expresses a hope in ideational expressions having the effect of "fulfilling the emancipatory promise of liberalism to overcome subjugation, repression, oppression, and misery" (ibid.: 15). It is the unambiguous connection between emancipation and liberalism expressed by Boettke and others that leads us to ask another question: What makes liberalism an emancipative doctrine? To be more precise, are there any aspects of liberal philosophy that allow its adherents to proclaim emancipation as a fundamental commitment and, if so, what are those aspects? As will be explained shortly, the *liberal basis* of emancipation seems crucial to explore and articulate when various alternative, and contending, philosophies and ideologies also lay claim to the emancipation mantle.

Having outlined the objectives and key questions of the book, we shall outline the structure of this introductory chapter. The next section will set forth to explain the concept of emancipation, exploring the etymological properties of the term as well as its definitional treatment in social-scientific literature. Following this, we discuss the conceptual and empirical properties of emancipation as a specifically liberal commitment, which wraps emancipation as a combinatorial process involving individual and collective agency, amelioration of legal and policy restrictions including upon the exercise of such agency, and socio-cultural dignification of previously dominated or marginalized groups. Next, the structure of the book will be described indicating the theoretical and applied insights made by the contributors.

What Is Emancipation?

Like many other terms that animate social-scientific research, and in reflection of the non-teleological and relatively open-ended character of language, "emancipation" is a polysemous concept encompassing a variety of contested meanings. The sources of contestation over the definition and implications of emancipation are not only associated with developments within the social sciences (e.g., Caillé et al., 2016), particularly the increasing specialization of disciplines and how these affect changes in the meanings and understandings surrounding terms. The lack of universal agreement over what is defined by emancipation may also reflect other intellectual trends such as the modern interest to contextually situate the human emancipative experience according to time and place and bearing in mind the likes of unique socio-cultural and political conditions (Rebughini, 2015). The complexification surrounding the concept has led some figures to decry emancipation as either "overused" (Caillé et al., 2016), or otherwise bears running the risk of being conceptually "incoherent" in the face of demands to explain worldly trends (Laclau, 1996).

It is not our purpose to arbitrate over definitional disputations over emancipation, but we will take a step in a certain direction to assert that there exists a sufficient degree of agreement among scholars to at least commence a productive discussion about its meaning as well as relevance. Susen (2015) indicates that the historical etymology of the emancipation term traces back to the Latin word *emancipare*, which effectively means "to take from the hand" or, as Rebughini (2015: 270) says, "to be 'out of someone else's control'." Intellectual developments in defining the concept, coupled with historical experiences of emancipation globally, have played their part in a variety of modern definitions of a reasonably similar basis. A dictionary definition offered by Brown et al. (2018) refers to emancipation as "the act of process of being set free from political, economic, cultural, and social restrictions and structures." Others have referred to emancipation as the removal of differing constraints, whether they be economic, socio-cultural, or political by nature (Buchanan & Powell, 2017; Welzel, 2013). Susen (2015: 1024) describes emancipation as "an entity's liberation from control, dependence, restraint, confinement, restriction, repression, slavery, or domination," contrasting emancipation with various antonym descriptors.

Studies into the attributes and implications of emancipation serve to deepen understanding of the concept, in a way that illuminates the multifaceted aspects which apply to it. Political theorist Marta Wojciechowska (2022) presents three categories of intellectual positionality when it comes to emancipation.[2] There is an "internal" *versus* "external" dimension of emancipation, with the former referring to conditions within a given actor's capacity to change (including those arising from that actor's abilities or desires) and the latter referring refer to conditions (including decision-making processes) which transcend the actor or, otherwise, which an actor is implicated only in part (ibid.: 160–161). An external dimension of emancipation is likely to relate to situations in which formal (and informal) institutions impose significant constraints upon a given actor's ability to be, do, or know. Another emancipation dimension distinguishes between the "negative" removal or absence of a particular (constraining) condition or phenomenon, and the "positive" aspect of emancipation describing the presence or introduction of a (liberating or freeing) condition or phenomenon. Finally, Wojciechowska states that emancipation can be furthermore distinguished as either an "end-state" condition or as a "process."[3] Under the former circumstance a person or group may find themselves as in an emancipated state, while under the latter a process is being undertaken to hopefully arrive at an emancipated state. As an example of emancipation as a process, "a group which is in the process of securing or acquiring, for example, individual rights or opportunities is in *the process* of becoming emancipated" (ibid.: 160).

An attractive feature of depicting emancipation as a *process*, of being freed or liberated from an unwanted-yet-significant constraint, is that the process perspective arguably invites a consideration of the roles and contributions that actors play in generating and promoting emancipation. Susen (2015) adopts an ontology reminiscent of the evolutionary thinking of Dopfer and Potts (2008) in highlighting an actor (as an individual or collective entity) as a "carrier" of emancipative belief or purpose.

These actors *qua* emancipation carriers are striving to overcome what Susen describes as modes of control constituting barriers or obstacles to emancipation. Although left unstated, acts of striving by emancipation carriers implies the coexistence of carriers of *non*-emancipative commitments or intuitions, essentially actors who prefer, and might well have the capacity to enforce, the *status quo* of certain constraints upon the exercise of agency.

Emanating from a consideration of the activities and motives of actors with variegated perspectives about emancipation, and its worthiness, comes an interactive process that does not necessarily deliver emancipative outcomes in a linear or deterministic fashion. Writing in the mid-1960s, Herbert Collins presents modern scholars with a preemptive taste of the character of emancipation processes when he describes that:

> ... one of the characteristics of complex societies is the attention and consideration voted to people, their relations with each other, and the feasibility altering traditionally binding relations. Candidacy for emancipatory action usually has been extended to minority, subordinate, deviant and exceptional people who are socially restricted by customs and laws. It is in the interplay of the public recognition of the relational aspects of social life and the public acceptance of the revision of special statuses that emancipation should be considered. (Collins, 1965: 148)

A processual account of emancipation, which we believe to be provided by liberal scholarship on the issues, alludes to various kinds of strivings (if not struggles) in the quest to secure greater freedoms and rights. The "process-range" of emancipation may refer to micro-level processes (e.g., entrepreneurship, exhibiting charismatic leadership), meso-level processes (e.g., social movement activity, and actions by public and private sector entities), and macro-level processes (e.g., shifting cultural, economic, political, and social structures), and any combination therein. Again, that the process of emancipation is wrapped up in combinatorial and coevolving individual agency and collective action by both proponents and opponents of change indicates that emancipation cannot be modeled as a deterministic assurance or lineal guarantee. That the emancipation process retains the characteristics of spatiality and temporality only affirms the need for detailed studies of emancipative projects and their effects in historical and contemporary contexts.[4]

The expansion of human freedom that is entailed by an emancipative process may be further distinguished as to whether the process attends to either formal or informal dimensions of freedom (or to both dimensions, at least to some extent). Achievement of emancipation in its formal dimension refers to the elimination of codified restraints against certain economic, political, and social activities that are granted to certain individuals (or groups) but not others, as well as the codification of expanded rights and liberties to the benefit of either previously marginalized or oppressed groups, or for an entire population. The codification pertaining to emancipation in the formal sense may be represented in institutional artifacts as constitutions, legislative statutes, judicial rulings, and public policies. Securing emancipative outcomes in the informal context refers to changes to conventions, customs, folkways, practices, and traditions having the consequence of expanding the envelope of individual- or group-based conceptions of liberties, rights, and freedoms. The informal dimension of freedom may be argued to more closely attend to desires to secure emancipation in the sense of greater psychological freedom to exercise one's own agency and will (Schmidtz & Brennan, 2010: ch. 6), although it is also clear that emancipation in its formal sense may affect, as well as be affected by, mental perceptions surrounding the appropriateness of exercising various kinds of freedoms.

Distinguishing between formal and informal emancipation alludes to potential disjunctions between these two dimensions, that have been the subject of ongoing discussions among academics, activists, and other participants implicated in emancipative processes. Consider, for example, the long and often fraught evolutionary pathways of American racial history. It has been commonly noted that the codification of racially emancipative intent through formal means, especially constitutional guarantees of equality and non-discrimination based upon race, did not achieve adequate results because of, in no small part, the lack of enforcement of rights to vote, to access public accommodations and facilities, and to live without racially inspired violence. This disjunction was especially evident throughout the American South, even in the aftermath of the Civil War. Drawing upon Martin Luther King's lamentations concerning the condition of freedom for African Americans during the twentieth century, Haider (2021) points to a divergence between formal ("political") emancipation and a "real" emancipation that would be consistent with ensuring informal environments characterized by equality of dignity, respect, and treatment between the races. The Chicago School economist

Frank Knight articulated similar concerns when stating that the ideal of equality before the law "was dishonored in the breach rather than honored in the observance for some time into the age of liberalism, notably by this country in the matter of racial discrimination" (Knight, 1960: 137).

The (incompletely achieved) case of racial emancipation in the U.S. and elsewhere in the world poignantly demonstrates the significance of power dynamics shaping an interactive process between (in this case, racialized) groups. In this regard, it is important to trace which parties have the capacity—formally and informally—to command or direct others to conduct themselves (or to possess a status) that those directed parties would otherwise prefer not to do (or to have). The conflictive element of emancipative process seems to rest, in no small part, upon perceived incongruities between the formal political authority to place certain groups under conditions of domination and subjection as opposed to informal understandings of disagreeability, if not unease and antipathy, on the part of those who experience the multiple disadvantages of domination and subjection.

We see from this admittedly selective discussion that emancipation is both a complex and versatile concept to describe important facets of the human condition. Emancipation as a concept is significant for it can serve as an *evaluative criterion* to critically assess and compare conditions of the world, both historically and in modern times, regarding the extent to which people are able to enjoy equal freedoms without undue and arbitrary constraints. Emancipation is also important because it serves as a *normative project* that inspires marginalized and oppressed peoples, and their supporters elsewhere in a society, to mobilize and press for the removal of specific restraints while simultaneously respecting the equal agency, dignity, and worth of others. As has been noted, emancipation may be considered as an *intellectual idea* amenable to philosophical and other forms of contemplation or as a *practical pursuit* with tangible outcomes (whether they be successful or not). In addition to these considerations of emancipation is, as will be discussed in the next section, an understanding of emancipation and the emancipative process as a fundamental *commitment of liberalism*.

Liberal Emancipation in Theory

Since its modern genesis in Europe from the Middle Ages followed by the Enlightenment period, liberalism has developed into one of the major ideological and philosophical doctrines that has not only informed the intellectual life of humankind but inspired seismic economic, political, and social change. Liberal ideas of freedom and individual rights are also evident in non-Western thought, as chronicled by the likes of Boaz (1997) and Klein et al.'s (2023) three volumes (to date) of liberal thought by country. Aside from the value of its underlying key commitments, part of the appeal of liberalism has been its intellectual and practical flexibilities in response to contextual circumstances, although it should also be admitted that the adaptability of liberal thinking has created nuances, if not certain ambiguities, that have long elicited vigorous expressions of support *and* opposition over the generations.

Liberalism is a living, rather than fixed, project, which, as indicated, necessarily bequeaths it a certain sense of elasticity (e.g., Courtland et al., 2022; Fawcett, 2014; Merquior, 1991). Notwithstanding the change in the intellectual character of liberal thought over time, it remains possible to identify several conceptual, methodological, empirical, and normative commitments which indicating that liberalism has withstood as a reasonably coherent body of thought. We may commence our generic description of liberalism's core attributes by considering its moral foundations. Liberalism indicates that all individuals are possessed of a fundamental dignity given their common status as human beings and that, furthermore, every individual is endowed with certain inalienable rights including (as is stated in the American Declaration of Independence) to the maintenance of life, enjoyment, and protection of liberty, and the agential pursuit of activities and projects conducive to attaining happiness. The liberal conception of justice, articulated by the likes of Hebert Spencer, John Stuart Mill, and others, rests upon an "equal liberty" provision in that a given person has the right to choose and act so long as the same right is extended to everyone else (Smith, 2013). These interconnected considerations give rise to the liberal presumption of value in individuals exploring and undertaking voluntary actions, and inclinations against the exercise in coercion in forcing people to act, or be placed in situations, they would otherwise not choose.

A non-trivial basis for the evolutionary growth and development of liberalism as an ideological and philosophical position is the tendency of its adherents to extend the logics of liberal morality to various domains of human action. Liberals have been forthright in their defense of economic freedom ever since their early critiques of feudalism, mercantilism, and colonialism, upholding the inherent right of individuals to engage in economic exchange with one another, and to experiment in terms of production and consumption activity. Liberal economists have conceptually and empirically articulated the benefits of owning, using, and transferring private properties, and of trade within and across political borders, all of which may be institutionally secured by property rights protections as well as the freedom to devise and uphold contracts.

Far from the assertions of critics that economic liberalism somehow promotes win-loss, zero-sum game arrangements that degrade human relations, thinkers such as Ludwig von Mises and Friedrich Hayek have insisted that liberties in the economic arena complement, if not reinforce, a host of social freedoms. Liberals have suggested that freely consummated economic activities correspond with social values such as freedom of association and expression, toleration and pluralism, and peace. It is also clear that these social values matter on their own basis, and are certainly important to the extent that individuals want to freely and peacefully choose with whom they wish to affiliate and identify. Indeed, liberal life is not reducible to economic transactions but encompasses a broader view in favor of flourishing group life through civil society (which, *inter alia*, stands as a bulwark against economic and political domination). Social progress is consistent with the extent to which human associations are freely chosen: "[b]y minimizing the scope of the mandatory, liberalism maximizes the domain of the voluntary. That, of course, includes voluntary association. ... Groups will wax and wane in response to the desires of the individuals who enter into them or defect" (Lomasky, 2002: 64, 65).

The liberal proponent tends to be a forthright defender of individualism and the economic and social liberties seen as sustaining the material prosperity and vibrant communalism upon which human life depends. But liberal theory is also prominent on account of its distinctive political doctrines, fashioned not only by intellectual inquiry but by the historical experiences of public governance across different environments. The liberal political mindset is a fundamentally democratic one in that it asserts the primacy of political equality between citizen-voters and those political actors occupying the formal offices and positions of state, which is coupled with the crucial addition that political proposals can only be given assent by the explicit and clear consent of citizen-voters to be governed by them (Buchanan & Tullock, [1962] 1999). To ameliorate the risk that political decisions are carried without the consent of the governed not only are regular democratic elections of public sector offices are to be conducted, but that the affairs of government are to be organized and constrained in accordance with constitutional limitations and the rule of law. Contrary to sentiments to the effect that constitutions and the rule of law contravene democratic values, their intention is to avoid principal-agent problems by ensuring better alignment between the private interests of political actors and public interests of the governed community.

As has been already indicated, Peter Boettke (2021: 235) is a liberal scholar who clearly equates liberalism with emancipation: "[l]iberalism is liberal. It is an emancipation philosophy, and a joyous celebration of the creative energy of diverse people near and far." Another modern liberal, Erwin Dekker (2019), whose work is represented in this volume, asserts that post-1940s liberalism is characterized by a relative absence of emancipatory spirit animated by values such as self-governance and respect for diversity. The implication of Dekker's suggestion, *contra* Boettke, is that liberalism was once fashioned by emancipatory values but not necessarily these days, but that this condition is not irremediable because liberalism can repossess its emancipatory mantle if its adherents so choose to do so. Putting aside one's position on the veracity of claims concerning the endurance, or otherwise, of emancipation as a core commitment of liberalism, our purpose is arguably to address a more fundamental question: *what is emancipatory about liberalism as an ideological and philosophical system?*

The association of emancipation with liberalism can be simply explained with reference to a shared commitment to freedom. Liberalism embraces an ethos of freedom and the moral integrity and worth of every individual, irrespective of their background or status, and, as explained previously, emancipation *qua* process refers to efforts aiming at freeing individuals from the bonds of oppression and restraint. The emancipation-liberalism association is therefore clear. Nonetheless, it is useful to briefly explore the nature of the connection between the two concepts with reference to the emancipating functions of liberal commitments to economic, social, and political freedoms.

Liberals agree that markets are highly effective institutions to coordinate economic exchange activities between heterogeneous agents, as demonstrated by the material betterment experienced in those societies allowing for a substantial measure of market activity. Crucially, living standards and opportunities for those in lower socio-economic status positions appear to be much improved within market-oriented economic environments (e.g., Callais & Geloso, 2023).[5] Part of the explanation for these results is that robust, market-based economies provide pathways for individuals to use their talents, either through entrepreneurship or participation in the labor force. "Rather than workers being limited in their choice of work by class or social status, greater freedom of entry and exit is *liberating* due to greater social mobility. Rather than being barred from certain occupations based on class or status, the son of a barber or pipefitter *might* rise to become a professor" (Boettke & Candela, 2017: 150). As explained by Gary Becker and others (Becker, 1971; Pager, 2016), economic growth and development increases the relative costs of discriminating against minority groups thereby providing a basis for conceiving markets as *pro-abundance* and *pro-emancipation* in their effects. Whereas a debate has persisted surrounding the extent to which economic conditions dominate, or otherwise oppress, workers (e.g., Anderson, 2017), the generic liberal position is that an increasing array of opportunities presented by vibrant markets can assist with emancipation insofar as they provide oppressed and marginalized individuals and groups with important kinds of "exit options" from unsatisfying scenarios (Taylor, 2017).

Support for markets within liberalism is grounded in an understanding that freely consummated and mutually beneficial economic exchanges serve as a basis for social cooperation. Entrepreneurs are incentivized under competitive and open economic conditions, including those presented by free and global trade, to produce goods and services that better meet the needs of consumers. Samuel Brittan (1973) suggests that profit-seeking entrepreneurs are likely to strive to satisfy even the demands of minorities whose unorthodox preferences that might not otherwise be catered for if stifling conventions are to hold. Indeed, markets are significant based on "allowing people to do, to the maximum feasible extent, what they feel inclined to do rather than conform to the wishes of authority, custom or convention" (ibid.: 1). While effective and efficient entrepreneurs can certainly meet the material demands of the "moral majority," the "profit motive will always be kicking against … restraints and seeking to widen the range of what is permissible – whether it is a nineteenth century publisher launching an attack on orthodox religion or a twentieth century theatrical or film producer challenging conventional concepts and decency and decorum" (ibid.: 2). It is through the inclination of entrepreneurs to cater to the "permissive" tastes of the public that the market economy becomes "a powerful agent for disrupting existing class barriers and official hierarchies" (ibid.).

Proponents of liberal ideas generally recognize that markets alone are insufficient to secure emancipative outcomes. This recognition arises from an appreciation of the existence of socio-cultural constraints upon the ability of certain individuals and groups to engage in civic life, and to enjoy equal opportunities, on the same basis as others. Discrimination and prejudicial attitudes relying upon such factors as gender, race, age, ethnicity, and so on, may be deeply ingrained within societies, and these pathologies in turn are typically undergirded by behaviors and practices such as stigmatization of minorities coupled with arguments justifying one's own elevated position within social status hierarchies (e.g., Grynaviski & Munger, 2017). The informal norms that constitute socio-cultural activities may lend credence to tribalist stratifications having the effect of circumscribing the ability of marginalized and oppressed people from fully exercising their liberties. Indeed, it is conceivable that marginalized and oppressed people may effectively "internalize" the negative attitudes and stereotypes that they encounter on an everyday basis thus limiting their appetite to achieve self-actualization, as the liberal feminist Mary Wollstonecraft ([1790] 1996) suggested in respect to the effects of patriarchal norms upon women's self-expectations of liberty.

Liberals are praiseworthy of civil society as a communal sphere, populated with arrangements, logics, and practices of variegated formalities and intimacies, that allow individuals to select their preferred terms of association with others according to mutual interest. Hayek ([1960] 2011) indicated that an important value for civil society, and its constituent entities such as families, clubs, and associations, is that it enables individuals to be free and secure from political domination. This insight is arguably most evident in the case of sub-altern communities facilitating the congregation of marginalized and oppressed groups in the relative (although not complete) absence of the inspectorial gaze of the rest of the community, but the project of liberal emancipation would seem to demand more than an ability of the unemancipated to huddle together in the face of majoritarian opposition and denigration. In essence, liberal emancipation has typically required a degree of active socio-cultural laboring to sustainably change community attitudes, and to bring the marginalized and oppressed into a broader community of equal dignity and regard.

Social movement mobilization has increasingly been understood as a key, but not necessarily determinative, strategy in driving cultural and social changes toward emancipation (Novak, 2021; Rojas & Stern, 2024). Within liberal societies that respect freedom of association and toleration of diverse beliefs and perspectives, activists are afforded the autonomy to collectively organize with others to, *inter alia*, overcome the basis of their social subordination and to articulate proposals for emancipative change. It is often assumed that social movements aim to challenge hegemonic authority, irrespective of whether the latter is defending formal or informal institutions and will tend to communicatively publicize normative right-claims for freedom and liberty as interpreted by participant activists. Even if it is the case that social movements are motivated by non-liberal ideals, their *peaceful*-yet-contentious activities are supposed to represent the embodiment of the social struggles that Boettke (2021) has identified as the core of the liberal emancipation agenda.

We finally turn to the political element of liberal emancipation. There is regrettably a long history of governmental oppression and marginalization of certain individuals and minority groups, a history which extends even to modern times in the cases of authoritarian and totalitarian regimes. The ill-treatment of those deemed politically unworthy of enjoying emancipated status has consisted of the punishment strategies of incarceration, exile, torture, and genocide, coupled with the use of statistical classification and other "legibility" techniques to discriminate against, and oppress, dissidents, and other identified adversaries of state interest (Bernstein, 2022; Scott, 1998). A pivotal conceptual move within liberal theory is to advocate for institutional changes that constrain the appetites of rulers to dominate over the ruled, including rules preventing the discriminatory (or otherwise exploitative) use of fiscal, legal, and regulatory policy instruments (Buchanan & Congleton, [1998] 2003; Hayek, [1960] 2011). The development of constitutions to guard against political exploitation have been coupled in liberal theory with support for democratization, the latter enabling all individuals irrespective of their status a say in the affairs of public governance. Historians and political economist have indicated that the advent of constitutional democracy is consistent with the development of "open access orders" that have emancipative reach in that government is conducted impartially for the benefit of all citizen-voters (North et al., 2009).

A source of controversy among liberal circles, including libertarians intrinsically opposed to a broad swathe of government interventions, surrounds the appropriateness of legal and regulatory specifications of rights as an aspect of emancipative process. To be clear about the nature of the controversy, it is assumed that there would be little, if any, opposition among liberal scholars and activists concerning the elimination of statutes and government policies that interfere with the abilities of individuals and groups to exercise a broad array of liberties.[6] Whereas some thinkers may express uneasiness about group-based emancipation projects of a formal character, it has been noted (e.g., Ferguson & Witcher, 2022; Geloso & Peng, 2024; Lemke, 2015) that governments often discriminate, or otherwise impose restraints on the ability to exercise freedoms, against groups. The elimination of group partiality in the conduct of political affairs—including through the delineation of constitutional terms and conditions limiting governmental scope, as well as democratic and other procedural specifications ameliorating political domination—is to be regarded as a cornerstone of the agenda of liberal emancipation.

More recent concerns about the role of government in the emancipative process have to do with the use of legislative and judicial powers to codify, and consequently enforce, a host of advantages, privileges, or rights in the name of emancipation. These initiatives come under a variety of names, including affirmative action, diversity, equity, and inclusion (DEI), and social justice. Some of these measures have been justified to redress perceived historical infringements against the liberties of marginalized and oppressed groups or have been advanced on the assumption that formal relaxations of illiberal restrictions are, unlikely in themselves, to ensure emancipative outcomes particularly if discriminatory and prejudicial group-norms are deeply interwoven within cultural conditions and social practices. Such efforts at so-called "positive discrimination" have been lambasted by some liberals (e.g., Epstein, 1992, 2014) on the grounds of undermining freedom of association, as well as the rule of law which demands equal treatment of all individuals. Similarly, other liberal critics have opposed a governmental role of the nature described here on account of its violation of political neutrality with respect to interests or broader conceptions of the good. A related concern of liberals would be that a reliance upon the state to secure specific emancipation outcomes risks "crowding out" the socio-cultural work necessary by non-state actors to dampen discrimination and prevent stigmatization toward marginalized or oppressed individuals or groups.

Based on the preceding discussion, liberal emancipation could be functionally regarded as a triple co-embedded process involving elements of economic, social, and political freedom for evermore numbers of people. By no means is this functionalist lens separable from the normative claims that continues to animate calls for emancipation on liberal grounds, including the identification by Dekker (2020) and McCloskey (2019) of emancipation as a humane project. However, it should be squarely acknowledged that other ideological and philosophical dispositions exist that challenge the preeminence of liberal claims as an emancipatory creed. Marxists have proclaimed an alternative model of emancipation that focuses upon the nondomination of the proletariat (working) classes by the bourgeoisie (capitalists) (Marx, [1848] 2020). The audacious historical determinist claim of Marxism is that nothing less than a revolution, consequently enshrining a "dictatorship of the proletariat," is necessary to eliminate the capitalist exploitation of the surplus labor value generated by immiserated workers.

In recent decades, an assortment of critical theorists has lambasted liberal emancipation on several fronts. For example, it is asserted that the liberal focus upon formal equality and the rule of law presents a mere smokescreen for distributional inequalities and other broad-ranging ills such as colonialism, structural racism, patriarchy, and heteronormativity, and even problems such as environmental degradation (Benson, 2021). Another set of intellectual challenges to liberalism have emerged in the form of so-called "post-liberalism," whose adherents suggest that the promise of liberal emancipation have delivered, *inter alia*, a cavalcade of bewildering options in life that have epistemically and morally exhausted communities rather than enabling individuals to achieve self-actualization in any meaningful way (Deneen, 2018).

Although space does not allow us to adjudicate the relative merits of the arguments, both old and new, against liberalism or liberal emancipation, it is worthwhile to outline the principles that are more likely to inform liberal responses to their critics. The reality of modern socialist systems of government that have organized and operated in the name of Marx is that they failed to deliver the material prosperity necessary to secure satisfactory upward mobility outcomes for those situated in the lower rungs of society. Lack of economic emancipation for the masses under socialism coincided with concentrated privileges amassed by the political class, including leadership positions, (state) enterprise ownership, access to Western goods, and so on (Henderson et al., 2005). Furthermore, social and political life under the Soviet Union and other socialist regimes—including contemporary China, Cubs, and North

Korea—consistently featured severe intolerance and repression of ethnic, religious, and other minorities. Socialism has not been the emancipatory idyll that its proponents have promised.

As for the objections of the post-liberals, two key counterclaims may be submitted. It may be true, following our earlier discussion of Samuel Brittain's complementarity between markets and permissiveness, that liberalism may produce upsetting outcomes and patterns that certain traditionalists may find disagreeable. But there is nothing within liberal theory, let alone its practice in the world, that nullifies or even fails to valorize traditional family life, the *Gemeinschaft* of tightly woven communities, or even antiquarian economic choices, for as long as any activities and pursuits by individuals and groups are freely chosen by them. Another objection that may be directed toward post-liberals equally applies to socialists of varying kinds. The liberal presumption of free expression allows non-liberal values (such as those of post-liberalism) to contend with those of liberalism for the affections of men and women, but the risk is ever-present that the political instantiation of post-liberal ideals would necessarily lead to the coercive adjudication of the good by so-called "moral betters" who self-perceive to possess better standards of living for themselves *and for others*. Under a socialist or post-liberal polity, the possibilities for emergent emancipative discoveries by individuals seeking to improve their own situations, including in mutually beneficial ways with their consenting peers, is highly likely to be exhausted.

Liberal Emancipation in Practice

Liberal emancipation is a doctrine that firmly embraces its historical achievements and recognizes the quintessentially intertemporal character of emancipative processes. Individuals and groups of individuals who themselves believe to be experiencing conditions of marginalization or oppression, which in turn is grounded in a lack of liberty, clearly need time to formulate and articulate their desire for emancipation, and to take concrete steps to advance their emancipationist agenda. Establishing such agendas would appear to be predicated at least upon the combination of socially epistemic sensemaking among people dissatisfied with their condition and status; the development of logistical and organizational capabilities, including strategic alertness to identify cultural, economic, political, or social opportunities; and the accumulation of resources of varying kinds (cultural, economic, financial, political, etc.). If these prerequisites for reform are successfully attained, it is probable (but not guaranteed) that a trajectory of "emancipative demand" can unfold as those desiring greater liberties mobilize in an effort to establish their objectives.

As discussed, a liberal emancipation theory also needs to incorporate the agonistic quality of striving for more freedom including in the form of the actions, capacities, and prerogatives of individuals and collectives who seek not to support, *but to oppose*, emancipative demands. At the very least, liberal theoretic accounting for human agency suggests that opponents of emancipation might be just as strategic and resources as (and perhaps more so, depending upon the circumstances, than) individuals and groups who want to expand freedom of action, expression, and identity, all of which are assumed to ensue from an emancipating process. Contestation will unfold between pro-emancipation and anti-emancipation cleavages and constituencies, but the character of contestation, let alone outcomes stemming from disagreement between different parties, will take time to reveal themselves. To the extent that emancipation has political effects it is supposed that legal, public policy, and regulatory responses to emancipative proposals will typically involve considerable lags. The formulation of new rules of living together that stem from emancipation may well be endogenous in character, but they again require time to bear fruit.

Activism within and across several domains of human action have been identified as having historically produced emancipative outcomes. These episodes have been variously described in social science literature as an "emancipation sequence" (Welzel, 2013), a "rights revolution" (Pinker, 2011), or a "moral arc" (Shermer, 2015). Welzel describes the key features of the historicized emancipation sequence in the following terms:

> ... Human empowerment is the emancipation of people from external domination. Emancipation requires equal freedoms, and such freedoms are granted through citizen rights. Ironically, as large as the theme of citizen rights loom in our time, it has literally been absent throughout most of history. But since the onset of preindustrial capitalism, starting with the abolition of slavery and feudal privileges, history takes a new turn: the granting of rights to common people, the steady differentiation

> of these rights, and their continuous extension to new groups and territories becoming a major trend of development—indeed a signature theme of modernity itself. (Welzel, 2013: 278)

Our contention is that some of the key historical episodes of emancipation have either been inspired by liberal ideas—such as an emphasis upon individual rights, the equal moral dignity and regard for all people, and equal treatment under the law—or have emanated from events that have had the effect (even if unintentional) of producing outcomes consistent with liberal precepts. The latter scenario, pertaining to the functional achievement of a liberal emancipation, is important, for it incorporates the live possibility in existing societies that pro-emancipatory activists need not necessarily subscribe to liberal ideological beliefs or philosophical principles for emancipation to take place. It may be argued, for example, that politically emancipative achievement of women's suffrage in the United Kingdom of the early twentieth century occurred in spite of the militancy of Pankhurst and the suffragettes, but because of selective political concession to appeal to feminist moderates on the question of voting rights (Novak, 2021). There appear to be numerous additional examples of emancipative concessions made to "moderate" rather than "radical" or "extremist" campaigners for change (e.g., Haines, 1988). More generally, certain non-liberals may agitate for emancipation and may succeed in achieving outcomes that liberals would find agreeable (or, at least, unopposed considering the given circumstances).

Significantly, these historical processes have either been inspired by liberal ideas—such as an emphasis upon individual rights, equal moral dignity for all people, and equal treatment under the law—or have had the effect (even if unintended) of having produced outcomes consistent with liberal ideas. The latter scenario, pertaining to the functional achievement of liberal emancipation, is important for it incorporates the possibility that pro-emancipatory activists need not necessarily subscribe to liberal ideological or philosophical beliefs for emancipation to take place.

Novak (2018) provides a rough categorization of the historical sequence of emancipative moves that have been especially evident in Western countries over the past three centuries or so. Liberal figures have been directly or indirectly involved in some of the key elements of emancipation:

- *Freedom of conscience*: Figures such as Desiderus Erasmus, Martin Luther, Jean Bodin, and Roger Williams argued that people should be free to exercise their own spiritual beliefs, without fear of persecution by the state or by adherents of other religious orders and belief systems. Following violent religious conflicts spanning centuries, Britain and continental Europe granted political rights and civil liberties to Roman Catholics and Jews during the eighteenth and nineteenth centuries. Demands against military conscription led to key reforms in the U.S. and elsewhere for the introduction of voluntary armies.
- *Freedom of expression*: The English essayist John Milton and philosopher John Stuart Mill both argued for freedom of speech to facilitate the discovery of better ideas, and stressed the importance of preventing press censorship and other prohibitions against free expression. The First Amendment of the U.S. Constitution enshrined protections for free speech and a free press, as well as guarantees for peaceful public assembly and the right to petition public officials. Commencing in Western countries, a process of democratization has gradually diffused around the world enabling individuals to participate in political activities.
- *Freedom to create economicvalue*: Adam Smith argued for the elimination of economic privileges advantaging certain producers, noting that empowering sellers and buyers to cooperate with each other fuels economic growth and improves material conditions for those less well-off. Richard Cobden and John Bright campaigned against agricultural tariffs in England during the nineteenth century, and anti-tax campaigners in the U.S. and other countries have occasionally succeeded in persuading governments to limit certain tax increases as well as introduce formal tax-and-expenditure limitations.
- *Freedom fromslavery*: Liberal arguments featured in demands to eliminate feudal relations on European landed estates, featuring the domination of serfs by nobles and lords. Numerous thinkers of a classical liberal persuasion, including William Wilberforce, John Stuart Mill, William Lloyd Garrison, and Frederick Douglass, also strenuously opposed servitude on racialist lines as a deprivation of fundamental individual liberties, including with respect to bodily integrity. The British Parliament formally abolished slavery in the 1830s, as did the U.S. during the 1860s, which has been followed by

similar abolition efforts on a global scale throughout the twentieth century.

- *Freedom for women*: Beginning with the writings of Britain's Mary Wollstonecraft, classical liberal activists and scholars called for equality between women and men, including the abolition of discriminatory legal treatments and the subversion of cultural norms reinforcing a false stereotype of female inferiority. From the early decades of the nineteenth century to the twentieth, a host of advances in the status of women were achieved including the ability to own and exchange property, to vote in general elections and, later, the easing of restrictions against divorce, criminalization of marital rape, and gender anti-discrimination laws.
- *Freedom to express sexual orientation*: During the eighteenth century, English philosopher Jeremy Bentham and the Italian legal scholar Cesare Beccaria wrote against state punishments against gay men engaging in mutually consenting sexual conduct. The twentieth century and the early twenty-first century saw significant improvements in the liberties and rights attained by gay men and lesbian women, for example through the anti-criminalization of sodomy, anti-discrimination provisions in employment and access to services, and, more recently, the ability of same-sex couples to marry.

Additional chronologies indicating the (albeit imperfect) pathway toward emancipation have been articulated by liberal thinkers. For example, Richard Ebeling (2019) traces the history of liberalism through several "crusades" by intellectuals, activists, and political figures to expand the boundaries of freedom and the delineation of individual rights from demands to abolish slavery, through to demands for civil liberties followed by economic freedom, political freedom, and international peace. Jim Powell (2000) describes the historical role of charismatic ideational, public, and other entrepreneurs in building support for waves of liberal emancipative achievement in the form of respecting natural rights, supporting toleration and peace, upholding individualism, promoting economic liberty, and implementing political and other safeguards for emancipative episodes that had the effect of promoting individual liberties. In more recent times one of the outstanding features of Western social change has been the relatively rapid extension of emancipation to an array of classes, groups, and identities, for example transgender and other gender non-conforming individuals and people with disabilities.

It is notable in this regard that Welzel's (2013) theory of emancipation emphasizes a sequence of material empowerment for populations followed by the realization of post-materialist emancipative values and civic entitlements, a sequence which appears to have unfolded at least in Western societies. Even so, and consistent with the significance that we place upon emancipation as a non-deterministic and non-linear process, it is observable that the trajectory of emancipation may become stalled or even regress. For example, Western societies have recently experienced backlash dynamics on questions of sexual orientation and gender identity, as well as against immigration rights and the freedom of movement for goods and capital. An appraisal of emancipation historically adhering to a sequence should also account for the stark regional differences in individual liberties around the world—in general terms—the relatively lowest levels of human freedom (implying a relative lack of emancipative achievement) have been attained by countries in the Middle East, North Africa, sub-Saharan Africa, and South Asia (Vásquez et al., 2023).

Structure of the Book

Excluding this introductory chapter and the conclusion, this book consists of nine chapters prepared by economists, political scientists, and sociologists on themes concerning the theory and (historical and contemporary) practices of liberal emancipation. Although most chapters succeed in intertwining conceptual and empirical dimensions of emancipation, the book may be roughly read in two parts. Chapter 2–6 inclusive are primarily conceptual in orientation, referring largely (but not exclusively) to what has been dubbed as the "mainline" approach to political economy. This approach represents a blending of Austrian, Bloomington, and Virginia schools of political economy to exemplify the importance of entrepreneurial decision-making, economic (as well as social and political) processes, and institutional constraints in generating knowledge and promoting coordination (Boettke, 2012; Boettke et al., 2016). Chapters 7–10 may be interpreted as largely presenting specific applications or cases of liberal emancipation with respect to the status of ethnic and other minorities, to issues of racial and gender equality as well as lesbian, gay, bisexual, transgender, and queer (LGBTQ) rights, although interdependencies between ideas and practices of emancipation are also evident throughout these latter chapters.

Rosolino Candela (Chapter 2) draws upon economics and "mainline" political economy literatures to articulate a case for the emancipatory effects of market processes as constituted by institutions such as property rights protections, flexible relative prices, and credible profit-and-loss signals. The capacity of markets to facilitate economic emancipation, most notably in terms of improving economic welfare experienced by minorities and lower socio-economic status groups, is appreciated through an understanding of private property rights as a social obligation to entrepreneurially search for value-added means of production and exchange that benefit trading counterparties. The dualistic disciplinary and productive incentives of individuals to acquire, use, and dispose of property in a welfare-enhancing manner is emergently implicated in the materially abundant economic scenario of "generalizing increasing returns" that realizes mass emancipatory outcomes.

The positive sum implications of property rights protection and generalizing increasing returns serves as the basis for Candela's critique of the "New History of Capitalism" literature that seeks to repudiate the market process as an emancipatory system. Candela's investigations challenge the proposition that the long-run development of the U.S. economy rested in the maintenance of what Candela identifies as both the morally odious and economically unproductive regime of slavery. In support of this position, a conceptual blending of Austrian economics (represented by Kirzner), property rights economics (Alchian, Demsetz), and James Buchanan's treatment of generalizing increasing returns is offered by Candela to appraise the historically emancipatory effects of African American entrepreneurship within an increasingly productive U.S. economy.

Alain Marciano and John Meadowcroft (Chapter 3) detail the contribution of Nobel Prize laureate in Economics, James M. Buchanan, to the theory of emancipation. Buchanan is known for his contributions to the economics of politics, otherwise known as "public choice," as well as to fields such as public finance and contractarian political philosophy. An important and original aspect of Buchanan's approach to economies lies in the sophisticated view of human nature he had, which is illustrated in the distinction he made between a "natural" and "artifactual" man. Marciano and Meadowcroft show how and why Buchanan's model of artifactuality provides the basis for a theory of emancipation, while his natural conception of individuals is the benchmark for a theory of alienation. Natural man is constrained by biological, cultural, political, and other conditions or, otherwise, guided by fixed and well-known economic preferences. On the other hand, artifactual man is emancipated because he can make creative and imaginative, as well as ethical and responsible, choices while interacting with others.

An important point raised by Marciano and Meadowcroft is to link Buchanan's distinction between artifactual man (an individual who is emancipated) and natural man (the individual who is alienated) to the rest of his work. The authors show that the natural-artifactual distinction is rooted in Buchanan's work on clubs, groups, and rules or constitutions. Marciano and Meadowcroft show that emancipation is impossible without a certain type of rules, therefore connecting Buchanan's theory of artifactuality and liberal constitutionalism.

Otto Lehto (Chapter 4) extends the conceptual architecture of liberal emancipation by relying upon evolutionary theory, a tradition within the social sciences that arguably stretches back to at least the Scottish Enlightenment period (Marciano & Pelissier, 2000). The liberal evolutionary paradigm that Lehto articulates is that of creative agency on the part of individuals that is, in turn, implicated in open-ended forms of economic and social changes. While the indeterminacy of evolution may imply a non-teleological vision of change whose results cannot be normatively appraised *ex ante*, or as some critics suggest, Lehto's framework is inclusive of a moralized account of human agency wherein individuals (including in interactive, collective action situations) are motivated to enact changes to their environments in pursuance of some normative or valuational aim. As Lehto indicates, such an aim may include emancipation for people whose interests have somehow been systematically compromised during previous episodes of change.

Lehto extends arguments over the emancipatory potential of evolution to questions of institutional and public policy framing and design. As he states, liberals should open-mindedly "acknowledge and tackle the downsides of unguided evolution and set up (or, where possible, grow and let evolve) institutions and rules (both formal and informal) to remedy or soften them." Within this, a potential role is given to policies such as a universal basic income (UBI) to further empower disadvantaged and marginalized persons as creative evolutionary agents. The UBI is posited as a facilitative means of emancipation, to the extent it enables individuals to discover ways to help overcome their historical or systemic oppression, together with a supportive financial basis to more intensively explore their ambitious, hopes, and desires.

Emily Chamlee-Wright and Mikayla Novak (Chapter 5) build upon the themes touched on in previous chapters to investigate the potential for emancipatory outcomes within liberal systems of social learning. Using a "four corners of liberalism" framework previously introduced by Chamlee-Wright (2022), the authors illustrate that emancipation is a complex and lengthy process involving some combination of reformist policy, economic entrepreneurship, intellectual effort, and social movement advocacy for economic, political, or social change. The idea that emancipative outcomes is a by-product of changes in the domains of economic, political, civic, and intellectual liberalism is, in part, intended to draw out the ever-present tensions that exist when individuals and groups partake in efforts to ameliorate experiences of marginalization and oppression, as well as indicating the potential for temporal backslidings of emancipative processes due to "backlash" effects and similar regressions.

Chamlee-Wright and Novak apply the four corners approach to the experiences of racial equality in the U.S., and improvements in the status of minorities on the basis of sexual orientation and gender identity. Instances are discernible in which reform-oriented groups successfully accumulated material and non-material resources to agitate for changes to formal and informal institutions. These processes emerged in conjunction with the formation of epistemic communities dedicated to racial equality and LGBTQ rights that spurred reasonably cohesive reformist identities that, in turn, helped to overcome collective action problems surrounding the push for emancipative legal and institutional changes.

Alongside Hayek and Buchanan, Vincent and Elinor Ostrom were prominent in the modern revival of classical liberal thought. The Ostroms provided important intellectual contributions in fields such as collective action theory, common goods management, governance studies, public administration, and public economy, and those contributions were suitably recognized through Elinor Ostrom's awarding of the 2009 Nobel Prize in Economics. Chapter 6, authored by Roberta Herzberg, a former collaborator and student of the Ostroms, introduces Vincent and Elinor Ostrom as key intellectual figures in the liberal conception of human emancipation.

Key to Herzberg's interpretation of the emancipatory instincts of Vincent and Elinor Ostrom is the capacity of polycentric systems to provide self-governing spaces with like-minded others. A central paradox of governance is that formal institutions coupled with coercive practices are widely presumed necessary to foster socio-political cooperation, but that these same arrangements have the capacity to coerce into submission, and to dominate, those unwilling to be governed by them. How does society escape such a paradox? According to Herzberg's reading of the Ostroms, the existence of multiple centers of decision-making ("polycentricity") is a necessary condition empowering disempowered, marginalized, or unsatisfied individuals and groups to exit away from unsatisfactory governance standards to those they find preferable. In addition to exit rights as an emancipative force, polycentric sorting reinforces emancipation by enabling diversity to socio-politically operationalize as a feasible way of life. Through Ostromian polycentricity, people who are otherwise harmed by the yoke of oppression can build self-sustaining and high-trust communities with robust self-governing properties.

Erwin Dekker (Chapter 7) presents an account of a distinctive, pro-emancipative "Chicago School" of sociology that emerged between the early to middle decades of the twentieth century. Dekker indicates that scholarly figures such as William I. Thomas, Robert E. Park, and Ernest Burgess, among others, provided novel methodological, analytical, and empirical contributions in respect of examining the conditions and experiences of marginalized communities in Chicago urban areas.

In his chapter, Dekker illustrates how the Chicago school of sociology developed the foundations of a social-scientific scholarship that has become increasingly receptive to emancipation arguments. One contribution by Chicagoan sociologists was through fieldwork research techniques, providing academics and policymakers alike with unique "windows" into the everyday lives of outsiders, such as immigrant communities, racial minorities, and others whose behaviors and practices were stereotyped as "deviant." The other major contribution is that Chicago sociology laid the groundwork for empathic inquiry, as well as a normatively emancipative agenda, affording dignity and voice to the urbanite downtrodden and maligned. By outlining these contributions, Dekker raises the profile of the arguably underappreciated "Chicago School" of sociology in comparison with its more vaunted economic counterpart.

Fabio Rojas (Chapter 8) engages with the now-voluminous critical race theory (CRT) literature from the classical liberal perspective. Arguably originating in the post-Civil Rights period of legal reforms in the U.S. during the mid-1960s, CRT represents both a theoretical system and explanatory framework intersecting socially constructed notions of race with systemically discriminatory patterns in law, public policy, and social norms. Associated with the writings of scholars and activists such as Derrick Bell, Patricia Hill Collins, Kimberlie Crenshaw, and Ibram X. Kendi, CRT's explication of the structural basis of racism poses as a refutation of the liberal position of emancipation through the promotion of individual freedoms and rights, as well as ethical commitments such as colorblindness and a non-racialized common humanity (Hughes, 2024; Lukianoff & Haidt, 2018).

Rojas's chapter serves as a defense of the liberal principle of anti-racism, especially the emancipatory implications of liberal institutions. Not only do liberal institutions incentivize material prosperity that give economic dignity to human lives irrespective of race, but that oppressed minorities can use these resources to press for expanded rights and liberties. Another virtue of liberalism is that its institutions allow for toleration and pluralism, that can help weaken the barriers to group emancipation. Significantly, marginalized groups can build a constituency for emancipation by galvanizing shared senses of identity against socio-political oppressors. The pluralistic properties of liberal institutions, according to Rojas, are further reinforced by checks and balances as presented by polycentric (rather than monocentric) authority structures. To be certain, these arguments do not refute the correctness of CRT claims concerning the historical injustices of colonialism, slavery, and formal discriminations (such as the "Jim Crow" provisions of the American South) but that minorities can use liberal institutions to help ameliorate the harms of history and to promote racial equality.

Jayme Lemke (Chapter 9) enquires into the implications for emancipatory efforts in societies wherein subjective choices and values about being, doing, and knowing are constrained by cultural, legal, and social provisions. There is little question that government legislation and policy provisions can have the effect of distorting the ability of certain individuals and groups from exercising their agency in terms of choice, but what Lemke's chapter illustrates is that choices may also be powerfully limited by the effects of culture in filtering perceptions as to appropriate behaviors and choices. It has been thoroughly elucidated in feminist literature that gendered norms have had the effect of preventing women from exercising a range of choice options ordinarily available to men. The subject of gender-related choice constraints affecting emancipative trajectories within a society is at the center of Lemke's chapter.

The historical significance of Lemke's contribution is indicated by her recounting the lessons of "first-wave" feminists, such as Mary Wollstonecraft. As Lemke indicates, Wollstonecraft and other early feminists not only chastized men for seeking to uphold patriarchal relations of gendered domination and subjection but demanded women critically interrogate the determinants of their own lack of emancipation. On this basis, emancipation may be understood as valuational and practical efforts to empower marginalized or oppressed individuals and groups to directly and meaningfully participate in processes of choice along meaningful margins.

As already hinted in this introductory chapter, another important emancipatory wave that has ensued in the modern world, especially in developed countries, has been trend improvements in the status of individuals based on their sexual orientation and gender identity. The emancipative process as experienced by the LGBTQ community is the subject of Nathan Goodman's Chapter 10. As Goodman notes, LGBTQ community members have been historically subjected to state harassment, including victimization by law enforcement personnel, which had been given legitimacy by a complicated web of social norms that have normalized heteronormative and cisnormative modes of behavior, expression, and identity. The gradual process of LGBTQ emancipation has rested in the tireless efforts of community activists and their supporters that, in turn, have brought about a greater sense of support and dignification benefiting queer individuals and groups.

A distinctive approach pursued by Goodman is his embrace of a "radical liberal" orientation to inquiry, which draws upon left-wing market anarchism (LWMA) theory but remains highly complementary to mainline economic approaches of entrepreneurial agency and institutional change. The radical liberal position allows Goodman to be receptive to critics of queer liberalism on issues of power and the cultural bases of LGBTQ oppression, while constructively illustrating how sexual and gender minorities help overcome (both formal and informal) bases of oppression through a combination of strategic agency at both individual and collective levels combined with endogenous and emergent governance practices. The record of modern LGBTQ emancipation attests to the significance of these effects in rendering economic, political, and social change.

Chapter 11 is the concluding chapter of the book. It provides a summary of the key arguments and themes conveyed throughout the book, and it offers several suggestions regarding future research on emancipative processes through a liberal conceptual lens. It is anticipated that the contributions provided in this book will not only provide a spur for additional intellectual inquiries into the liberal foundations of emancipation processes, but inspire practical emancipative projects within and across cultural, economic, political, and social realms that seem increasingly necessary in a world wherein individual freedoms are under increasing threat.

Notes

1. Throughout this book the term "liberalism" is treated as being synonymous with classical liberalism, unless otherwise specified in ways that recognize the existence of differing strands of liberal thought (e.g., Hobhousian social liberalism, Rawlsian liberal egalitarianism, etc.).
2. Wojciechowska (2022) limits her discussion to that of political emancipation, however it is supposed the categories to which emancipation pertains may be applied to other domains of human action.
3. However, it is noted the use of the Latin suffix *ion* in emancipation may reflect both a process and a state of affairs (Wojciechowska, 2022: 160).
4. Thulani Davis (2022) intriguingly refers to an "emancipation circuit" applicable to the American experience of racial equality, in which a grassroots Black southern resistance to racism emerged and operated on the combinatorial basis of geographic connectivity and deep social networks.
5. Researchers have also suggested that wealthier societies tend to be more capable in providing welfare and other social supports to vulnerable individuals and groups, including through not-for-profit associations and government agencies (e.g., Lindert, 2004).
6. Freedom from interference, or the absence of formal constraints, affecting an individual or a collective is referred to by Isaiah Berlin (1969) as "negative liberty."

References

Anderson, E. (2017). *Private Government: How Employers Rule Our Lives (and Why We Don't Talk About It)*. Princeton University Press.

Becker, G. S. (1971). *The Economics of Discrimination* (2nd ed.). University of Chicago Press.

Benson, D. (2021). Introduction. In D. Benson (Ed.), *Domination and Emancipation: Remaking Critique* (pp. xi–xxii). Rowman & Littlefield.

Berlin, I. (1969). Two Concepts of Liberty. In *Four Essays on Liberty* (pp. 118–172). Oxford University Press.

Bernstein, D. E. (2022). *Classified: The Untold Story of Racial Classification in America*. Bombardier Books.

Boaz, D. (1997). *The Libertarian Reader: Classic and Contemporary Readings from Lao-tzu to Milton Friedman*. Free Press.

Boettke, P. J. (2012). *Living Economics: Yesterday, Today, and Tomorrow*. Independent Institute.

Boettke, P. J. (2021). *The Struggle for a Better World*. Mercatus Center at George Mason University.

Boettke, P. J., & Candela, R. A. (2017). The Liberty of Progress: Increasing Returns, Institutions, and Entrepreneurship. *Social Philosophy and Policy, 34*(2), 136–163.

Boettke, P. J., Haeffele-Balch, S., & Storr, V. H. (2016). *Mainline Economics: Six Nobel Lectures in the Tradition of Adam Smith*. Mercatus Center at George Mason University.

Brittan, S. (1973). *Capitalism and the Permissive Society*. Macmillan.

Brown, G. W., McLean, I., & McMillan, A. (2018). *A Concise Oxford Dictionary of Politics and International Relations*. Oxford University Press.

Buchanan, A., & Powell, R. (2017). De-moralization as Emancipation: Liberty, Progress, and the Evolution of Invalid Moral Norms. *Social Philosophy and Policy, 34*(2), 108–135.

Buchanan, J. M., & Congleton, R. D. ([1998] 2003). *Politics by Principle, Not Interest: Toward Nondiscriminatory Democracy*. In G. Brennan, H. Kliemt, & R. D. Tollison (Eds.), *The Collected Works of James M. Buchanan: Volume 11*. Liberty Fund.

Buchanan, J. M., & Tullock, G. ([1962] 1999). *The Calculus of Consent: Logical Foundations of Constitutional Democracy*. In G. Brennan, H. Kliemt, & R. D. Tollison (Eds.), *The Collected Works of James M. Buchanan: Volume 3*. Liberty Fund.

Caillé, A., Chanial, P., & Tarragoni, F. (2016). Emancipate Oneself, Yes, but from What? *Revue du Mauss, 48*(2), 5–28.

Callais, J. T., & Geloso, V. (2023). Intergenerational Income Mobility and Economic Freedom. *Southern Economic Journal, 89*(3), 732–753.

Chamlee-Wright, E. (2022, January 31). The Four Corners of Liberalism: Mapping Out a Common Ground. Archbridge Institute. *Profectus Magazine*. https://profectusmag.com/the-four-corners-of-liberalism-mapping-out-a-common-ground

Collins, H. (1965). Sociology of Emancipation. *Phylon, 26*(2), 148–161.

Courtland, S. D., Gaus, G., & Schmidtz, D. (2022). Liberalism. In *Stanford Encyclopedia of Philosophy*. https://plato.stanford.edu/entries/liberalism

Davis, T. (2022). *The Emancipation Circuit: Black Activism Forging a Culture of Freedom*. Duke University Press.

Dekker, E. (2019). Is There an Agenda of Neoliberal Emancipation? *Journal of Contextual Economics, 139*(2–4), 213–224.

Dekker, E. (2020). On Emancipators, Engineers, and Students: The Appropriate Attitude of the Economist. *Review of Austrian Economics, 33*(1), 55–68.

Deneen, P. J. (2018). *Why Liberalism Failed*. Yale University Press.

Dopfer, K., & Potts, J. (2008). *The General Theory of Economic Evolution*. Routledge.

Ebeling, R. (2019). *For a New Liberalism*. American Institute for Economic Research.

Epstein, R. A. (1992). *Forbidden Grounds: The Case Against Employment Discrimination Laws*. Harvard University Press.

Epstein, R. A. (2014). *The Classical Liberal Constitution: The Uncertain Quest for Limited Government*. Harvard University Press.

Fawcett, E. (2014). *Liberalism: The Life of an Idea*. Princeton University Press.

Ferguson, R. S., & Witcher, M. M. (2022). *Black Liberation Through the Marketplace: Hope, Heartbreak, and the Promise of America*. Emancipation Books.

Geloso, V., & Peng, L. (2024). Postbellum Electoral Politics in California and the Genesis of the Chinese Exclusion Act of 1882. *European Journal of Law and Economics, 57*(3), 403–434.

Grynaviski, J. D., & Munger, M. C. (2017). Reconstructing Racism: Transforming Racial Hierarchy from "Necessary Evil" into "Positive Good." *Social Philosophy and Policy, 34*(1), 144–163.

Haider, A. (2021). Emancipation, Political, and Real. In D. Benson (Ed.), *Domination and Emancipation: Remaking Critique* (pp. 69–88). Rowman & Littlefield.

Haines, H. H. (1988). *Black Radicals and the Civil Rights Mainstream, 1954–1970*. University of Tennessee Press.

Hayek, F. A. ([1960] 2011). *The Constitution of Liberty: The Definitive Edition*. In R. Hamowy (Ed.), *The Collected Works of F. A. Hayek: Volume 17*. University of Chicago Press.

Henderson, D. R., McNab, R. M., & Rózsás. (2005). The Hidden Inequality in Socialism. *Independent Review,9*(3), 389–412.

Hughes, C. (2024). *The End of Race Politics: Arguments for a Colorblind America* (Thesis). New York.
Klein, D. B., Briggeman, J., & Stroup, J. S. (2023). *Classical Liberalism by Country* (Vols. I, II, and III). CL Press.
Knight, F. J. (1960). *Intelligence and Democratic Action.* Harvard University Press.
Laclau, E. (1996). *Emancipation(s).* Verso.
Lemke, J. S. (2015). An Austrian Approach to Class Structure. *Advances in Austrian Economics, 19*, 167–192.
Lindert, P. H. (2004). *Growing Public: Social Spending and Economic Growth Since the Eighteenth Century.* Cambridge University Press.
Lomasky, L. (2002). Classical Liberalism and Civil Society. In S. Chambers & W. Kymlicka (Eds.), *Alternative Conceptions of Civil Society* (pp. 50–68). Princeton University Press.
Lukianoff, G., & Haidt, J. (2018). *The Coddling of the American Mind: How Good Intentions and Bad Ideas Are Setting Up a Generation for Failure.* Penguin Press.
Marciano, A., & Pelissier, M. (2000). The Influence of Scottish Enlightenment on Darwin's Theory of Cultural Evolution. *Journal of the History of Economic Thought, 22*(2), 239–249.
Marx, K. ([1848] 2020). *The Communist Manifesto.* Oxford University Press.
McCloskey, D. N. (2019). *Why Liberalism Works: How True Liberal Values Produce a Freer, More Equal, Prosperous World for All.* Yale University Press.
Merquior, J. G. (1991). *Liberalism, Old and New.* Twayne Publishers.
North, D. C., Wallis, J. J., & Weingast, B. R. (2009). *Violence and Social Orders: A Conceptual Framework for Interpreting Recorded Human History.* Cambridge University Press.
Novak, M. (2018). *Inequality: An Entangled Political Economy Perspective.* Palgrave Macmillan.
Novak, M. (2021). *Freedom in Contention: Social Movements and Liberal Political Economy.* Lexington Books.
Pager, D. (2016). Are Firms That Discriminate More Likely to Go Out of Business? *Sociological Science, 3*(36), 849–859.
Pinker, S. (2011). *The Better Angels of Our Nature: The Decline of Violence in History and Its Causes.* Allen Lane.
Powell, J. (2000). *The Triumph of Liberty: A 2,000-Year History, Told through the Lives of Freedom's Greatest Champions.* Free Press.
Rebughini, P. (2015). Framing Emancipations. *Journal of Classical Sociology, 15*(3), 270–285.
Rojas, F., & Stern, C. (2024). *Sociology and Classical Liberalism in Dialogue: Freedom is Something We Do Together*. Lexington Books.
Schmidtz, D., & Brennan, J. (2010). *A Brief History of Liberty.* Wiley-Blackwell.

Scott, J. C. (1998). *Seeing Like a State: How Certain Schemes to Improve the Human Condition Have Failed*. Yale University Press.

Shermer, M. (2015). *The Moral Arc: How Science and Reason Lead Humanity Toward Truth, Justice, and Freedom*. Henry Holt and Co.

Smith, G. H. (2013). *The System of Liberty: Themes in the History of Classical Liberalism*. Cambridge University Press.

Susen, S. (2015). Emancipation. In M. T. Gibbons, D. Coole, E. Ellis, & K. Ferguson (Eds.), *The Encylopedia of Political Thought* (pp. 1024–1038). Wiley Blackwell.

Taylor, R. S. (2017). *Exit Left: Markets and Mobility in Republican Thought*. Oxford University Press.

Vásquez, I., McMahon, F., Murphy, R., & Schneider, G. S. (2023). *The Human Freedom Index 2023: A Global Measurement of Personal, Civil, and Economic Freedom*. Cato Institute and Fraser Institute.

Welzel, C. (2013). *Freedom Rising: Human Empowerment and the Quest for Emancipation*. Cambridge University Press.

Wojciechowska, M. (2022). Participation Is Not Enough: An Argument for Emancipation as a Foundation of Participatory Theorising. *Representation, 58*(2), 155–168.

Wollstonecraft, M. ([1790] 1996). *A Vindication of the Rights of Men*. Prometheus Books.

CHAPTER 2

Property Rights and the Liberating Effect of Generalized Increasing Returns: A Reassessment of the New History of Capitalism and the Economics of Slavery

Rosolino Candela

> The essence of the liberal position, however, *is the denial of all privilege*, if privilege is understood in its proper and original meaning of the state granting and protecting rights to some which are not available on equal terms to others.
> —F.A. Hayek, *The Road to Serfdom* ([1944] 1994: xxxvi; emphasis added)

> It is because we do not know how individuals will use their freedom that it is so important.
> —F.A. Hayek, *The Constitution of Liberty* (1960: 31)

R. Candela (✉)
Mercatus Center at George Mason University, Fairfax, VA, USA
e-mail: rcandela@mercatus.gmu.edu

M. Novak (ed.), *Liberal Emancipation*, Mercatus Studies in Political and Social Economy, https://doi.org/10.1007/978-3-031-94406-2_2

Frédéric Bastiat once stated that "the worst thing that can happen to a good cause is, not to be skillfully attacked, but to be ineptly defended" (Bastiat, 1996: 107). In recent years, the literature on the New History of Capitalism has challenged the positive-sum nature of private property rights and market processes. Among its strongest criticisms of capitalism is the notion that the economic development of the United States was caused by the institution of slavery, upon which cotton and textile production was based prior to the Civil War. The implication of this argument is that rise of Western economic development has been predicated on a zero-sum game, whereby slavery and other associated institutional arrangements of coercion (i.e., colonialism and imperialism) were the driving force for a coercive transfer of wealth upon which Western capitalism is based (Baptist, 2014; Beckert, 2014; Blackburn, 2011). The purpose of this chapter is to reassess this claim in a twofold manner. I do so by clarifying the distinction between the concepts of private property and privilege in economic theory that are too often conflated, not as a matter of reassessing the conclusions of the New History of Capitalism per se, but as an opportunity to reestablish the basis for a more effective defense of the emancipatory effects of a liberal market order.

A liberal market order is emancipatory by expanding the set of choices available for individuals to realize human flourishing. The emancipatory effects of a liberal market order can be understood in terms of a dual level of analysis: (1) a "lower-level" analysis of social interaction within a set of rules; and (2) a "higher-level" of analysis over alternative sets of rules and their corresponding effect, either positive-sum or negative-sum, on social interaction. Within a framework of political-legal rules, governed by private property and freedom of contract under the rule of law, individuals become emancipated from the constraints imposed by nature by realizing the gains from productive specialization, technological innovation, and exchange. This has allowed human beings to live longer, healthier, and more prosperous lives.

The focus of this chapter, however, is a "higher-level" of analysis how individuals become emancipated *from constraints imposed by other human beings*, such as the case in which individuals are precluded by institutions, both formal and informal, from realizing their creative talent because of their race, creed, gender, or sexual orientation. The historical case studies of two African Americans, Elijah McCoy and Dr. Daniel Hale Williams, are illustrative of this emancipatory process. McCoy, an engineer, and Williams, a medical doctor, were both pioneers by overcaming barriers imposed by nature and stretched the boundaries, technologically speaking, of what had been possible in science and medicine, but also by overcoming racial discrimination and changing what white Americans considered to be possible from black Americans. However, the exploits of McCoy, Williams, and other black Americans, would not have been possible had they been enslaved, whereby their labor would have been the privilege of another human being. Thus, the emancipation of humankind has been fundamentally marked by an institutional transition, from a framework that defines one's legal status and personal destiny in society by privilege, to a framework of private property that emancipates an individual to realize their own creative talent and human flourishing. However, the "application of the term 'privilege' to property as such," according to F. A. Hayek, has resulted in an unfortunate "consequent abuse" of these terms ([1944] 1994: 89), the correction of which motivates this chapter.

The next section begins by establishing the broader intellectual context in the history of economic thought in order to situate the origins of the New History of Capitalism. Here I argue that the conclusions of New History of Capitalism are premised on a conflation between private property and privilege, which are mutually exclusive institutional concepts. This conflation begets an additional conflation between rent-seeking (i.e., competition over privileges) and profit-seeking processes (i.e., competition over property rights). By failing to identify slavery (as well colonialism and imperialism) with rent-seeking, the New History of Capitalism fails to realize its negative-sum effects, rendering its narrative about Western economic development vacuous.

I follow this discussion by revisiting the distinction in economic theory between economics of scale and what James Buchanan and Yong Yoon refer to as *generalized increasing returns* (Buchanan & Yoon, 1995, 2000).[1] Stated briefly, economies of scale refer to a *technical* relationship between the value of output and the variance of the units of valued inputs in a particular productive activity. Increasing (or decreasing) returns to scale refer to disproportionate increases (or decreases) in the value of output from increases in the quantity of valued inputs in production, such as land, labor, or capital allocated toward finer-grained specialization in a particular productive activity. This is distinct from generalized increasing returns, which refers to an economic relationship between the size of a particular market (hence the scope of market exchange), and the economic viability of specialization across various productive activities.

Viewed in this way, increasing (or decreasing) returns to scale emerge as a by-product of expansions (or contractions) in the scope of productive specialization and exchange (Candela, 2022: 329).

I draw this distinction to disentangle an implicit conflation in the New History of Capitalism to argue that while privileges may realize *economics of scale*, they cannot realize generalized increasing returns because, in the best-case scenario, there is an inevitable onset of diminishing returns to scale in production that results from slavery. In the more likely scenario, the welfare costs associated with the lost productive potential of human beings being precluded from participating in an ever-widening scope of entrepreneurial discovery will only generate a negative-sum game. Thus, this implication of this conflation misdirects away attention from the emancipatory effects of the generalized increasing returns, which can only be realized within a framework of private property rights. The section that follows, through a set of historical case studies of black Americans in the United States, demonstrates the emancipatory effects of generalized returns, in terms of unleashing capital accumulation, technological innovation, and productive entrepreneurship, by harnessing the creative powers of human beings through productive specialization under the division of labor.

I later conclude this chapter with implications for future research. The implications of my argument are that a proper understanding of the nature of *property rights as a social liability, not a private privilege*, results in a positive-sum and emancipatory effect on society. Its emancipatory effect is premised on giving rise to generalized increasing returns to productive specialization and social cooperation under the division of labor. Understood this way, liberty coevolved with generalized increasing returns, gradually transforming the political process from a means to confine individuals based on legal status, into a means by which to emancipate individuals according to contract.

Private Property Rights, Privileges, and the New History of Capitalism: A Reassessment

Since at least the publication of Adam Smith's *An Inquiry into the Nature and Causes of the Wealth of Nations* ([1776] 1981), political economists sitting in the seat of Adam Smith have argued against the notion that slavery was ever a positive-sum driving force for economic development, and more importantly, has always delivered negative-sum outcomes across societies. It is for this reason that economics would later become dubbed as the "dismal science" in the 1840s by the Scottish philosopher and historian, Thomas Carlyle. As recounted by economist David Levy (2001a, 2001b), Carlyle's characterization of economic science was not against the gloomy predictions of Thomas Malthus, who had predicted that the rate of human population growth would always exceed that of food, thereby trapping humankind in a vicious circle of poverty from which it would never break out. Rather, Carlyle was attacking British political economists, particularly John Stuart Mill, not only for their role in defending the emancipation of West Indian slaves in the 1830s, but also for arguing that it was institutions, not race, that explained why some nations were rich and others poor. The case *for* private property among British classical political economists did not reflect a conservative political posture, but rather a *progressive* and *emancipatory* one against slavery.[2] As Levy states this point, "scholars who do not know the Carlyle-Mill debate and its context all too often infer that since modern economists occupy a rightist position, the attack came on classical economics from their left. No. The attack on economics for which the term 'dismal science' was coined a weapon came from their right...the classical British economists, generally speaking, favored property in things and opposed property in people" (Levy, 2001a: 6).

With this intellectual background in context, how can we explain the more recent assertions among the New Historians of Capitalism, which postulates the direct opposite of what political economists in the classical liberal tradition have argued? Two reasons can explain this intellectual trajectory, one more proximate, and the other more fundamental that goes beyond the New History of Capitalism. The proximate reason, as Geloso and Gluck (2021) suggest, for the rise of this discipline can be partially attributed to the divide that emerged after the 1970s between the empirical methods deployed by historians and economists regarding the economic effects of slavery. The increasing application of quantitative evidence, grounded in economic theory, among economic historians in the field of "cliometrics," drew an increasing wedge between economic historians in economics departments and the methods of historians in history departments, the latter being drawn away from applying economy theory or quantitative evidence in their historical narrative. This wedge was particularly widened after conclusions drawn by Robert Fogel and Stanley Engerman ([1974a] 1989, [1974b] 1989) in the two-part study of American slavery, entitled *Time on the Cross*, which provide evidence to support the claim that slave agriculture in the American antebellum South was more efficient relative to agriculture in the North. For example, Fogel and Engerman state that "[s]outhern agriculture as a whole was about 35 percent more efficient than northern agriculture in 1860" in terms of producing output given the same amounts of land, labor, and capital ([1974a] 1989: 192).

These considerations, however, do not imply that the scholars associated with the New History of Capitalism would necessarily reject them. Citing the conclusions of Fogel and Engerman that "slavery was profitable is now widely accepted" (Blackburn, 2011: 309, fn. 68), historian Robin Blackburn (2011: 308–309) has argued "[m]odern research has shown that slave plantations were still highly profitable before emancipation, and hence there was no purely economic reason to abolish slavery." Eric Hilt, in a critical survey of the New History of Capitalism, argues that unlike economic history, "[w]ith few exceptions, the literature is not concerned with the early origins or deep institutional foundations of capitalism, and it does not seek to analyze the full evolution of capitalism over time. *None of the books even define what is meant by capitalism*" (Hilt, 2017: 512; emphasis added), and "rather than adopting the approach of the field of economic history, which seeks to analyze historical economic behavior, historians of capitalism aspire to something closer to social criticism" (ibid.). If all facts are theory-laden, and if, as Hilt suggests, the New History of Capitalism lacks an explicit and well-defined theory upon which its empirical conclusions are based, then an attempt to render explicit the underlying assumptions of its analysis presents an opportunity to establish a more robust understanding of not only how a liberal market order works, but also its emancipatory implications.

Therefore, my point here is not to adjudicate why the New History of Capitalism has emerged as a field of study, nor to draw any comparisons or contrasts between their conclusions and those made by cliometricians regarding the economics of slavery. Rather, by motivating our attention back to John Stuart Mill, particularly over the relationship between private property and the economic effects of slavery, what I want to suggest is that much confusion over the economic consequences of slavery has deeper roots in conflating slavery with private property over the labor of another human being, when in fact slavery refers to a *privilege* over the labor of another human being, the benefits of which are concentrated upon a slaveowner, but the costs of which are dispersed across society. My point here is not to suggest that Mill (or other economists for that matter) were unaware of this distinction, nor to suggest that Mill has directly led to the conceptual confusions held by the New Historians of Capitalism. Rather, by using Mill's arguments over the economics of slavery as representative of this conflation, and by disentangling this distinction, economists and historians alike can *conceptually* clarify the economic effects of slavery by avoiding semantic confusions.

In Chapter V of Mill's *Principles of Political Economy*, entitled "On Slavery," Mill writes, "after allowing the full value of these considerations, it remains certain that slavery is incompatible with any high state of the arts of life, and any great efficiency of labour. For all products which require much skill, slave countries are usually dependent on foreigners. Hopeless slavery effectually brutifies the intellect; and intelligence in the slaves" (Mill, [1848] 2006: 247). As Mill furthers this point, "[h]ired labour is generally so much more efficient than slave labour, that the employer can pay a considerably greater value in wages, than the maintenance of his slaves cost him before, and yet be a gainer by the change" (ibid.: 249).

There is no doubt, therefore, that John Stuart Mill, one of the greatest political economists of his time, shared similar conclusions about the economic effects of slavery with other classical political economists going back to Adam Smith. However, his description of slavery as "an institution of property" generates an ambiguity that misdirects attention from the fact that slavery is an institution of *privilege*. To be fair, Mill elsewhere discusses "rights of property in abuses" (Mill, [1848] 2006: 232) and singles out "at the head of them, is property in human beings" (ibid.: 233). There, he states further that it "is almost superfluous to observe, that this institution can have no place in any society even pretending to be founded on justice, or on fellowship between human creatures." However, through his word choice, the unfair reader may conclude that calling slavery an institution of property justified compensation for its elimination, after the British Parliament had legislated to abolish slavery in 1833. As Mill states, "iniquitous as it is, yet when the state has expressly legalized it, and human beings, for generations, have been bought, sold, and inherited under sanction of law, it another wrong, in abolishing the property, not to make full compensation. This wrong was avoided by the great measure of justice in 1833, one of the most virtuous acts, as well as the most practically beneficent, ever done collectively by a nation" (ibid.).

In what way can we reconcile what seems to be a contradiction between Mill's abolitionist credentials and deeming compensation to slaveholders a "great measure of justice"? Once we draw this distinction and appropriately label slavery as an institution of privilege, we can better understand that the attempt to abolish slavery by government decree, without compensation, would have only incited further rent-seeking on the part of slaveholders to lobby against such legislation and prevent a transfer of wealth vested in the privilege of holding individuals in bondage.[3]

What would seem to be a tension can be chalked up to the fact that what Mill means by slavery as property is the physical assignment of a "good," in the case another human being's labor, or as Fogel and Engerman put it, another human being's human capital (Fogel & Engerman [1974a] 1989: 233). The conflation of privileges with property, therefore, conflates the physical assignment of a good with *the assignment of consequences of one's choices exercised over that good*, the latter of which is the fundamental purpose of private property—namely, to tie consequences to one's action (Candela, 2021). Ludwig von Mises identifies this distinction as one between a "physical *having*" and a "social *having*" of resources, which corresponds to the distinction between the right to an object and the right to an action (von Mises, [1922] 1981: 30; emphasis in original). By creating a focal point that concentrates both the *full* costs *and* benefits of choice upon a decision-maker, private property creates a *social liability* (von Mises, [1949] 2007: 311), and because a "primary function of property rights is that of guiding incentives to achieve a greater internalization of externalities" (Demsetz, 1967: 348), Robert Wright (2017) has correctly critiqued the New History of Capitalism, and other scholars defending the economic benefits of slavery, by associating slavery with a negative externality, which implies the *absence* of private property and the existence of a privilege.[4]

The inefficiencies that Mill identifies with slavery are analogous to the costs of rent-seeking (Hummel, 1996; Tullock, 1967a).[5] Holding individuals in bondage implies that in the process of coercively transferring wealth, such as the value of a slave's labor, costs are incurred by the slaveholder attempting to appropriate this wealth as well as the fact that slaves themselves are incurring costs attempting to avert this coerced transfer of wealth, either by shirking or fleeing. Moreover, entrepreneurial talent that could have been exercised by those individuals in bondage is redirected toward unproductive entrepreneurial activity (Baumol, 1990) or otherwise evasive entrepreneurial activity (Coyne & Leeson, 2004), both of which redirect labor and human capital of slaves solely to prevent the transfer of existing wealth, both in pecuniary and non-pecuniary form (i.e., leisure). Resources that could have otherwise been utilized to create new wealth become dissipated in the transfer of wealth, generating a negative-sum game. The consequences of such wealth dissipation are involuntarily borne by society, which is left poorer than if slavery did not exist.

Moreover, drawing this distinction between property and privilege further clarifies what is a paradoxical conclusion drawn by the New History of Capitalism, namely that economic development, which implies a creation of wealth across society based on private property, is according to their analysis predicated on the privilege of slave owning, and therefore a zero-sum game. This is not to deny the seen effect that slavery had by enriching a landed elite in the antebellum South, but enriching a concentrated interest group in the form of a landed elite is not synonymous with economic development. Moreover, because such concentration of wealth was predicated not on private property, but on private privilege, the unseen effect of slavery are the costs dispersed upon slaves *as well as* the masses of the population in terms of foregone wealth from those individuals failing to realize their full potential. This implies a negative-sum outcome resulting from slavery, rather than a zero-sum outcome that the New History of Capitalism would conclude.

Putting aside the rent-seeking costs associated with slavery, Eric Hilt writes that:

> … most [New Historians of Capitalism] seem aware of Robert Fogel and Stanley Engerman's *Time on the Cross* (1974), and some repeat its arguments about the profitability of slavery or the efficiency of slave plantations. But they do not seem to have taken seriously the debates among economic historians that followed the publication of that book (e.g., David & Temin, 1974, 1979). Some of the literature has challenged Fogel and Engerman's claims regarding scale economies in plantation agriculture and the role of gang labor (Hilt, 2017: 520).

In the next section, we will engage the points raised by Hilt by reframing them in terms of the another conceptual distinction between *generalized increasing returns* and *increasing returns to scale* that has been completely overlooked not only by the New Historians of Capitalism, but also economists as well.

Constitutional Implications of Alternative Models of Increasing Returns for the New History of Capitalism

Up until now, one may be dismissive of the distinction drawn between private property and privilege as semantic, with little, if any, positive implications for making welfare comparisons between a liberal market order, constituted by free labor, and market for the labor of human beings (i.e., slavery). After all, under slavery, title over human beings were being exchanged in slave markets, thereby fulfilling the distinguishing characteristic of private property from other forms of property, namely the ability to exchange (Alchian, 1965). Therefore, the potential objection that could be raised here is that there is only a semantic difference being drawn over *different initial assignments of title* over private property in labor, or property in free labor assigned in terms of self-ownership, and slavery assigned in terms of one individual being assigned ownership over another's labor (and human capital). Moreover, this might also imply that private property rights have little to do, fundamentally, with explaining the positive-sum and emancipatory effects of increasing the scope of voluntary exchange between individuals. Then on what theoretical basis can we object to the implicit assumption by New Historians of Capitalism that capitalism is a zero-sum game predicated on transfers of wealth from the institution of slavery? Moreover, if the conclusion that economic growth in the United States and the West as a whole is premised on the superior efficiency of the institution of slavery relative to free labor, then upon what welfare criterion can we falsify this conclusion?

Although not writing in the context of engaging the literature on the New History of Capitalism, an important but much neglected article by Lawrence White (2008) on the economics of slavery provides an answer that has important positive implications for the conclusions drawn by the New History of Capitalism. Writing in the context of the literature responding to Fogel and Engerman that slavery is in fact less economically efficient than free labor (David & Temin, 1974, 1979; David et al., 1976; Hummel, 1996; Tullock, 1967b; Wright, 2017), White explains that the use of the term "efficiency" has provoked much confusion over the welfare economics of slavery.

According to standard welfare economics, the first fundamental welfare theorem states that, given an initial set of endowments, any economy in general competitive equilibrium is Pareto-efficient. The second fundamental welfare theorem states that a Pareto-efficient outcome could be achieved through the decentralized market mechanism with transfers of endowments (Boettke, 2012: 274–275; Mas-Collel et al., 1995: 549, 551). Thus, a Pareto-efficient outcome implies that, *given* an initial assignment of property rights over endowments, in this case over labor and human capital, all the potential gains from trade will be exhausted (White, 2008: 329). Based upon Pareto efficiency criterion, or Kaldor-Hicks criterion,[6] according to White, he correctly identifies that such allocative efficiency criteria are not about comparisons between initial sets of property rights assignments (in the case between free labor and slave labor) before exchange, but comparisons between *outcomes* of exchange. Taking an initial assignment of property rights as a set of *constraints*, then maximizing behavior will imply that all potential gains from trade will be exhausted, such that all parties within such constraints will be incentivized to minimize rent dissipation, net of transaction costs. Therefore, *from the standpoint of the givenproperty rights assignments*, it cannot be said that a slave-owning property rights assignment is no less efficient than a self-ownership property right assignment (ibid.: 328).

White's conclusion must be qualified in three important respects, which have important *constitutional* implications for the distinction between *increasing returns to scale* and *generalized increasing returns*. First, the claim that a system of free labor and slave labor are both allocatively efficient, given their constraints, does not deny moral objections to slavery. As White states, by "denying initial self-ownership, slavery dehumanizes the slave. Under slavery, owned humans have the property status of owned horses. There are ample moral objections to be raised against such a system. Finding it *Pareto inefficient* is not one of them. That some men have no initial self-ownership rights (but instead owned by other men as chattels) is no more a matter of *Pareto inefficiency* than that some men are less endowed than others with land or any resource" (ibid.: 331; emphasis in original). Second, none of this implies that enforcing the institutional arrangements of slavery does not entail rent-seeking wastes associated with expenditures by slaveowners to prevent escape or coerce work effort *when compared to* an initial assignment of property rights in self-ownership of one's labor (ibid.: 333). However, from "a slave-owning system's *own* terms, these are wastes only by the 'nirvana' standard of a world in which property titles are costlessly enforced" (ibid.: 336; emphasis original). Judging from within the initial constraints, the notion that enforcement of property rights in slave labor are rent-seeking costs "are no more wasteful with respect to human slaves than with respect to horses" (ibid.).

Third, and most importantly for my argument here, the relevance of any welfare criterion, Pareto optimality, is not based upon welfare assessments between different sets distributions or allocations of resources, but upon different sets of *rules* or institutional arrangements that generate different patterns of distribution and allocation of resources (Buchanan, 1962). This final point is directly related to the distinction between the increasing returns to scale and generalized increasing returns, which is the focal point of my argument. Within the context of slavery, the relative efficiency of slave labor, according to Fogel and Engerman, and which the New Historians of Capitalism has implicitly accepted, is that the productive efficiency of slave labor in the antebellum South was predicated on: (1) increasing returns to scale, or "economies of scale" as they put it; and (2) the relative inelasticity of demand for slave labor in agriculture (Fogel & Engerman, [1974a] 1989: 234). The first point suggests, as they've written later clarifying their position, was based on greater intensity of labor per hour, not more hours of labor per day nor more days of labor per year, nor even more intensive use of land (Fogel & Engerman, 1977: 293). Even if their productivity estimates are not correct, then *given the absence of self-ownership*, the fact that "free labor was a very poor substitute for slave labor" (Fogel & Engerman, [1974a] 1989: 235) implies that a slave's leisure time is lower in *market* value than for a free laborer, given not only the compensating differential that the slave-owners would have to pay to bid free laborers to bid them away from their freedom, but also the inability of a slaves to bid for their own leisure in the market compared to as a free laborer. The economic logic therefore implies that longer working hours for slaves are not only consistent with allocative efficiency, but also consistent with the notion that American capitalism is predicated on economies of scale realized through slave labor in agriculture. Moreover, assessments over the relative efficiency of slavery are about distributions and allocations of resources *within a given set of constraints*.

However, an institution, whether it is deliberately constructed at a moment in time, or has evolved and been modified over time, is based on a the fundamental element of human choice, even if not by human design. The institution of slavery is not an artifact of given constraints endowed by nature, but a particular set of social relations, the existence of which is *variable* and therefore predicated on human choice, not on the part of the enslaved of course, but on the part of the enslavers to perpetuate this system. This raises an additional technical economic point that is overlooked, and must be made explicit, regarding the economic benefits associated with economies of scale. In order for economies of scale to become generalized increasing returns, *then this means that all factors of production must actually be variable, including the extent of the market itself*.

This directs our attention to the economics of slavery from a standpoint of constitutional political economy. Up until now, the welfare analysis has been based upon an analysis of human interaction within an initial assignment of property rights, but constitutional political economy entails a "higher-level" of analysis regarding *choice* over the rules themselves, in this case rules governing choice over the assignment of property rights *and* the consequences of their allocation. If, as James Buchanan argues, that the Pareto-optimality criterion rests fundamentally on unanimous agreement over the choice of rules, then in the case of slavery, to the extent that the *choice* of this particular rule governing the exchange of property rights is not unanimously selected, will by definition create negative externalities, as Tullock (1967b) and Wright (2017) argue. The associated negative externalities are due to the fact that too many resources, in this case coerced labor, are being utilized to realize increasing returns to scale, at the unseen cost of such resources (labor and human capital) not realizing generalized increasing returns to extending the scope of the market through *self-directed* entrepreneurship of one's own labor and human capital. In other words, the negative externalities associated with choosing to assign *privileges* in the form of slave labor are the social costs of which slaveowners are not liable, and involuntarily borne by future generations of individuals that are not party to that choice and will not benefit from the benefits of generalized increasing returns. Restrictions in the ability to exchange among individuals held in bondage must therefore come at the unseen cost of contracting the scope of market exchange, forgoing the realization of increasing returns to widening the scope of exchange between individuals.

The Emancipatory Effect of Generalized Increasing Returns: A Historical Account

"Although African Americans were largely excluded from the booming industrial sector of the late-nineteenth-century economy," historian Joe William Trotter Jr. (2000: 21), states, "they nonetheless used their newly won freedom to participate in the proliferation of mechanical innovations during the industrial era. Under the impact of emancipation, civil rights laws, and constitutional amendments, African Americans made the transition from slave to citizen and gained the right to patent their own inventions."

This political transition from slave to citizen can best be understood through the emancipatory effect of generalizing increasing returns, which entails an economic transition from privilege to private property, the cosmopolitan by-products of which include the promotion of mutual toleration among heterogenous individuals and their emancipation from being privileged or confined by arbitrary discretion based on legal status, race, creed, gender, or sexual orientation (Pipes, 1999).[7] Generalized increasing returns depends upon on ever-widening scope of exchange that does not preclude individuals from productively specializing under the division of labor. This does not deny that private property creates exclusionary boundaries around non-owners of a good or service, including one's own labor, but such boundaries are a means by which to create a focal point of decision-making in order for individuals to *learn how* to socially cooperate under the division of labor by reinforcing norms of trust, honesty, and integrity (Choi & Storr, 2022; Storr & Choi, 2019). Thus, whereas private property rights provide a framework for the *possibility* of emancipation, generalized increasing returns is the mechanism for its *realization*.

The realization of generalized increasing returns is both radically individualizing and radically social. By harnessing the collective knowledge among the millions of minds of individuals through social cooperation of the division of labor, generalized increasing returns allows individuals to discover opportunities for self-directed human flourishing that would not otherwise exist independent of such social interaction, and that the individual could not otherwise anticipate for himself or herself. Restrictions in the ability to exchange among individuals held in bondage must therefore come at the unseen cost of contracting the scope of market exchange, forgoing the realization of increasing returns to widening the scope of exchange between individuals. This is because, as illustrated in the historical case studies below, what is foregone by individuals continuing to be held in bondage is the realization of their creativity and talent through productive specialization and exchange. This is illustrated in the historical case studies of Elijah McCoy and Dr. Daniel Hale Williams.

The "Real McCoy": The Story of Elijah McCoy

Generalized increasing returns not only unleashes economic prosperity by tapping into the entrepreneurial talent of marginalized individuals who, without private property in their labor and entrepreneurial talent, would have been precluded from the division of labor. That entrepreneurial market process, in turn, expands the scope of market exchange among individuals who would otherwise be precluded from the benefits of commerce based upon their race, creed, gender, or sexual orientation. The case of Elijah McCoy, an inventor who revolutionized the railroad industry, is demonstrative of the emancipatory effects of commerce. Born the son of recently escaped slaves in Colchester, a town in Ontario, Canada, on May 2, 1843, McCoy's family would later return to the United States, settling in Ypsilanti, Michigan, just west of Detroit. From a young age, McCoy demonstrated great potential in his understanding and tinkering of machinery, beginning his career as a mechanical engineer with an apprenticeship in Edinburgh, Scotland (Folsom, 1999: 29).

Upon returning to the United States, in spite of his education and training, racial discrimination would relegate him to finding employment as a locomotive fireman for the Michigan Central Railroad, in which he shoveled coal into the firebox of locomotive steam engines (Cross, 2014: 77). The profit motive in the railroad industry did not prevent the injustice of racial discrimination, resulting in a market failure to realize the potential gains from utilizing McCoy's talent. The potential for generalized increasing returns, however, created the basis for McCloy to realize a future profit opportunity by first productively specializing his knowledge in locomotives, the by-product of which was to discover a pioneering technological innovation.

One of the features of realizing generalized increasing returns, according to Adam Smith, is that a "great part of the machines made use of in those manufactures in which labour is most subdivided, were originally the inventions of common workmen, who, being each of them employed in some very simple operation, naturally turned their thoughts towards finding out easier and readier methods of performing it" (Smith, [1776] 1981: 20). Illustrative of this observation by Smith, McCoy would come to realize the solution to a problem in the form of a technological breakthrough that revolutionized the railroad industry. Besides shoveling coal as a locomotive fireman, McCoy was also tasked to oiling the steam engine in order keep it running from wear and tear, as well as to prevent overheating. However, this lubrication process required trains to make frequent stops. This technological inefficiency resulted in McCoy discovering an invention, which was "a lubricating cup consisting of a piston set inside an oil-filled constrainer" (Spangenburg & Moser, 2003: 177). This allowed for a regular and steady supply of oil that kept the steam engine lubricated without stopping.

This invention, which would become known as the "McCoy Lubricator" patented in 1872, is also the origin of the phrase "the real McCoy" for reasons explained below. Railroad companies, at first, "refused to have anything to do with a device invented by a black man, no matter how useful it might be" (Spangenburg & Moser, 2003: 177–178). As a result, others tried to imitate his invention, but to no avail. Both because his original design was of such high quality, and his constant adaption and improvement of his design to steam engines and other machines outside the railroad industry, from ocean liners to factories, this caused concerned buyers to ask, "is this the real McCoy?", to make sure they were not purchasing inferior substitutes of McCoy's invention (ibid.). Whereas, at the beginning of his career, McCoy had to overcome racial discrimination from whites, by the end of his life, McCoy's technological innovation created a market for lubrication devices, the demand for which prompted him to open in 1920, at the age of 77, the Elijah McCoy Manufacturing Company, formed with the financial backing by investors.

In the words of Montesquieu, "[c]ommerce cures destructive prejudices, and it is an almost general rule that everywhere there are gentle mores, there is commerce and that everywhere there is commerce, there are gentle mores" ([1748] 1989: 338). While secure private property and freedom of contract under the rule of law precludes arbitrary discretion, they do not guarantee that all mutually beneficial trades will not go unrealized due to intolerance, bigotry, or outright hate. While individuals may not be color blind, the case of Elijah McCoy illustrates that commerce cannot turn a blind eye to outstanding human potential, regardless of a person's race. Moreover, McCoy's exploits also illustrate is that generalized increasing returns *depends upon* the emancipation of marginalized groups of individuals in society, and facilitates its realization by promoting tolerance and raising the cost of discriminating against previously unknown trading partners.

Dr. Daniel Hale Williams and the First Open-Heart Surgery

"The difference of natural talents in different men is," according to Adam Smith, "in reality, much less than we are aware of; and the very different genius which appears to distinguish men of different professions, when grown up to maturity, *is not upon many occasions so much the cause as the effect of the divisionof labour*" (Smith, [1776] 1981: 28; emphasis added). One example used by Buchanan to illustrate this point is the emergence of barbers and surgeons as separate professions as a by-product of generalized increasing returns (Buchanan, 1994: 14). For example, in the Middle Ages, there was no distinction between the profession of a barber and that of a surgeon, both of which had been practiced as a single profession. However, an expanding market increases the returns to specialization that has generated a sharp differentiation between the two professions. Moreover, as Smith suggests, generalized increasing returns is emancipatory by expanding the choice of professions available to individuals, regardless of their race, creed, gender, or sexual orientation, leaving individuals free to productively specialize through their own effort.

The incredible story of Dr. Daniel Hale Williams, affectionately known as "Dr. Dan," exemplifies this point as an individual who started out as a barber and would later become a well-respected surgeon, particularly famous as a pioneer in modern medicine, when he successfully performed open heart surgery in 1893. That same year, he would save the life of President Grover Cleveland, who was diagnosed with a rapidly progressing form of cancer known as *verrucous carcinoma*, by successfully removing the tumor from his mouth, a feat still marveled by doctors today.[8]

Born to free blacks of mixed white, black, and Indian ancestry, Williams was born on January 18, 1856, in Hollidaysburg, Pennsylvania. His father, Daniel Williams, who unfortunately died when Dr. Dan was 11-year-old boy, had been a barber by profession. Eventually, Dr. Dan would also take up his father's profession. Working in Janesville, Wisconsin, for a barber named Charles Anderson, who recognized the skill and dexterity that Daniel had with his hands, he was encouraged to continue his education. But by no means, however, did this predestine him to become a surgeon. It was working for Charles Anderson that he met a local doctor, Dr. Henry Palmer, a Union Army surgeon that eventually became the Surgeon General in Wisconsin. Palmer would also recognize Daniel's intelligence and agile hands. It was through Palmer's discussions as he cut his hair that Williams would decide to pursue a medical profession. Beginning first as Dr. Palmer's assistant, Williams would eventually receive his medical degree from Northwestern University in 1883, where he remained an instructor of anatomy (Spangenburg & Moser, 2003: 223). This was a testament of his exceptional ability, as it was highly unusual to appoint black instructors at the time (Tokunage, 1955: 153). It was during his studies that surgery would become his area of specialization, and he became one of Chicago most sought-after surgeons.

In the course of his career, Dr. Dan utilized his talent and professional reputation to break color barriers and create opportunities to benefit individuals of color in the medical profession. In 1891, Dr. Dan realized his dream of opening Provident Hospital in Chicago, noted not only for admitting patients of all colors and staffed by black and white doctors, but also for providing the first training school for black nurses in the United States. In 1894, he was appointed by President Grover Cleveland as Surgeon-in-Chief of Freedman's General Hospital in Washington, D.C., a hospital originally established after the Civil War to provide medical care to freed slaves (Spangenburg & Moser, 2003: 224).

What this implies is that the source of differences in specialization, and hence of choice of profession, is not based on differences in color. "Even in a world of equals," Buchanan and Yoon state, "trade offers mutuality of gain. There is no need for participants in the economic nexus to differ one from another" (Buchanan & Yoon, 2000: 43). Generalized increasing returns are emancipatory in the sense no individual's profession is predestined by legal status, let alone their race, creed, gender, or sexual orientation. Moreover, nothing about Dr. Dan preordained him to remain a barber or become a doctor. Rather, the choice of his profession was realized in the process of productive specialization itself. Yet, had Williams (or McCoy) been born slaves, we may have never benefited from the realization of their own potential.

Conclusion

The liberal project of emancipation, based upon the right to private property and emancipatory effects of generalized increasing returns, is an "imperfect" project. However, continued misunderstandings with respect to the economics of slavery and criticisms of capitalism made by the New History of Capitalism have completely negated this emancipatory story. The answer to such criticisms is not to reframe the emancipatory message of liberalism but to reflect on what it means for the project to be "imperfect." Whereas the New Historians of Capitalism see capitalism to be imperfect in the sense of being hopelessly flawed by the institution of private property, my argument here is that such misunderstandings have been based on a conflation between private property and privilege. The very feature of the liberal project of emancipation is that it is indeed imperfect, but in the sense of being *incomplete* or *not thoroughly done* and therefore in constant realization of untapped human potential. The emancipatory effects of capitalism based on the institutionalization of private property, and the erosion of privilege, which has liberated human beings from the physical constraints imposed upon us by nature in the form of scarcity, and from the social and political constraints imposed upon individuals through discrimination, arbitrary discretion, and privilege. Generalized increasing returns explains why economic development can only occur by emancipating the most marginalized individuals in society and harnessing their creative powers through an ever-widening scope of productive specialization and exchange.

Acknowledgements Special thanks to Mikalya Novak and the anonymous referees for their valuable feedback and comments, which significantly improved an earlier draft of this chapter. Any remaining errors are entirely my own.

Notes

1. See also Boettke and Candela (2017).
2. To illustrate the conservative, anti-capitalist defenses of slavery at the time, consider the arguments made by George Fitzhugh, a Virginian not of affluence but tied to the Southern planter class, who, in his book *Cannibals All!* ([1857] 1960), defends slavery not only as a "positive good," but as a universally necessary institution stating: "Southern slavery has become a benign and protective institution,

and our negroes are professedly better than any free laboring population in the world" (ibid.: 201). In his defense of slavery, Fitzhugh utilized Marxist socialist doctrine in his disdain for capitalism and for his regard of slavery as protective and humane institution. From the title of his book, "cannibals" refers to those who attempt to exploit the labor of others, which would refer to everyone, implying that individuals live in Hobbesian state of nature. He therefore considers slavery as a protective instruction, appealing to the notion of Southern slavery as neo-feudal social order, in which masters are lords providing protection to his serfs.

3. For a broader theory that explains this transition point, but encompasses monopoly privileges more generally, see Tollison and Wagner (1991).
4. For an earlier exposition of this conceptual point, see Tullock (1967b).
5. For an excellent overview on Gordon Tullock's contributions to the economics of slavery, see also Magness et al. (2023).
6. An allocation of resources is said to be Kaldor-Hicks efficient "when no reallocation remains unmade in which the gainers could in principle fully compensate the losers" (White, 2008: 329).
7. For an empirical case study illustrative of this notion of property rights as human rights (Novak, 2023).
8. Unbeknownst to him, as a matter of secrecy, Williams was not informed of Cleveland's identity, and therefore made the operation in complete anonymity. See Reed (2021).

References

Alchian, A. A. (1965). Some Economics of Property Rights. *Il Politico, 30*(4), 816–829.

Baptist, E. E. (2014). *The Half Has Never Been Told: Slavery and the Making of American Capitalism.* Basic Books.

Bastiat, F. (1996). *Economic Sophisms.* Foundation for Economic Education.

Baumol, W. J. (1990). Entrepreneurship: Productive, Unproductive, and Destructive. *Journal of Political Economy, 98*(5), 893–921.

Beckert, S. (2014). *Empire of Cotton: A Global History.* Knopf.

Blackburn, R. (2011). *The American Crucible: Slavery, Emancipation and Human Rights.* Verso.

Boettke, P. J. (2012). *Living Economics: Yesterday, Today, and Tomorrow*. Independent Institute.

Boettke, P. J., & Candela, R. A. (2017). The Liberty of Progress: Increasing Returns, Institutions, and Entrepreneurship. *Social Philosophy and Policy, 34*(2), 136–163.

Buchanan, J. M. (1962). The Relevance of Pareto Optimality. *Journal of Conflict Resolution, 6*(4), 341–354.

Buchanan, J. M. (1994). *Ethics and Economic Progress*. University of Oklahoma Press.

Buchanan, J. M., & Yoon, Y. J. (1995). Constitutional Implications of Alternative Models of Increasing Returns. *Constitutional Political Economy, 6*(2), 191–196.

Buchanan, J. M., & Yoon, Y. J. (2000). A Smithian Perspective on Increasing Returns. *Journal of the History of Economic Thought, 22*(1), 43–48.

Candela, R. A. (2021). Steve Pejovich's Insights into Property Rights, Capitalism, Socialism and Freedom. *Independent Review, 26*(2), 307–313.

Candela, R. A. (2022). The Division of Labor and Knowledge Is Limited by the Division of Ownership Over the Ultimate Resource: The Role of Economies of Scope in Julian Simon. *Review of Austrian Economics, 35*(3), 323–341.

Choi, G. S., & Storr, V. H. (2022). The Market as a Process for the Discovery of Whom Not to Trust. *Journal of Institutional Economics, 18*(3), 467–482.

Coyne, C. J., & Leeson, P. T. (2004). The Plight of Underdeveloped Countries. *Cato Journal, 24*(3), 235–249.

Cross, K. J. (2014). The Impact of African American Engineers on Contemporary Life: Remembering Who We Are. *Black History Bulletin, 77*(2), 22–27.

David, P. A., Gutman, H. G., Sutch, R., Temin, P., Wright, G., & Stampp, K. M. (1976). *Reckoning with Slavery: A Critical Study in the Quantitative History of American Negro Slavery*. Oxford University Press.

David, P. A., & Temin, P. (1974). Slavery: The Progressive Institution? *Journal of Economic History, 34*(3), 739–783.

David, P. A., & Temin, P. (1979). Explaining the Relative Efficiency of Slave Agriculture in the Antebellum South: A Comment. *American Economic Review, 69*(1), 213–218.

Demsetz, H. (1967). Toward a Theory of Property Rights. *American Economic Review, 57*(2), 347–359.

Fitzhugh, G. ([1857] 1960). *Cannibals All! Or, Slaves Without Masters*. Belknap Press.

Fogel, R. W., & Engerman, S. F. ([1974a] 1989). *Time on the Cross: The Economics of American Negro Slavery*. W. W. Norton.

Fogel, R. W., & Engerman, S. F. ([1974b] 1989). *Time on the Cross: Evidence and Methods, a Supplement*. W. W. Norton.

Fogel, R. W., & Engerman, S. L. (1977). Explaining the Relative Efficiency of Slave Agriculture in the Antebellum South. *American Economic Review, 67*(3), 275–296.

Folsom, B. (1999). Elijah McCoy and Berry Gordy: Ingenuity Overcomes. *The Freeman: Ideas on Liberty, 49*(1), 29–31.

Geloso, V., & Glock, J. (2021). The New History of Capitalism and the Methodologies of Economic History. *Essays in Economic & Business History, 39*, 207–221.

Hayek, F. A. (1960). *The Constitution of Liberty*. University of Chicago Press.

Hayek, F. A. ([1944] 1994). *The Road to Serfdom: Fiftieth Anniversary Edition*. University of Chicago Press.

Hilt, E. (2017). Economic History, Historical Analysis, and the 'New History of Capitalism.' *Journal of Economic History, 77*(2), 511–536.

Hummel, J. R. (1996). *Emancipating Slaves, Enslaving Free Men: A History of the American Civil War*. Open Court.

Levy, D. M. (2001a). How the Dismal Science Got Its Name: Debating Racial Quackery. *Journal of the History of Economic Thought, 23*(1), 5–35.

Levy, D. M. (2001b). *How the Dismal Science Got Its Name: Classical Economics and the Ur-Text of Racial Politics*. University of Michigan Press.

Magness, P. W., Carden, A., & Murtazashvili, I. (2023). Gordon Tullock and the Economics of Slavery. *Public Choice, 197*(1–2), 185–199.

Mas-Collel, A., Whinston, M. D., & Green, J. R. (1995). *Microeconomic Theory*. Oxford University Press.

Mill, J. S. ([1848] 2006). *Collected Works of John Stuart Mill, Vol. II: Principles of Political Economy*. Liberty Fund.

Montesquieu, C. L. de S. ([1748] 1989). *The Spirit of the Laws*. Cambridge University Press.

Novak, M. (2023). Constitutional Catallaxy and Indigenous Rights: The Australian Case. *Journal of Institutional Economics, 19*(1), 36–51.

Pipes, R. (1999). *Property and Freedom: The Story of How Through the Centuries Private Ownership Has Promoted Liberty and the Rule of Law*. Knopf.

Reed, L. W. (2021, February 10). *Two Miraculous Surgeries of 1893: A Successful Human Heart Operation and Removing a President's Tumor*. Foundation for Economic Education. https://fee.org/articles/two-historic-surgeries-of-1893-the-first-successful-human-heart-operation-and-removing-a-presidents-tumor

Smith, A. ([1776] 1981). *An Inquiry into the Nature and Causes of the Wealth of Nations*. Liberty Fund.

Spangenburg, R., & Moser, K. (2003). *African Americans in Science, Math, and Invention*. Facts on File.

Storr, V. H., & Choi, G. S. (2019). *Do Markets Corrupt Our Morals?* Palgrave Macmillan.

Tokunage, M. (1955). Contribution of the Negro to Science and Invention. *Negro History Bulletin,18*(7), 153–154, 172.
Tollison, R. D., & Wagner, R. E. (1991). Romance, Realism and Economic Reform. *Kyklos, 44*(1), 57–70.
Trotter, J. W., Jr. (2000). African Americans and the Industrial Revolution. *OAH Magazine of History, 15*(1), 19–23.
Tullock, G. (1967a). The Welfare Costs of Tariffs, Monopolies and Theft. *Western Economic Journal, 5*(3), 224–232.
Tullock, G. (1967b). The Economics of Slavery. *Left and Right, 3*(2), 5–16.
von Mises, L. ([1922] 1981). *Socialism: An Economic and Sociological Analysis*. Liberty Fund.
von Mises, L. ([1949] 2007). *Human Action: A Treatise on Economics* (4th ed.). Liberty Fund.
White, L. H. (2008). Can Economics Rank Slavery Against Free Labor in Terms of Efficiency? *Politics, Philosophy & Economics, 7*(3), 327–340.
Wright, R. E. (2017). *The Poverty of Slavery: How Unfree Labor Pollutes the Economy*. Palgrave Macmillan.

CHAPTER 3

Buchanan's Theory of Emancipation: Artifactual Man in Perspective

Alain Marciano and John Meadowcroft

From the perspective of a narrow, but basic, definition of emancipation as freedom from oppression, James Buchanan would seem to qualify as an emancipatory thinker since he retained Frank Knight's definition of "freedom as the absence of coercion" (Buchanan, 1954: 340). On the other hand, however, Buchanan also defended free markets, in general and, more specifically, as means of promoting freedom and, by extension, as an important guarantee of the emancipation of individuals.[1] For the many critics of free markets and liberalism, who view markets as means

A. Marciano (✉)
Department of Economics and Statistics, University of Turin, Turin, Italy
e-mail: alain.marciano@unito.it

Karl Mittermaier Centre for Philosophy of Economics, University of Johannesburg, Johannesburg, South Africa

Mercatus Center at George Mason University, Fairfax, USA

J. Meadowcroft
King's College London, London, UK
e-mail: john.meadowcroft@kcl.ac.uk

M. Novak (ed.), *Liberal Emancipation*, Mercatus Studies in Political and Social Economy, https://doi.org/10.1007/978-3-031-94406-2_3

of oppression, rather than emancipation, this suggests Buchanan's work is hardly the place to find a genuine account of emancipation. Its disqualification might be settled once and for all by recalling, in case it has been forgotten, that Buchanan was one of the economists who invented the economic analysis of politics (public choice) and pioneered economic imperialism: to think of democracy, political participation, and elections in terms of self-interested utility-maximization does not seem obviously compatible with emancipation.

Yet, we aim to demonstrate in this chapter that one can find a real defence of emancipation in Buchanan's work. Our argument is that Buchanan cannot be said to defend emancipation merely because of his definition of freedom. His view on emancipation does not rest on a narrow definition of the concept. Hence, his contribution to the theory of freedom is not linguistic or semantic, but rather an expansive one that is perfectly captured by the distinction he made in an article published in 1979 between what he termed "artifactual" and "natural" man.

Buchanan claimed that individuals can adopt two distinct types of behaviours, or alternatively, that "man's behaviour" can be divided into two parts. First, what Buchanan called "natural" man. The behaviours he attributed to "natural man" are consistent with the behaviour an animal—a "dog" or a "squirrel" Buchanan wrote in his 1979 article—or perhaps a robot exhibits. More precisely, a natural individual or an individual behaving naturally does not consciously reject or accept the biological, genetic and also cultural constraints that weigh on his behaviour; he simply endures them and behaves within the frame they impose. Therefore, these constraints "rigidly" prevent natural man from becoming anything other than what he or she currently is, natural man cannot transcend what or who they are. Buchanan contends that an individual whose choices are set by their biological inheritance and cultural environment cannot be free, nor emancipated. He or she is an alienated human being—natural man is detached from their true nature as a human person.

There are circumstances, situations, that cannot be avoided, in which people must behave naturally. Therefore, some of the behaviours that human beings adopt are natural. They take place within constraints that are not or cannot be removed, such as the physical limits of the human body. This does not mean, however, that individuals must be completely alienated. If natural man thus "exist[s] in the human psyche," it is "along with many other men" (Buchanan, [1976b] 1979: 207). Natural man "need not reign supreme over other men" (ibid.). Emancipation is indeed possible, according to Buchanan. Human beings can behave as "artifactual man", which is Buchanan's account of the emancipated individual. For Buchanan, emancipation involved transcending one's biological and cultural inheritance.

"Artifactual man", on other hand, is a man who wants to become a "different" or "better" person than the person he is (Buchanan, 1979: 96–97). He has a "sense of becoming", and a willingness of "becoming different from what he is" (ibid.: 94). He is thus capable of imagining himself beyond what he is presently, and then to act in order to become what he imagines he could be. This explains the term artifact that Buchanan uses to characterize this type of individual: artifactual man "constructs himself through his own choices" (ibid.: 110). Therefore, in this perspective, artifactual man does not take all constraints as given or inescapable, constraints may be part of a process of construction; artifactual man may accept or reject constraints, but always in an active way. In other words, artifactual man is capable of choosing—and freeing himself from—the constraints that frame his life.

If we take natural man to be the alienated version of man, and artifactual man to be the emancipated one, then an understanding of Buchanan's theory of emancipation requires two steps. First, we need to understand what it takes for an individual to be an artifactual man, to escape the determinism of natural and cultural constraints. These conditions have already been briefly sketched out in the previous paragraph—the willingness and capacity to construct oneself and the capacity to escape constraints, freedom or "*liberty to become the man he wants to become*" (ibid.: 112; italics in original), but also responsibility towards oneself and towards others. Then, in a second step, we need to know how these conditions are implemented. Indeed, if emancipation is partly based on what the individuals want, the institutions that allow an individual to behave artifactually are particularly important. Hence, Buchanan's theory of emancipation has an institutional dimension.

By emphasizing both cultural and biological constraints, and the ability to free oneself from both, Buchanan's theory of emancipation stands squarely in the classical liberal tradition of John Stuart Mill (1859) who saw the opinions, values and judgements of others (what we might call "culture") as an important source of unfreedom. But Buchanan's emphasis on freedom from our biological inheritance pushes his theory beyond this and may refer to his ambiguous conception of human nature in which people are neither irredeemably bad nor entirely good (Buchanan, 1975b: 82–83). The natural-artifactual distinction suggests emancipation involves choosing to act on one's better nature, for example by writing a constitution that protects the liberty of all, rather than using politics to pursue one's own distributional advantage at the expense of others.

In the rest of this chapter, we discuss Buchanan's characterization of what it takes for a person to become an artifactual being in more detail, enriching Buchanan's views of the emancipated version of man, and then we discuss the institutional dimension in the second part of the chapter.

Behaviour *Versus* (Genuine) Choice

The first aspect of Buchanan's theory of emancipation, the first dimension that makes it possible to distinguish between natural and artifactual man, is the way in which each acts: natural man adopts behaviours from his biological or cultural inheritance; artifactual man is capable of making choices as to the life he lives. This theory is scattered in the various methodological works Buchanan wrote in the 1960s and early 1970s (Buchanan, 1964, 1966, 1969a, 1969b, 1976a, 1976b). These texts were mainly concerned with defining economics and delineating its subject matter. In the course of this analysis, Buchanan reached a point where he realized that economists need a theory of human behaviour. He therefore started to discuss how the different definitions of economics he identified rested on a specific theory of human behaviour. Buchanan (1964), as is well known, argued that economics was the science of exchange, rather than the science of choice, and that it should not be reduced to "an abstract science of human behaviour" (Buchanan, 1969a, 1969b). The individual of Buchanan's science of exchange is not the individual of the science of choice, the former being emancipated and the latter alienated (Marciano, 2009; Meadowcroft, 2023).

The individual that inhabits the models and theories of Buchanan's exchange paradigm is the individual who *behaves* as *homo œconomicus* or whose "psyche" is dominated by homo œconomicus (Buchanan, [1976b] 1979: 207). Buchanan was clear that in the economic-abstract-science-of-human-behaviour, "[w]hat we now confront is *behavior*, not choice" (Buchanan, [1969a] 1979: 44).

In economics as a science of choice, Buchanan explained, behaviour "implies acting but there is no reference to conscious selection from among alternatives" (ibid.: 40). This is consistent with the idea that "[b]ehavior can be predetermined" (ibid.), and therefore, obviously, "purely mechanical" (Buchanan, 1964: 218). A behaviour, i.e. the way of acting of natural man and *homo œconomicus,* is "programmed". It therefore consists of "direct response to stimuli" (ibid.: 44)—one therefore understands why Buchanan claims that this kind of behaviour is similar to that of an animal (or a robot). Or, another possible and significant illustration of the behaviour of natural man is the behaviour of a "consumer in a supermarket": an individual who is confined to a particular place, with a limited number of goods to choose from, and has therefore a problem to solve: select the best possible set of goods given his constraints (Buchanan, 1964: 216, 217). It is also, another of Buchanan's examples, the behaviour of a poker player who "choos[es] and implement[s] strategies within the rules that define the game" (Buchanan, 1991a: 154). Or it is the behaviour of any individual playing a game according to existing rules who chooses from the strategies to him. Natural man, or *homo œconomicus*, is the one "who must, when confronted with alternatives, select that which stands highest on his preference ranking, as evaluated in terms of a *numeraire*" (Buchanan, 1969a: 44).

Even if this behaviour gives the individual his or her highest possible level of utility, it is not emancipatory. Natural man, *homo œconomicus*, tries to solve a problem in which everything is given. First, the preferences—or the utility function—"known in advance", or the cost function to minimize, are given. This obviously implies that individuals cannot become something other than what they are; they cannot imagine themselves as being different from what or who they currently are. Second, the set of alternatives within which choice is made is also given, which means that individuals can (and have to) choose within this set. Typically, natural man cannot imagine a solution that is outside the set of given alternatives, like a non-human animal—"Given his constraints, and his utility function, the squirrel is not, and cannot be concerned with the size of his 'choice' set, with the existence or nonexistence of his rejected alternatives" (Buchanan, 1979: 111).

Therefore, the solution to the (economic) problem that this type of individual tries to solve is given, and it exists independently of the actual choice itself—even if the individual does not choose the best possible basket of goods, the unchosen goods remain the best possible basket of goods. But, if natural man wants to choose it, he must accept it. He cannot even *imagine* a different solution, that is a solution not given by the problem. He cannot *imagine* choosing from another supermarket, or playing poker with different rules that demand a different strategy. Even if the solution were "within the limits imposed by purely physical or natural constraints", natural man would not be able to envisage it; it would be "beyond the boundaries of behavioral feasibility" (Buchanan, 1995: 145). An individual facing this kind of problem is obviously alienated by the conditions of the choice—he must choose from a given set of alternatives that are outside his control. Hence, everything natural man does is perfectly predictable—the "acting unit responds to environmental stimuli in predictably unique fashion" (Buchanan, [1969a] : 45)—predictable by any external observer who has the tools and means to observe individuals, so "behavior ... is subject to conceptually predictable laws" (ibid.: 44).

Artifactual man, Buchanan's emancipated version of man, differs from natural man in that he or she makes "genuine choice[s]" (Buchanan, [1969a] 1979: 44).[2] Buchanan is not particularly forthcoming about the nature of these choices. We mainly derive their content from what Buchanan said about the behaviour of natural man. Genuine choices, then, are those choices that are not obviously predetermined or predictable: "Choice, by its nature, cannot be predetermined and remain choice" (ibid.: 40). Or, in other words, a "genuine choice is confronted only in world of uncertainty" (Buchanan, 1969: 89). Uncertainty because the elements that make up the choice—the set of alternatives and the preferences or utility function—are not given in advance. Artifactual man does not only respond to stimuli. Or, to use similar words as above, artifactual man is not trying to solve an economic problem of the allocation of scarce resources.

Utility functions, for one thing, are not given because they do not "exist independently from the acting-choosing process" (Buchanan, [1976a] 1979: 88). Similarly, values and costs cannot be estimated independently of the act of choice itself (Buchanan, 1969). Therefore, making genuine choices cannot consist in maximizing a given utility function; it does not mean "act[ing] as if... maximizing a utility function subject to constraints" ([1976a] 1979: 87). Making genuine choices means escaping "the automatic routine that utility maximization, as normally presented, seems to embody" (Buchanan, 1979: 100). But this does not imply that artifactual man behaves irrationally. Rather, rationality assumes a different form. Natural man, as seen above, is rational because he maximizes a utility function under various constraints. Artifactual man is rational because he is *purposive*. He is "making ordinary choices for more rather than less" (Buchanan, [1966] 1979: 120). He is guided by the ends and goals that he is striving to achieve,[3] ends and goals that are however not given. Artifactual man is therefore capable of imagining having different preferences from those he has now. It is significant that one of Buchanan's original examples of the actions of an artifactual man was the decision of a smoker to stop smoking and become a different person—to imagine adopting the identity of and then acting to become a non-smoker (Buchanan, 1979: 253).

Indeed, if artifactual man is the individual who constructs himself—i.e. in other words, an individual capable of *self-construction*—then he has to be "autonomous"—capable of choosing his own ends and goals—and therefore capable of "self-governance" (Buchanan, 2006: 12–14). The point is important: self-governance also means the capacity to choose the constraints in which choices are made. The absence of a given objective function to maximize, therefore the capacity to change one's preferences, would not be emancipatory if artifactual man still chose from a set of given alternatives, that is if the constraints were given. Buchanan insisted on this aspect of human agency. To Buchanan, an individual who makes choices "has a clear interest in seeing that the choice set ... remains as open as is naturally possible, and, if constrained, then the constraints be also of his own choosing" (Buchanan, 1979: 111). Making genuine choices implies a capacity and willingness to "choose their own constraints" including a capacity and willingness "to impose constraints or limits on their own behavior" (Buchanan, 1990: 3).[4]

Obviously, making genuine choices—and therefore to be or behave as an artifactual man—does not and cannot imply escaping *all* constraints, only some. Buchanan described choosing one's own constraints "at least to a degree and within some limits" (Buchanan, 1990: 3). Buchanan mentioned this aspect in particular in reference to some "social states" that could "be imagined by people" but that "cannot be brought into existence as emergent outcomes under any possible assignment of rights" (ibid.). But one must think of Shackle, who influenced Buchanan when he wrote "Natural and Artifactual Man" and for whom choice depends on imagination (Buchanan, 1979: 101; also Lewis & Dold, 2020: 1164). This means what is imagined has to be possible. Choices, in Shackle's mind, though creative/non-deterministic, are nevertheless bounded by constraints, what Shackle called "the imagined, deemed possible" (Lewis, 2017: 5, 19).[5]

This view of the capacity of artifactual men to make choices that lead to new alternatives from which future choices will be made logically leads to Buchanan's dynamic conceptualization of economics and politics as mediums of exchange from which emerge hitherto unforeseen outcomes that become new bases for future exchanges. Two unequal individuals may agree an "exchange" of rights that enables the stronger to capture most of the product of the weaker, for example, but it also offers the basis for a new agreement that may enable the weaker to keep more of his produce if the stronger also benefits from increased future productivity. Hence, exchange was a dynamic process in which both parties tried to change the alternatives available in the future (Buchanan, 1975b, 1975c, 1977; Congleton, 2014; Meadowcroft, 2023).

This is particularly important in Buchanan's analysis of individual behaviour and how it relates to constitutional agreement: emancipated individuals make choices, but they do not so much choose the goods and objects they will consume than choose the means to select these goods. Individuals are therefore emancipated when their choice bears on the availability of alternatives rather than on the alternatives themselves. In the constitutional context, Buchanan is clear: "each of us, as a citizen, has an *ethical obligation* to enter directly and/or indirectly into an ongoing and continuing constitutional dialogue" (Buchanan, 1991a: 154). When individuals make *constitutional* choices that relate to the available alternatives and the rules of the game, they behave as artifactual men and are therefore emancipated.[6]

Independence *Versus* Interdependence

Emancipation necessarily has a social or collective dimension. Whether or not individuals can choose the available alternatives, that is being alienation and emancipation, has consequences for the way individuals relate to and interact with each other. Related to the distinction between choice of and between alternatives is the distinction between two modes of interaction with others.

The first mode, which is alienating, is the consequence of how natural man behaves. An individual with given preferences, which he seeks to satisfy by choosing items (goods or objects) from a given set of alternatives, is himself a tool that produces satisfaction. This individual-tool treats others as tools, too. Natural man, thus, treats others as suppliers of goods and therefore as part of the environment, of nature. He relates to them in an "instrumental way" (Khalil & Marciano, 2021), in the sense that he treats them as tools to achieve an end. They are external to him. In this sense, it can be said that natural man needs others, he is interested in others but not as persons, only because of the goods or objects they have that enable him to reach his ends. Other people do not really exist as other human beings but as suppliers of goods and objects. It might be interesting here to frame the discussion in the terms and concepts used by Martin Buber (1937) in his dialogic philosophy of human relationships. We could say that an individual—the "I"—engages with others as "it" (Khalil & Marciano, 2021).[7]

It is precisely because of this externality that natural man does not (and cannot) recognize the existence of interdependencies that bind him to others. He, natural man does not or cannot understand why he should adapt his behaviour to what others do, any more than he adapts his behaviour to the presence of others. He just uses them. In Buchanan's words, natural man behaves in a "non-strategic" way. In that case, each individual becomes a part of the others' maximization problem and, one might add, *not* part of the solution. This leads each natural man to treat others as means that can be used to achieve his ends (see Marciano & Meadowcroft, 2024). Natural man can be said to be a-social, in that he ignores others as human beings. The consumer in a supermarket, the poker player, the individual playing a game, do not care about others; they are instances of the typical natural man, the typical non-emancipated man: Robinson Crusoe. The latter, Buchanan explained:

> ... reacts to his natural habitat in a strictly scientific manner; he tries to maximize his own well-being, or utility, by bending nature to his will where possible. When Friday is present, we may model Crusoe's behavior to be motivationally unchanged. Crusoe might treat Friday as a new factor in his natural environment, a new subject to be utilized with the objective of enhancing Crusoe's well-being. (Buchanan, 2006: 14)

As Brough and Simmons (2023: 403) explain, the I-it relationship is fragmented, and therefore the "*I* can never relate to the *It* with the wholeness of his or her being". Therefore, they add, "there is no room for growth or development", and the I-it relationship is "static" (ibid.). In our terms, this kind of relationship is alienating. The *I* remains a natural man, a prisoner of the constraints within which he is born.

By contrast, and as described above, emancipation results from making genuine choices, which includes, as also mentioned, being able to choose one's preferences (one's ends), the constraints that limit our set of choices, and the rules of the game (which are the constitutional constraints). In this perspective, others are not external to the individual (to artifactual man). Individuals are no longer independent of others but, on the contrary, become *inter*dependent. Individuals "cannot treat other individuals as they can the physical environment" (Buchanan [1966] 1979: 120). The *I*, when he is an artifactual man, no longer relates to others as an it, as an external object, or in an instrumental way. He relates to others as what Buber called a "thou". Thus, to go back to Buchanan, when two individuals, Robinson Crusoe and Friday for instance, engage in a I-thou relationship, they recognize that they are "economically" and "ethically" interdependent (Buchanan, 1991b: 181). Being economically interdependent means that each individual understands that "[n]either person, acting on his or her own and independently, can do as well as he or she could do by engaging the other in exchange or trade" (ibid.). And being ethically interdependent implies that "[t]he separate behavior of one person… affects the utility of the other person unilaterally" (ibid.). This *I-thou* relationship is emancipatory because it is complete, rather than fragmented, in the sense that the *I* and the *thou*, the two individuals, treat each other as subjects. Their relationship is "existential" (Khalil & Marciano, 2021); they build their ends and how to reach them together. As Brough and Simmons (2023: 403) write, "[i]t is through a process of encounter in which individuals meet each other in mutuality that our full humanity is made manifest".

Robinson Crusoe and Friday, when they are caught in this "catallactic" emancipatory relationship necessarily change their behaviour. They begin to behave "strategically", that is, to take other people into account and adapt their behaviour to what others do. They no longer behave as if they have to solve an optimization problem in which the solution is actually given. They no longer treat others as means; the other individual becomes part of the solution. Each individual understands that the set of possible alternatives has increased because they can now both exchange with the other to improve their situation. The "artifactual" man is therefore a profoundly social being who constructs the set of alternatives with others via a process of exchange, and from this process he will choose what to consume.

Ethics and Ethical Behaviour

An important aspect of interacting with others is that individuals have the opportunity to trade and they are also connected to others. The presence of others implies interdependencies between their respective utility or production functions. The way individuals deal with these interdependencies is potentially alienating, or liberating, emancipatory. Buchanan distinguished between two types of behaviour that individuals can adopt, strategic (emancipatory) and non-strategic (alienating).

Non-strategic behaviour is alienating because it means that the individual follows his self-interest in the "narrow" (narrowest) or "pure" sense of the word. He follows, as Buchanan put it, "the private maxim" or "the expediency criterion" (Buchanan, 1965: 2). This meant "retain[ing] full freedom to act on the basis of expedient considerations in each particular instance that arises" (ibid.). This is exactly how Robison Crusoe treats Friday, as part of his environment, as described above. Buchanan explicitly states that this kind of behaviour was anti- or non-Kantian, because Robinson Crusoe treats Friday as a means—"In Kantian terms, Crusoe might treat Friday strictly as a means toward furtherance of his own ends" (Buchanan, 2006: 15). Thus, when Robinson Crusoe, or any individual for that matter, behaves independently from others, he behaves non-ethically. It can thus be said that natural man, *homo œconomicus*, the alienated man, behaves non-ethically.

By contrast, artifactual man behaves ethically. Artifactual man recognizes the interdependencies that exist and link each individual to others and therefore she takes others into account; as explained above, she adapts her behaviour to what others do—she behaves strategically. This means, to Buchanan, following "moral or ethical principles" (Buchanan, 1961: 340), or what Buchanan calls "the moral law" (Buchanan, 1965: 2). He described such behaviour in this way:

> ... By selecting the first, the individual commits himself to act in subsequent situations on the basis of something like the generalization principle. That is, he will not act in ways other than those which allow his particular action to be universalized, regardless of the specific consequences. (ibid.)

An emancipated individual follows, in Buchanan's parlance, a Kantian rule of action.

Responsibility

Buchanan's views on human nature, on the natural and artifactual man, are closely related to freedom and liberty. The natural man is not and cannot be free, his behaviour is determined by genetic and social constraints—"To rationalize or to explain choices in terms of either genetic endowments or social environment removes the elements of freedom and of responsibility" (Buchanan, 1979: 109). By contrast, the "artifactual" man needs and also "*wants liberty to become the man he wantsto become*" (Buchanan, 1979: 112; italics in original). Buchanan always defended individual freedom as a normative imperative. Freedom is crucial to guarantee the emancipation of human beings; in the absence of freedom, it is impossible to become an artifactual, emancipated man. But being free also implies responsibility.

This responsibility is, to start with, a responsibility towards oneself. This is the consequence of artifactual man's capacity to make genuine choices. Being autonomous and capable of self-governance, as discussed above, means having responsibility for oneself.

Individual responsibility necessarily extends to the choice of constitutions and constitutional rules at the social or collective level. For, if "we do not consciously choose… among structures or rules, how can we be responsible?" (Buchanan, 1991a: 153). And if we are not responsible, then "we acquiesce in the regime under which we live and simply do our best to behave rationally as we confront the pragmatically generated choices that emerge" (ibid.: 154). That is, put in the terms of the argument in this chapter, individuals who do not choose constitutional rules, the collective constraints that frame their lives, simply react to these constraints and therefore behave as natural men. An individual living in a political system who passively accepts the given rules and makes no attempt to engage in constitution-making is alienated.

This constitutional responsibility—what Buchanan called the "ethic of constitutional citizenship" (Buchanan, 1991a: 156)—obviously has a collective dimension but must not be confused with the responsibility towards others and the adoption of an "ethical behavior in interactions with other persons within the constraints imposed by the rules of an existing regime" (ibid.). Rules, to Buchanan, are no substitute for behaving ethically and following the Kantian principle of treating others as ends not means.[8] Rules, to be more precise, replace ethical principles when the latter no longer exist.

The importance of responsibility towards others, and its role in emancipation, can be illustrated by Buchanan's (1975a) analysis in "The Samaritan's Dilemma". In this essay, Buchanan explained that individuals, in the 1970s, have become weak and "soft"—"modern man has 'gone soft'" (ibid.: 75). This meant, Buchanan argued, that people had become weak in wanting to help people in need as soon as such a need was observed. The Samaritan, having identified a person in need, decides mechanically to help that person. He adopts a "pragmatic or independent behavioural *response* to the choice situation he faces" (ibid.: 72; emphasis added). It was a *response* because the Samaritan reacts to a stimulus; he follows the strategies of the game, choosing a strategy within the given rules of the game without trying to change the rules.

Thus, if one accepts the idea that mechanical choices are those of an alienated natural man, then the pragmatic, non-strategic behaviour of "modern man" is clearly the behaviour of an alienated individual. The Samaritan cannot be an "artifactual man" when and/or because he refuses to assume the responsibility that goes with being a Samaritan, that is the courage of not giving in to the "gratification of immediate desires" (ibid.: 83). To a certain extent, the Samaritan is afraid to be responsible. Complementarily, the Samaritan's help also alienates the recipient of his assistance because the person in need does not try to change his behaviour to bring about a change in his situation. Rather, the Samaritan's actions trap both individuals in an equilibrium of mutual dependence. The short-term benefits of the Samaritan's behaviour are outweighed by the long-term costs to both. The recipient becomes dependent on the Samaritan—the "softness" of the Samaritan creates a culture of dependency (Marciano & Meadowcroft, 2024: 831–839).

Both the Samaritan and the recipient are examples of individuals who are "afraid to be free" (Buchanan, 2005), and thus are afraid to be emancipated. They prefer to "escape, evade and even deny personal responsibilities" (ibid.: 19). Buchanan (ibid.) was indeed conscious that people were often reluctant to act on this personal responsibility, to incur short-term costs to ensure long-term benefits for themselves and others. Buchanan predicted that socialism would endure into the twenty-first century, not because people believed in the socialist project of material equality, but because socialism offered protection against the sometimes painful consequences of individual responsibility for others.

Emancipatory behaviour therefore consists in following an "ethics of responsibility ... akin to the Kantian generalization principle" (ibid.: 80).

Emancipatory, indeed, because the responsibility ethic precisely implies "fully recogniz[ing] the interdependence among behavior patterns" (ibid.). Such an ethic precisely means not succumbing to the gratification of instant desires—even the desire to help those in need. It is very similar to what Buchanan called a "Puritan ethic" (ibid.: 83). An ethic that allows the emancipation of the natural man and enables the shift towards the artifactual man because it implies making efforts to become a better person.

Institutions, Alienation and Emancipation

There is no doubt that, for Buchanan, the most obvious example of an alienated society was the USA of the early 1970s. Buchanan viewed it as an example of generalized Samaritan's dilemma that manifested itself both at the constitutional and at the post-constitutional level. No one, he thought, assumed the responsibilities that went with being what he would come to call artifactual man. The pathologies of American society were the consequence of a "loss of constitutional wisdom", of the "erosion of the ethical principal of constitutional responsibility" that then characterized his country (Buchanan, 1991b: 156).

Buchanan referred to this situation as a form of "anarchy", either "constitutional" (Buchanan, 1973, 1975c, 1991b) or "moral" (Buchanan, 1981). In those years, Buchanan did not use the term "anarchy" to characterize a peaceful situation, but rather the Hobbesian sense of the word (Buchanan 1973, 1975b, 1975c). To him, American society had become a "jungle" (Buchanan, 1975a: 45; 1975b: 19; 1978b: 31; 2006: 96). This did not mean a situation without rules, for rules did exist in the USA at this time, but a place where there was little respect for the existing rules. Buchanan linked "the emergence of anarchy in civil society" (Buchanan, 1986: 12) to a "mounting behavioral disorder" (ibid.). Anarchy was the consequence of how individuals were observed—Buchanan used the term several times—to behave without regard to the existence of others as ends in their own right. A few years later, he made this clear: "In moral anarchy, each person treats other persons exclusively as means to further his own ends or objectives" (Buchanan, 1981: 190).

The connection with the earlier discussion should be clear: this kind of behaviour means that individuals treat others as a means to satisfy their own ends because they focus on themselves, ignore the interdependencies that link them with others, and maximize their narrowly defined self-interest. They limit themselves to selecting what is "best" for themselves individually—"either in the terms of the individual's own interest or in terms of the individual's own version of some general interest" (Buchanan, 1991a: 156). In other words, they behave as natural man would. The implication is immediate. As natural men, American citizens were not (no longer) capable of reasoning in terms of constitutional rules—they act "without understanding, or even of consideration, of the rules that define the constitutional order" (ibid.: 157)—were thinking only in pragmatic terms—"restrict[ing] their attention to policy options within rules" (ibid.: 156). The moral anarchy, and then the constitutional anarchy, that Buchanan observed in America in the early 1970s, was therefore characteristic of a society of alienated men and women.

The first to behave as natural men were the elected officials, politicians and judges, who devised public policies without taking into account the effects on the political and constitutional structure. Public policies were instead based on the "*accidental* preferences of politicians in judicial, legislative and executive positions of power" (Buchanan, 1973: 6; 1975b: 19; italics added). "Accidental" meant that individuals, and their "rights", were "subject to the whims of politicians" (Buchanan, 1975b: 206). The term was also used to designate the fact that politicians were now responding to citizens' "demands for more public goods and services" (Buchanan, 1973: 7) without thinking of the constitutional aspects of the demands and the answers provided. It evidenced, Buchanan argued, a "pragmatic drift" (Buchanan, 1977: 287)—"the piecemeal adjustments made to situations as they are confronted without attention to the design of the structure as a whole, either in a backward looking or a forward-looking direction" (ibid.: 296). Politicians, as decision-makers, were now all utility maximizers (Buchanan, 1978a).

This led to an increase in government spending, a growth in the size of the government, of the Leviathan. This state expansion was supported both by the elites, those who were wealthy enough to pay for redistribution, and by the citizens who benefited from it. The former, "the scions of the rich ... of the wealthy" (Buchanan, 1975b: 25) were less confident, "less secure in their roles of custodians of wealth than were their forebears" (ibid.), and therefore they easily gave in to the redistributive demands of the less rich and less wealthy without displaying any strategic courage. And the beneficiaries of these redistributive measures also behaved without strategic courage, asking for changes in the constitutional rules without understanding the long-term consequences of these demands. The result was that American society had ended up on one of the "off-diagonals" of the social game in which many individuals were subject to repeated, routine predation without prospect of amelioration (Lehto & Meadowcroft, 2021; Marciano & Meadowcroft, 2024). Individuals were not capable, or willing, to envisage leaving this diagonal.

Buchanan interpreted the situation as the result of an increase in population and a concentration of the population in urban areas (Buchanan, 1965: 8). In other words, it came about because the size of the group in which individuals lived had increased and, as a consequence, the number of individuals interacting with each other had also increased. Thus, alienation (and, therefore, emancipation) depended on the size of groups in which people made collective decisions.

Large groups are problematic because they prevent individuals from behaving as ethical citizens. Indeed, in large groups or "large-number settings" (Buchanan, 1965, 1991a, for instance), individuals understand that they will not be able to influence "the ultimate selection among sets of rules" (Buchanan, 1991a: 155). As a result, in this kind of environment, "there may exist little or no incentive for any single player to participate actively in any serious evaluation of the rules" (ibid.). Indeed, Buchanan insisted, "if the individual cannot ultimately influence the choice among regimes, it is not rational to participate actively in any discussion of constitutional change" (ibid.). Similarly, in large groups, and with respect to post-constitutional interpersonal relationships, individuals "react or adjust to the behaviour of 'others' in a manner similar to his reaction to the natural environment" (Buchanan, 1967: 113). Individuals maximize their utility in order to satisfy their self-interest in the narrow sense of the word. Or, as Buchanan put it, they follow "the private maxim" or "the expediency criterion" (Buchanan, 1965: 2). Choosing in large groups necessarily implies alienation because individuals treat others as part of their environment who cannot be influenced by strategic decision-making.

By contrast, Buchanan argued, individuals who find themselves in small groups tend to realize the interdependencies that link them to others and therefore do not follow their "narrowly defined self-interest" (Buchanan, 1978a: 366). Rather, they adopt "moral or ethical principles" (Buchanan, 1961: 340). More precisely, individuals in small groups adopt a Kantian rule of behaviour (see Buchanan, 1965, in particular). In small groups, therefore, individuals behave as artifactual man and therefore such groups are emancipatory.

Buchanan envisaged two forms of small groups. First, the "moral communities", that exist when individuals view themselves as members of "a collective unit… rather than conceive themselves to be independent, isolated individuals", characteristic of the commitment people might feel towards "the nuclear family, the extended family, the clan or tribe… ethnic, racial or religious cohorts, the trade union, the business firm, or, finally, with the nation-state". A moral community is therefore an example of an emancipated society. But a large-scale emancipated society might not be based on moral communities. Indeed, competing moral communities could give birth to an unstable society characterized by conflict that would require government intervention and limit emancipation.

Another example of such an emancipatory society is what Buchanan called a "moral order", which is a more impersonal set of social interactions among people who do not identify as a moral community but conceive of themselves and others as autonomous individuals worthy of mutual respect. Buchanan (1981: 189) wrote: "In a moral order, it is possible for a person to deal with other persons who are not members of his own community if both persons have agreed, explicitly or implicitly, to abide by the behavioral precepts required for reciprocal trust and confidence".

Therefore, to make our point more explicitly, we argue that Buchanan saw emancipation as flowing from non-economic institutions, in terms of moral communities or a moral order of individuals capable of writing a liberal constitution. Emancipation is not primarily a matter of economic exchange. Certainly, a free market economy may complement an emancipatory moral order; but it is not the cause of emancipation.

Conclusion

Unlike many liberal thinkers, Buchanan did not define or view emancipation simply as "freedom from coercion". Or, put differently, he was not a thinker of emancipation who sought to defend a negative view of freedom. Rather, Buchanan contributed to a theory (and defence) of emancipation in a more expansive and complete way. To Buchanan, emancipation means the realization of one's capabilities, leading to the achievement of a free life. It meant becoming an artifactual man, an individual making genuine choices, responsible and ethical. It meant pursuing one's ends, in a rather self-interested way, but by taking others into account. Buchanan's emancipated individual is far from the image of the neoliberal homo œconomicus that some have caricatured. Buchanan's vision of emancipation spoke to both the personal and the constitutional—it was an account of how individuals could realize freedom in their daily interactions with others and as political actors framing the rules of the game that governed their collective lives.

Acknowledgements We thank Paul Lewis, Mikayla Novak and an anonymous referee for extremely helpful comments. An earlier version of this chapter was presented at Second Colloquium on the History of Economic Thought at the Department of Political Economy, King's College London, on 4 July 2024.

Notes

1. Buchanan for instance wrote: "If consistency in individual behavior and individual freedom are highly regarded relative to other values, the market will tend to be favored" (1954: 342). Or, "[f]or those who place strong positive value on individual freedom of expression, on individual and personal liberty in their conception of the 'good society', the market offers major advantages over its collectivist counterpart" (1971: 234).
2. Buchanan also distinguished between "creative" and "reactive" choices, the former being those that create "a sequence of events... that did not exist prior to the choice and that was brought into being, literally, by the choice itself" ([1989] 1991: 218). This kind of choice gives birth of sequences of events that are "indeterminate": "[i]n creative choice, the behavior of the individual is not probabilistically predictable because such choice, it itself, *creates* alternatives from which the other individual choose" (ibid.: 219) By contrast, a reactive choice is "always predictable, at least within probabilistic limits" (ibid.). One form of such reactive choices is when "the individual actor is genetically programmed to respond uniquely and predictably to the alternatives that are confronted; in this limit, 'choice' in any meaningful sense disappears" (ibid.).
3. Striving could be distinguished from reaching goals, which would correspond to the actions of natural man. See Boettke (2022: 791) on Menger, for whom "[e]conomizing individuals strive to better their economic positions as much as possible".
4. One way a smoker may achieve this personal transformation is to "throw out all of his cigarette inventory and impose upon himself a

strict rule against further purchases" (Buchanan, 1979: 253). Hence, one way to stop smoking is via a personal constitution that forces a change in behaviour. As Paul Lewis and Malte Dold (2020: 1172) note, "Buchanan believe[d] in the capability of self-constitution".

5. We thank Paul Lewis for reminding us of this crucial point. Let us add that a tension might exist here, that Lewis and Dold (2020: 1172–1173) stress, between the capacity of emancipated individuals to choose their constraints and choices that are "shaped by pre-existing social structures" (ibid.: 1173).
6. The behaviours natural man adopt are not too different from how a slave behaves (Buchanan, 1995). Slaves, in Buchanan's description, do not "retain personal control over actions along at least some minimal set of dimensions of behavioral adjustment" (ibid.: 142).
7. Although Elias Khalil and Alain Marciano discuss Buber's philosophy, they do no try to connect it with Buchanan. This possible connection was studied by Tyler Brough and Randy Simmons (2023). Our purpose here is not to enter into the details of this connection, but rather to suggest that the I-it-instrumental relationship is alienating, while the I-thou-existential is emancipatory.
8. Buchanan stressed that this was a difference that existed between him and Gordon Tullock, who believed in "the substitutability between legal and ethical constraints" (Buchanan, 2006: 15). Buchanan thus wrote: "I can scarcely imagine an interaction setting in which persons refrain from cheating, stealing and keeping promises only because of some fear of punishment. There is surely a minimal level of voluntary adherence to the whole set of norms implied by the Kantian precept" (ibid.: 16).

References

Boettke, P. J. (2022). Menger and Contemporary Austrian Economics: Knowledge, Institutions and Liberalism. *European Journal of the History of Economic Thought, 29*(5), 788–800.

Buber, M. (1937). *I and Thou*, Trans RG. Smith. T. T. Clark.

Brough, T. J., & Simmons, R. T. (2023). Economics as Moral Exchange: James Buchanan Meets Martin Buber. *Public Choice, 194*(3), 395–420.

Buchanan, J. M. (1954). Individual choice in voting and the market. *Journal of Political Economy, 62*(4), 334–343.

Buchanan, J. M. (1961). Simple Majority Voting, Game Theory and Resource Use. *Canadian Journal of Economics and Political Science, 27*(3), 337–348.
Buchanan, J. M. (1964). What Should Economists Do? *Southern Economic Journal, 30*(3), 213–222.
Buchanan, J. M. (1965). Ethical Rules, Expected Values, and Large Numbers. *Ethics, 76*(1), 1–13.
Buchanan, J. M. ([1966] 1979). Economics and Its Scientific Neighbors. In J. M. Buchanan (Ed.), *What Should Economists Do?* (pp. 65–79). Liberty Fund.
Buchanan, J. M. (1967). Cooperation and Conflict in Public Goods Interactions. *Economic Inquiry, 5*(2), 109–121.
Buchanan, J. M. ([1969a] 1979). Is Economics the Science of Choice. In J. M. Buchanan (Ed.), *What Should Economists Do?* (pp. 39–63). Liberty Fund.
Buananan, J. M. ([1969b] 1979). Professor Alchian on Economic Method. In J. M. Buchanan (Ed.), *What Should Economists Do?* (pp. 65–79). Liberty Fund.
Buchanan, J. M. (1969). *Cost and Choice*. University of Chicago Press.
Buchanan, J. M. (1971). Equality as Fact and Norm. *Ethics, 81*(3), 228–240.
Buchanan, J. M. (1973). America's Third Century in Perspective. *Atlantic Economic Journal, 1*, 3–12.
Buchanan, J. M. (1975a). The Samaritan's Dilemma. In E. S. Phelps (Ed.), *Altruism, Morality and Economic Theory* (pp. 71–85). Russell Sage Foundation.
Buchanan, J. M. (1975b). *The Limits of Liberty. Between Anarchy and Leviathan*. Chicago University Press.
Buchanan, J. M. (1975c). Boundaries on Social Contract. *Reason Papers, 2*, 15–28.
Buchanan, J. M. ([1976a] 1979). General Implications of Subjectivism in Economics. In J. M. Buchanan (Ed.), *What Should Economists Do?* (pp. 81–91). Liberty Fund.
Buchanan, J. M. ([1976b] 1979). Methods and Morals in Economics. In J. M. Buchanan (Ed.), *What Should Economists Do?* (pp. 201–217). Liberty Fund.
Buchanan, J. M. (1977). *Freedom in Constitutional Contract. Perspectives of a Political Economist*. Texas A&M University Press.
Buchanan, J. M. (1978a). Markets, States, and the Extent of Morals. *American Economic Review, 68*(2), 364–368.
Buchanan, J. M. (1978b). A Contractarian Perspective on Anarchy. *Nomos, 19*, 29–42.
Buchanan, J. M. (1979). Natural and Artifactual Man. In J. M. Buchanan (Ed.), *What Should Economists Do?* (pp. 93–112). Liberty Fund.
Buchanan, J. M. ([1981] 1999). Moral Community, Moral Order, or Moral Anarchy. In G. Brennan, H. Kliemt, & R. D. Tollison (Eds.), *The Collected Works of James M. Buchanan: Volume 17* (pp. 187–202). Liberty Fund.

Buchanan, J. M. ([1986] 1992). *Better Than Ploughing and Other Personal Essays*. University of Chicago Press.
Buchanan, J. M. ([1989] 1991). Shackle and a Lecture in Pittsburgh. In J. M. Buchanan (Ed.), *The Economics and Ethics of Constitutional Order* (pp. 217–220). Edward Elgar.
Buchanan, J. M. (1990). The Domain of Constitutional Political Economy. *Constitutional Political Economy, 1*(1), 1–18.
Buchanan, J. M. (1991a). The Ethics of Constitutional Order. In J. M. Buchanan (Ed.), *The Economics and Ethics of Constitutional Order* (pp. 153–157). Edward Elgar.
Buchanan, J. M. (1991b). Economic Origins of Ethical Constraints. In J. M. Buchanan (Ed.), *The Economics and Ethics of Constitutional Order* (pp. 179–193). Edward Elgar.
Buchanan, J. M. (1995). Individual Rights, Emergent Social States, and Behavioral Feasibility. *Rationality and Society, 7*(2), 141–150.
Buchanan, J. M. (2005). Afraid to Be Free: Dependency as Desideratum. *Public Choice, 124*(1–2), 19–31.
Buchanan, J. M. (2006). *Why I, Too, Am Not a Conservative. The Normative Vision of Classical Liberalism*. Edward Elgar.
Congleton, R. D. (2014). The Contractarian Constitutional Political Economy of James Buchanan. *Constitutional Political Economy, 25*(1), 39–67.
Khalil, E. L., & Marciano, A. (2021). A Theory of Instrumental and Existential Rational Decisions: Smith, Weber, Mauss, Tönnies After Martin Buber. *Theory and Decision, 90*(1), 147–169.
Lehto, O., & Meadowcroft, J. (2021). Welfare Without Rent Seeking? Buchanan's Demogrant Proposal and the Possibility of a Constitutional Welfare State. *Constitutional Political Economy, 32*(2), 145–164.
Lewis, P. (2017). Shackle on Choice, Imagination and Creativity: Hayekian Foundations. *Cambridge Journal of Economics, 41*(1), 1–24.
Lewis, P., & Dold, M. (2020). James Buchanan on the Nature of Choice: Ontology, Artifactual Man and the Constitutional Moment in Political Economy. *Cambridge Journal of Economics, 44*(5), 1159–1179.
Marciano, A. (2009). Buchanan's Constitutional Political Economy: Exchange vs Choice in Economics and in Politics. *Constitutional Political Economy, 20*(1), 42–56.
Marciano, A., & Meadowcroft, J. (2024). Asymmetrical, Symmetrical and Artifactual Man: Group Size and Cooperation in James Buchanan's Constitutional Economics. *Cambridge Journal of Economics, 48*(5), 823–842.
Meadowcroft, J. (2023). Exchanges with and Without the Sword: Slavery, politics-as-exchange and freedom in James M. Buchanan's institutional economics. *Journal of Institutional Economics,19*(6), 787–801.
Mill, J. S. (1859). *On Liberty*. John Parker & Son.

CHAPTER 4

Power to the Powerless: Evolutionary Freedom as Emancipation

Otto Lehto

In his influential essay, *The Intellectuals and Socialism*, Hayek (1949) prophesied that the "revival of liberalism" must coincide with the resurgence of "the courage to be Utopian." Today, at a time when liberalism is under attack from multiple fronts, it seems that we need Hayekian courage more than ever:

> … What we lack is a liberal Utopia, a program which seems neither a mere defense of things as they are nor a diluted kind of socialism, but a truly liberal radicalism which does not spare the susceptibilities of the mighty (…) and which does not confine itself to what appears today as politically possible (Hayek, 1949: 432).

The rediscovery of the Utopian potential of liberalism coincides with going back to its roots. This chapter shows that classical liberalism, especially in its so-called "epistemic" or "evolutionary" branch, which

O. Lehto (✉)
School of Law, New York University, New York, USA
e-mail: otto.lehto@nyu.edu

M. Novak (ed.), *Liberal Emancipation*, Mercatus Studies in Political and Social Economy, https://doi.org/10.1007/978-3-031-94406-2_4

goes back at least to the Scottish Enlightenment (Gaus, 2016, 2021; Hayek, 1967, 1982, 2002, [1960] 2011; Lavoie, 1985; Mill, [1859] 2003; Popper, [1945] 1966; Smith, [1776] 2008; Spencer, 1851, 1896; Sumner, 1992), provides a platform for a "liberal radicalism" with the power to *emancipate poor, marginalised, and downtrodden people* from the shackles of poverty, misery, and oppression. Such an emancipatory paradigm is congruent with the "bleeding-heart libertarian" branch of liberalism that combines a robust commitment to liberty with a robust commitment to social justice (Tomasi, 2012; Zwolinski, 2015). Although some have questioned the wisdom of using the language of "progress" in the context of liberal evolution (Tebble, 2017), I shall defend the position that the liberal tradition merits the courage to proclaim itself progressive in the sense of containing the seeds of Utopian thinking.

Specifically, I believe that evolutionary liberalism provides a framework for "real Utopian" theory and practice, as defined by the Marxist sociologist Wright (2011, 2013). Wright defines real Utopianism as the marriage of the capacity to *imagine radically better social realities* with the discipline to be sober about *viable pathways* of getting there: "Real utopias capture the spirit of utopia but remain attentive to what it takes to bring those aspirations to life" (Wright, 2011: 37). Real utopias "enable us to make empirically and theoretically sound arguments about emancipatory possibilities," through the elaboration of "clear-headed, rigorous, and viable alternatives to existing social institutions that both embody our deepest aspirations for human flourishing and take seriously the problem of practical design" (ibid.). In this spirit, liberalism counts as a real Utopian theory. It has the capacity to realise radically transformative aspirations that combine a *general aspiration for human flourishing* with particular attention to the *overcoming of the circumstances of oppression and misery of the poor and the downtrodden*. Such a normative exploration and articulation of the emancipatory potential of classical liberal institutions reminds us that the "courage to be Utopian"—namely, "real Utopian"—is part and parcel of the liberal creed.

The structure of this chapter is as follows. The next section defends the normative appeal of evolutionary theory against the charge that it is immoral. This is followed by an exploration of evolutionary liberal pathways for social emancipation. I then explore ways to address the downsides of evolutionary selection. This is followed by a conclusion.

Evolution: Brute Facts, Endless Suffering, and Utopian Hope

Wildlife documentaries reveal the seeming cruelty of nature. But this is mostly projection. Evolutionary processes are themselves *amoral*. Wherever it occurs, the logic of evolutionary development follows its own course, unconstrained by moral laws except the ones that we impose—or better yet, cultivate—upon it. So, it may seem quaint to impose moral judgement on evolution. This remains so whether the judgements we make involve approval or disapproval. In order to understand how evolution (or what it produces) can be deemed "good" or "bad," we have to first understand how ethical judgements at all are possible in a world governed by evolutionary processes. In the end, I wish to defend the normative claim that we should facilitate certain types of evolutionary processes in social life.

In biology, evolution emerges out of the self-organising properties of the biochemical substrata of life (Kauffman, 1993, 2016). In social life, processes of cultural and economic evolution emerge *on top of*, *and out of*, biological evolution (Arthur, 2015; Wilson, 1975, 2019). This is why evolutionary approaches to social and moral theory, including those of evolutionary liberalism, must account for the complex interaction between biological and cultural evolution. As part of this process, morality and social order seem to emerge gradually through cultural evolution (Ferguson, [1767] 2001; Hume, 1777). At the same time, we are also endowed with reason, self-reflective capacities, and a moral sense that allow us to question, refine, and change our established moral judgements. So, we should not look to nature as the final moral legislator; ultimately, we have to take responsibility for ourselves.

Any ethical theory that reads social evolution in sweepingly moralistic terms is committing, at best, a category error (Tebble, 2017). Most evolutionary processes, even the ones that look like non-zero-sum games, have absolute and relative winners and losers who have justifiably different judgements about the merits and demerits of the evolutionary outcome. To the extent that we have access to alternative pathways of evolution, we also must take better account of the details of the evolutionary process: *Who benefits? In what way? Who bears the cost? In what way?* A willingness to overgeneralise and sometimes sweep such questions under the rug plagues many sweepingly optimistic theories such as Spencerian evolutionism (Spencer, 1851, 1896), but it also plagues sweepingly *pessimistic* theories, including Hofstadter's [1944] (1992) influential blanket denunciation of the application of evolutionary thinking into social theory.

Given the state of the discussion, it is not surprising that many people wince at the claim that "survival of the fittest" is good for society. And they become positively incredulous if you try to convince them that one of the primary tasks of social policy that cares for the poor should be facilitating evolutionary competition. This is understandable if people have images of "nature red in tooth and claw" in their minds. They might conflate evolutionary thinking with eugenics or cruelty towards the poor. It seems plausible that the process of evolutionary selection that is often ruthless and cruel in biology, would also be ruthless and cruel in society. The infelicitous phrase "Social Darwinism" was brought into popular consciousness with the publication of Hofstadter's [1944] (1992) firebrand denunciation of free market economics. The book denounced nineteenth-century laissez-faire capitalism in the same breath as eugenics and Nazism. Hofstadter saw both as little more than ideological justifications for inequalities of power and wealth based on misguided evolutionary analogies. However, modern critics like the evolutionary biologist David Sloan Wilson tend to find this link between evolutionary thinking with siding with the powerful a mere accident of history that can be overcome by *better* evolutionary theory:

> … Darwin's theory can and has been misused by some people. However, the same can be said for any theory and indeed for almost any tool of any sort. There is no evidence that Darwin's theory is especially prone to misuse, so using the term "social Darwinism" as a bogeyman has no place in serious scholarship or science (Wilson, 2019: 34).

Hofstadter's unfortunate conflation between laissez-faire liberalism and Nazi eugenics was inaccurate, as was his wholesale denunciation of evolutionary theory. However, unless the worries about "Social Darwinism" can be overcome, the suspicion that the application of evolutionary thinking to social and moral theory tends to favour the rich and the powerful seems warranted. This worry was already expressed in the nineteenth century by the founder of American pragmatism, C.S. Peirce, who denounced the evolutionary liberalism of his contemporaries, especially Herbert Spencer:

> ... the conviction of the nineteenth century is that progress takes place by virtue of every individual's striving for himself with all his might and trampling his neighbour under foot whenever he gets a chance to do so. This may accurately be called the Gospel of Greed (Peirce, 2022: 364).

Against such worries (which are reasonable enough), I offer a qualified normative defence of the "evolutionary viewpoint" in social theory in general, and evolutionary liberalism in particular. I argue that evolutionary liberalism is both a normatively appealing version of liberalism and a methodologically appealing version of evolutionary theory. With appropriate guidelines, it offers an institutionally robust program of social amelioration. To that end, this chapter offers a *normative justification* of the continued relevance of the "evolutionary" strands of classical liberal social theory. However, rather than a full-blown justification, it may be better to speak of a *conceptual reconstruction*, by which I mean an attempt at making evolutionary liberal theory legible and credible in light of modern evolutionary theory and modern sensibilities. It seeks to offer a normative vision that is compatible with the attempts of recent evolutionary theorists to "complete the Darwinian revolution" by extending evolutionary theory from biology to social affairs (Wilson, [1975] 2000). Indeed, evolutionary liberals in many ways pioneered "synthetic philosophy" at the intersection of life and society (Spencer, 1851; Hayek, 1967).

Although evolutionary liberalism, as a "real Utopian" theory, must ultimately concern itself with society *on the whole*, I am primarily concerned with answering a narrower, equally urgent question: *If* we especially care about the welfare of the underprivileged, poor, and marginalised people, do we have *prima facie* grounds for pursuing evolutionary liberalism? My primary desire is to defeat the accusation of "social Darwinism" (Hofstadter, [1944] 1992). For that reason, I will not attempt a pro tanto defence of liberalism against all its objections and weaknesses. Nor is it necessary to specify all the concrete pathways (markets, civil society, technological advancement, etc.) whereby an evolutionary liberal society achieves its purported capacities for solving problems, generating innovations, and boosting human flourishing. I simply want to establish a theoretically robust link between the advancement of evolutionary liberal institutions and the advancement of general social capacities for responding to the needs of the powerless and the underprivileged. Crucially, I seek to establish that *evolutionary mechanisms* do the work of *social emancipation*. Evolutionary liberalism benefits from the insights of contemporary complexity theory and evolutionary social theory to enrich its capacity for formal modelling and theoretical rigour (Arthur, 2015; Beinhocker, 2006, 2011; Beinhocker & Hanauer, 2014; Colander & Kupers, 2014; Hodgson, 2019; Hodgson & Knudsen, 2010; Holland, 1995; Hong & Page, 2004; Page, 2011).

The Evolutionary Liberal Pathway to Social Emancipation

Evolutionary liberalism, in the historical sense, is a diverse family tree of theories. Nonetheless, it is possible to isolate a mainline thread in the "spontaneous order" or "social evolution" lineage that stretches from the Scottish Enlightenment, through Spencer, to contemporary neo-Hayekian social theory. This is the lineage that I believe has done more than anyone to outline the concrete institutional trappings of evolutionary emancipation. However, in order to make it relevant, it needs to be updated with some of the insights of contemporary evolutionary and complexity theory. And fully justifying evolutionary liberalism requires understanding the close link between freedom, adaptation, innovation, and evolutionary selection.

My hypothesis can be broken down into two sub-hypotheses. My *first claim* is that *evolutionary liberalism* enriched by the contemporary insights of *complexity theory* offers a plausible model of *emancipatory,* "*real Utopian*" *imagination*. Evolutionary liberal institutions tend to generate processes that make poor and downtrodden people better off in ways that count as emancipatory. My *second claim* is that its emancipatory potential can be partially explained, and justified, on the basis of social *evolutionary mechanisms* that (a) exhibit similarities to biological evolution, and (b) are partly capturable by the typical evolutionary language of adaptation, mutation, innovation, selection, and diffusion. Since biological evolution has impressive real-world track records of solving complex evolutionary problems, we have *prima facie* reasons for assuming that any similar mechanism—whether in nature or society—will exhibit similar promise. And the evidence seems to bear it out.

The primary motivation guiding the evolutionary liberal hypothesis is that poor and disadvantaged people stand to benefit greatly from evolutionary processes that are steered and guided by liberal norms and rules. They benefit greatly from having access to evolutionary mechanisms that generate innovations that can improve their lives in qualitatively different and often radically transformative ways. This does not entail assuming that evolution always works for social emancipation, only that it has a robust chance of doing so and its downsides can be partly mitigated or thwarted by appropriate institutional measures. I will proceed on the assumption that evolution is, at least partly, subject to human guidance. Such an assumption avoids hubris as long as we keep in mind that our ability to control evolution is limited, distributed, and provisional. Although evolution can never be fully "tamed," diverse private and public actors can affect its course through their interlocking epistemic horizons.

Before proceeding further, I need to dispel one common misconception. The word "evolution" is sometimes used in political discourse to indicate "gradual change" in contradistinction to "revolutionary change." I am thinking of statements like the following: *Presidential candidate X favours gradual, evolutionary social change and opposes sudden, revolutionary change*. This makes evolutionary thinking seem aligned with conservatism and hostile to real Utopian thinking. This is not the sense of the word that I have in mind. In my sense of the term—which is just the dictionary definition of the term—evolution is not opposed to radical change. It is opposed to *design* and *planning*. Although the liberal project recommends certain rule-conservatism with regard to the basic rules of the Open Society (for which reason it sometimes strategically aligns itself with conservatism), the social change that it tolerates or facilitates *within* its liberal institutional structures is *not* subject to conservative caution. Social evolution within the liberal order is intermittently conservative or radical, reformist or revolutionary, gradual or sudden, slow or fast. Indeed, at the more emancipatory, radical side of the liberal spectrum, liberals like myself openly celebrate the *swiftness, profoundness, and radicalness* of the changes that the liberal society, through its evolutionary tentacles, generates. Anybody who cares about social emancipation should celebrate the rapid, profound, and indeed *revolutionary* acceptance of LGTBQ+ rights (despite ongoing struggle) in the Western world in recent decades. Equally emancipatory have been the technological advancements in internet access, mobile phones, and artificial intelligence, all of which can profoundly improve the lives of poor and marginalised people.

The examples could be multiplied, but these alone suffice to show that being "evolutionary" is *not* a prescription against radical, transformative, and profound social change. Indeed, this gradualist, conservative-leaning connotation of evolution should probably be dropped given what we know about how evolution works in the biological and sociological domains. There is, however, a second compelling reason to believe that the evolutionary liberal project is necessarily linked with some conservative attitudes. This is exemplified by Popper's [1945] (1966) famous "paradox of tolerance," according to which the liberal society must reserve the right to defend itself against intolerant forces even if this means acting intolerantly itself (see also Gaus, 2016, 2021). Those who take this paradox seriously (as I do) may be tempted to argue that gradual evolution might be the safer option, since it gives the Open Society more time to defend itself against its enemies. This strategy, however, is a double-edged sword. Gradualism also gives the enemies of liberalism more time to plan, attack, and regroup. Contrary to its conservative and liberal proponents, gradualism might lead to the gradual erosion of the Open Society. At the same time, rapid evolution—even seemingly "revolutionary" transformation in our habits and norms—might be required to disrupt the *status quo* and jolt society in an emancipatory direction. At this stage, the gradualism debate remains unsettled. What is obvious, however, is that evolution can be quite revolutionary.

Let me now unpack the mechanism of social evolution with minimal technical exposition. Much like in the biological world, evolution in the social world proceeds by way of mutations, adaptations, and the selective multiplication of successful experiments (Beinhocker, 2006; Colander & Kupers, 2014; Darwin, 1859, 1871; Hodgson, 2019; Nelson & Winter, 1982; Spencer, 1851, 1896). In the biological world, the unit of selection is usually the phenotype, the genotype, or even the social group (Darwin, 1859; Dawkins, [1976] 2006; Wilson, 2019). In the social world, the unit of selection is harder to define. Indeed, there are multiple units of selection operating on multiple levels and in multiple domains (Hodgson & Knudsen, 2010; Wilson, 2019). For example, in the business world alone (which obviously does not exhaust the social world), we can treat the *firms*, their *products*, their *routines*, their *business plans*, the *ideas* that motivate them, or the *people* who manage the firm, as units of selection (Beinhocker, 2011; Colander & Kupers, 2014; Nelson & Winter, 1982). For simplicity's sake, I have found it useful to treat all such diverse units of selection as "*innovations*." Specifically, the liberal evolutionary regime can be described as one of "permissionless innovation" (Thierer, 2014). *Innovations in goods and services* are the paradigmatic units of selection in the market economy (certainly in the era of entrepreneurial capitalism), but the logic also extends to other domains, so looking at market transactions is insufficient. In the culture, for example, innovations occur in the form of new habits, new ideas, new social norms, and new ways of life.

The link between *innovation* and *social emancipation* in the liberal order, although normatively compelling, is not straightforward or linear. Many innovations are banal, trivial, and seemingly non-emancipatory. New varieties of ice cream (however tasty), marginally improved latest models of cell phones (however convenient), and new street jokes (however funny) do not, under most considerations, rise up to the level of *truly emancipatory* social processes. True emancipation seems to require something more profound and substantial. I agree. However, even quite minor and forgettable innovations may contribute non-trivially to human happiness and wellbeing when aggregated over time and across large populations. A million human beings made marginally happier—certainly it counts for *something*? Perhaps even something *profound*? Even though the analogy between biology and social science should not be taken literally, it is helpful to model society as a highly complicated "ecosystem" where the complicated dance of millions, or even billions, of simultaneous mutual adjustments—composed of numerous, *individually minor and seemingly trivial*, steps—makes possible the simultaneous satisfaction of diverse tastes, desires, and adventures (including, crucially, the exploration of new ones). In the social order, *perhaps almost no single innovation appears transformative on its own*; it is frequently the emergent result of millions of innovations interacting in a dynamic process of discovery that constitutes profound social change.

Some pathways towards social emancipation are more obvious than others. This does not make them any less valuable. Market competition in a liberal economy (even if we accept that it comes with many imperfections) can be modelled as an evolutionary process that tends to produce more wealth, new markets, and qualitatively better products (Hayek, 2002; Nelson & Winter, 1982). As long as the fruits of the booming economy actually reach all the sectors of the society, economic growth remains one of the most promising (and well-understood) pathways to gradually eliminating several intransigent problems that stand in the way of social emancipation. Generating general opulence tends to correlate with increased ability to solve diverse social problems. *First*, mitigating resource scarcity leaves more resources available for solving more problems. *Second*, economic growth tends to go together with increased investments in human and social capital, which generates secondary advances in science, technology, and the arts. And *third*, growth tends to build on top of growth thanks to the peculiar nature of exponential growth. For such reasons, I agree with Cowen (2018: 41) that a "more rapidly growing economy will, at some point, bring about much higher levels of human well-being—and other plural values—on a consistent basis."

However, we should not reduce everything into a simple metric—whether growth, wealth, or happiness. Getting rich may be among the class of "universal" innovations that most people will predictably benefit from. To some extent, the same goes for having access to better quality housing and healthcare. However, we should be careful not to try to "second-guess" the evolutionary process by setting up lists of "necessary" or "basic" innovations (at least not too hastily), since even such seemingly "obvious" categories are subject to contestation, evolution, and disruption. Evolution is inherently *surprising*. Emancipatory pathways often emerge from unpredictable directions, so it is hard to know in advance what kinds of innovations those suffering from oppression, marginalisation, and poverty most desperately need. The general prescription that *innovations are conducive to social emancipation* must be agnostic as to the kind of innovations that are best suited to the job. This does *not* mean pretending to be completely ignorant of such elementary discoveries that, indeed, people generally need food to eat. We can take that much for granted. Nonetheless, *how* the food that people need to survive should be produced, stored, transported, sold, prepared, cooked, eaten, and culturally embedded cannot be known in advance. So, the evolutionary liberal program, as I see it, should focus on improving the general, all-purpose *adaptive efficiency* or "*evolvability*" of the society, in order to best cater to the diverse needs and rights of the downtrodden. "Evolvability" refers to the capacity of the system to evolve and innovate efficiently across multiple domains (Beinhocker & Hanauer, 2014; Dawkins, 2003; Hodgson, 2019). A higher rate of evolvability boosts the capacity of a robust evolutionary system to produce miraculous results "without miracles" (Cziko, 1995). So, *emancipation through evolution*, as we might call this liberal program, should focus on identifying and facilitating *innovation capacity*, or *evolvability*, in society.

The institutional dimension of the evolutionary liberal framework seeks to ensure that such outcomes are within the reach of the population. If the evolutionary hypothesis about social emancipation is correct, then poor, oppressed, and downtrodden people have a moral right to, and can be expected to benefit greatly from, *widespread freedom toexperiment* with new innovations (whether in technologies, ideas, habits, customs, goods, or services). Liberal institutions offer robust guarantees of individual autonomy and equal protection that uniquely guarantee people such freedoms. This does not necessarily mean that they have to limit their functions to libertarian "nightwatchman states." Indeed, the evolutionary liberal program is compatible with multiple degrees of government involvement in the economy as long as evolutionary competition is protected. Let us remember that most Western societies today are mixed liberal economies that incorporate significant elements of both liberal and non-liberal institutional design. At any rate, in a consistently evolutionary liberal regime, *innovation with the new* should generally take normative priority over *redistribution of the old*. The reason is that emancipation requires the discovery of surprising, creative pathways out of seemingly intractable and fatalistic conditions. Emancipatory theories that dare not dream of radically new social conditions and simultaneously facilitate mechanisms that can reliably get us there are not worthy of the name.

Let me offer a few more examples. Take the existence of the Black Death, for example. The bacterium *Y. pestis* has (literally) plagued society for millennia. Undoubtedly, historically speaking, poor, downtrodden, and oppressed people have, on average, suffered more from pandemics like the plague. This is a striking reminder why social emancipation is so important: to eradicate the sorts of unfair social hierarchies and class divisions that generate large-scale suffering and death. At the same time, until the discovery of modern medicine, *nobody was safe from the plague*. Today, (effectively) *nobody dies from the plague*. This seems quasi-miraculous, but is better understood as the inevitable result of medical, technological, and economic evolution (or, why not, *progress*). Not all of that improvement can be attributed to liberalism, but liberal institutions have certainly contributed to the incredible progress of modern medicine. The normative takeaway is twofold: (1) no amount of reshuffling of existing resources, however justified, can substitute for better innovations, and (2) evolutionary liberal institutions are exceptionally good at facilitating innovations across multiple domains.

Do not get me wrong: societies should not ignore their responsibility to also improve the allocative efficiency and distributive fairness among what already exists. Prioritising the "world to come" (*even if* we have high credence in its viability) can easily become an excuse to ignore the urgent needs of the world today. In today's world, there is still a lot of low-hanging fruit in the form of easily addressable poverty, disease, hunger, and misery. But we also misattribute the status of low-hanging fruit to many problems that actually require non-obvious, innovative, experimental solutions. Two more recent examples include the cost-effective use of virtual reality (VR) technology—initially designed for tech enthusiasts and gamers—to help train aeroplane pilots, surgeons, and architects, and the sudden popularity of online dating apps like Tinder and Grindr as (however imperfect) solutions to loneliness. Remarkably, such innovations enable even poor, downtrodden, and marginalised people to have access to diverse opportunities that were previously unavailable. Such radical innovations tend to become widespread even in societies that have more restrictive freedoms, but they are unlikely to originate in them. Indeed, most of the innovations that I have listed originate in relatively liberal countries.

To summarise, the crucial insight of the evolutionary perspective is that *most good solutions do not yet exist, so they have to be discovered*. No amount of reshuffling existing resources—the existing pool of potential solutions to human problems—is enough to guarantee robust mechanisms of social emancipation. Making real and permanent improvements in the repertoire of available solutions means exploring and expanding the possibility space of available innovations through institutional investments into evolution. This includes investing a significant portion of the available material and non-material resources (beyond what is needed for immediate consumption and short-term relief) into the construction and maintenance of institutional structures and regulatory measures that facilitate widespread evolutionary experimentation. The human world, consisting of overlapping domains of social evolution, adaptation, and innovation, thus increasingly takes on the function of an *experimental laboratory*. Advances in wealth, knowledge, and technology liberate an increasing proportion of scarce resources—including "the ultimate resource" that is the creative human mind (Simon, 1997)—from serving basic animal needs and zero-sum competition into more progressive, radical, and adventurous projects of positive-sum evolutionary emancipation.

To be sure, human evolutionary expansion comes with many potential downsides and ethical problems that require addressing, including environmental destruction, the mistreatment of animals, and the presence of catastrophic and existential risks like global warming and A.I. doom (Ord, 2020). Nonetheless, these downsides can be partially mitigated by innovations in our technologies, attitudes, customs, and institutional practices. And given the vast upside of the evolutionary trajectory—up to the gradual elimination of poverty, disease, and misery—even such significant costs *might* be worth bearing. That said, it seems ethically imperative to avoid imposing unnecessary costs on unwilling third parties, human or non-human. And social emancipation itself may call for strategies beyond laissez-faire liberalism to respond to some of the negative aspects of evolution and other social problems. Evolution can be a marvellous tool in the hands of the poor and the marginalised, but ensuring that it does not derail into "Social Darwinism" (or worse!) requires institutional guidance. In the next section, I explore such evolutionary governance.

Beyond Laissez-Faire: Updating Evolutionary Liberalism

In the previous section, I argued that the core institutional insights of nineteenth-century evolutionary liberalism, especially when combined with the insights of contemporary evolutionary theory, are a useful starting point for social emancipation today. The classical liberal institutions that protect individual liberty, private property, the rule of law, and a fair administration of justice tend to generate incentives for evolutionary progress in the service of human welfare and flourishing (Hayek, 1982, [1960] 2011; Smith, [1776] 2008). Nonetheless, evolutionary liberalism has sometimes paid insufficient attention to the inefficiencies, downsides, and market failures attending laissez-faire liberalism. So, in this section, I offer some preliminary thoughts on how to remedy this. Instead of getting bogged down in generic debates about market imperfections, I will focus on the specific problems associated with *evolutionary failure*, defined as the risk that an evolutionary system becomes misaligned with human flourishing. In the context of real Utopian theory, the specific evolutionary failures to keep in mind are those that threaten to undermine prospects for social emancipation.

The first false belief to overcome is the idea that evolution can never go wrong. Although nobody in the evolutionary liberal tradition has argued for such a caricatured position, laissez-faire liberals have tended to downplay the downsides of evolution. Nineteenth-century evolutionary liberalism, especially with Spencer (1851, 1896) and Sumner (1992), was connected to an optimistic vision of progress. The Scottish Enlightenment vision of the spontaneous order (Ferguson, 2001; Hume, 1777;

Smith, [1776] 2008), as picked up by Hayek (1982, [1960] 2011) offers a considerably less rosy and more nuanced picture of progress. So, although I am temperamentally attuned with the Utopian vision of Spencerian evolution, Smith and Hayek offer a better starting point for thinking about the downsides of evolution. Evolution has no necessary "telos." Even when goal-directed, it is always a messy business. Innovations tend to benefit some people while harming others. Competition has its winners and losers. So, if evolutionary liberalism seeks to embrace and emphasise the Utopian aspects of evolutionary politics (and thus be a viable competitor to, say, anarchist and socialist models of social emancipation), it is paramount to keep track of the distribution of the costs and benefits of evolution. To do so, it is not merely enough to be willing to accept that evolution can fail and cause problems. It is also necessary to accept that sometimes laissez-faire is not enough. This is always a tough pill to swallow for classical liberals who have done so much theoretical work to explain the limitations of human agency in the design of institutions. Some conservative learning liberal thinkers in the Fergusonian and Hayekian tradition are correct to emphasise that human societies frequently stumble into good solutions that were never their intention. They are also correct to worry about the limitations of planning. Indeed, evolution cannot be "designed" or "planned" from the top down; it can only be gently steered from the bottom-up, and no single agent or state can monopolise such an activity. Nonetheless, there remains an important role for conscious (political, cultural, and moral) agency in (re)shaping evolutionary processes.

It is, of course, true that the precise distribution of costs and benefits in the evolutionary system is, by definition, as radically uncertain as the gales of creative destruction themselves. And it is equally true that no agent—neither the proponents of the evolutionary proposal nor the proponents of the stagnation proposal—can be expected to possess sufficient knowledge to *fully* ascertain the evolutionary outcomes, positive or negative. However, none of these facts should obscure the fact that we must bear responsibility for the impact of our intentional action on the future states of the system to the extent that we *do possess* some knowledge, however imperfect and conjectural, of the *expected* (or *theorised*) outcomes of various policy options. If we choose, for example, to press on the evolutionary accelerator by removing barriers from the way of rapid socioeconomic evolution, we must take some responsibility for the social (re)distribution of costs and benefits that this entails. Political entrepreneurs must bear some moral responsibility for choosing one expected distributional pattern over another—even if the preferred distributional pattern is seemingly, for the most part, complex and "unpatterned."

The first lesson is: "*Let society evolve, but take part in reforming goodinstitutions*." Institutional reforms can mitigate the *destructive* and *maladaptive* side of the evolutionary process by improving the steering capacity of *evolutionaryinstitutions* (both formal and informal) in shaping the evolutionary process, including the distribution of its costs and benefits. This is a natural extension of the classical liberal principle that facilitating the capacity of the liberal order to serve all its members—and not just the rich, the lucky, the hard-working, the well-connected, and the ruthless—requires paying attention to the "rules of the game" (Hayek, [1960] 2011; Lavoie, 1985). In addition, the framework of evolutionary liberalism must pay special attention to how the rules of political economy can be reformed and tweaked to abolish privileges, hierarchies, and other forms of power and domination that stand in the way of widely shared social emancipation. This way, evolutionary liberalism is more aligned with social emancipation, and charges of "Social Darwinism" can be more effectively deflected.

This requires paying attention to the cost–benefit calculus of evolution. Although evolution has many expected benefits that potentially outweigh its costs, given a sufficient long-time frame, it is not a Panglossian process that produces the best of all possible worlds. Nor is it a Pareto-optimal process that leaves everybody better off at each step. The image of market competition as a "positive-sum game" is only approximately true. It remains true that, given some deceptively simple and noncontroversial assumptions (such as that people tend to do whatever makes them better off), every voluntary contractual transfer looks like a "win–win" proposition. Nonetheless, this should not be conflated with the stronger claim that there are no losers in the market process. Evolution is a process that is, metaphorically or figuratively, "red in tooth and claw," to the extent it always demands a metaphorical "blood sacrifice." By definition, something must be destroyed (or heavily discouraged) in order for evolutionary selection to play out. Some experiments must lead to failure or death. This is equally true in the social and economic realm as it is in the biological realm. Many companies, marriages, rock bands, and cities fail. The creative spirit of liberal emancipation is always accompanied by some level of destruction, whether local or global, limited or extensive, tolerable or intolerable. To that extent alone, the old bogeyman of Social Darwinism, much like any caricature, carries an element of truth to it. Evolutionary models can entail "harsh" measures. Even if we put in various safeguards of individual rights and opportunities, there are no fail-safe mechanisms available for preventing hardships. Hence, institutional rules must be designed so that the predictable costs of adjustment do not fall disproportionately on already disadvantaged people.

Although most of the critics of Social Darwinism failed to appreciate that evolutionary processes can be harnessed for the benefit of poor and disadvantaged people, they were not entirely wrong to detect the danger, potential callousness, and anti-sociality in the evolutionary method. Treating society as a platform for competitive forces exposes society, or at least some people in it, to the risk of being overrun by waste, destruction, and suffering. Whether left to the spontaneous forces of bottom-up socioeconomic evolution or guided by the conscious agency of top-down institutional intervention, the evolutionary process is a hazardous and messy social phenomenon that cannot be "tamed" by anyone. Recognising this fact remains important even if we accept the evolutionary liberal claim that the expected net benefits of its institutional program outweigh its expected costs. This means that we can recognise the positive contributions of the evolutionary method while trying to minimise its downsides through careful institutional interventions into the society's (formal and informal) "rules of the game."

The second lesson is: "*Embrace the upside but devise ways to minimise the harms of evolution*." What this should mean in practice is a more difficult question. Several bleeding-heart libertarians, myself included, have suggested that the provision of something like *Universal Basic Income* (UBI), although non-ideal, might be justified as a way to increase the emancipatory capacity of the liberal order (Lehto, 2021; Lehto & Meadowcroft, 2020; Van Parijs, 1995; Zwolinski, 2015). However, the precise mechanism suitable for this task remains outside the present analysis. A failure to engage seriously with such problems—especially when illiberal forces are on the rise—might undermine liberalism's appeal as a robust emancipatory paradigm.

Another, slightly different charge is that evolutionary liberalism is anti-egalitarian. Aside from *harsh competition*, evolutionary liberalism inherits the problematic legacy of Social Darwinism in its reliance on *unequal outcomes* as means of social emancipation. This challenges its egalitarian credentials. Although evolutionary liberalism is committed to egalitarianism in the form of equal rights and equal freedoms (what is sometimes called "liberal neutrality"), it must reject doctrines that prioritise the direct achievement of equal outcomes (or equity). Although one may even hope that the fruits of evolution become dispersed equally among the population, the pattern of social emancipation that flows out of evolution is necessarily unequal. Indeed, the function of the liberal framework is precisely to discover the *hiddeninequalities* (differences in their contribution to social welfare) between experimental pathways, to learn from them, and to make it count for social progress. If bird A has wing type W^1, and bird B has wing type W^2, it is impossible to promise that both wing types will lead to equal outcomes. Most likely, one of the wing types is more adaptive, which leads to increases in the population of birds who carry that wing type. Similarly, if person A tells a joke J^1, and person B tells a joke J^2, it is nigh impossible to ensure that both jokes will be equally well-received! (Indeed, even a veteran jokester will have a hard time knowing in advance which of their jokes will "kill" in front of a live audience before actually testing them out!).

So, *evolutionary emancipation* is committed to a form of *outcome inequality*. (This is what it means to have a selection mechanism.) It entails the (occasionally harsh and brutal) non-random selection of innovations according to an impersonal fitness function. The liberal doctrine of equality before the law should not be mistaken for the false belief that all evolutionary mutations are equally adaptive. Not all innovations contribute to wellbeing equally. On the contrary, even small differences matter, and all innovations can be ranked, in various competitive evolutionary arenas, as (relatively) "better" (fit) or "worse" (unfit), based on their adaptive capacity to improve welfare and solve various problems. However, fitness is always relative to the rules of the game, which includes both naturally imposed constraints and human made rules. Since the fitness function determines what gets selected, *getting the fitness function right* (to the extent that it lies in our power) is the only way to ensure that the evolutionary mechanism serves emancipatory (and universal) interests rather than reactionary (and factional) ones. Although we never have access to infallible Archimedean leverage points—or other imaginary "planning centres"—from which to tweak the society's fitness function(s), we do have access to more modest mechanisms of institutional, cultural, and moral reform.

The third lesson is thus: "*Encourage competitive selection but tweak the fitness function to ensure that the resulting inequalities reveal pathways for social emancipation.*" A good fitness function ensures that selection selects for the right things. If current rules cease to be functional, there is room for tweaking the rules. Large-scale evolutionary experimentation only contributes to social emancipation when evolution passes through appropriate *selection filters* that contribute to the differential survival of welfare-enhancing and problem-solving innovations over innovations that are welfare-decreasing and non-problem-solving (or even problem-causing).

Summing up, the doctrine of evolutionary liberalism is an emancipatory social program that seeks to improve the wellbeing of all citizens, but especially that of its most disadvantaged members, by boosting the evolvability (innovation generating capacity) of the social order. For evolutionary liberalism to be a viable competitor to other forms of radical, progressive, emancipatory politics, it must articulate its message better. But it must also make some changes to its institutional and political program. It must openly acknowledge and tackle the downsides of unguided evolution and *set up* (or, where possible, *grow* and *let evolve*) institutions and rules (both formal and informal) to remedy or soften them. Since it is impossible to employ evolutionary mechanisms without incurring some unwanted costs, any evolutionary policy program must bear moral and political responsibility for the creative destruction that it tolerates or encourages. I have deliberately not provided much concrete guidance on how to do this, since easy institutional blueprints can be misleading, panaceas tend not to exist, and much work still remains to be done before agreement reigns. Until then, evolutionary liberals can potentially achieve higher public legitimacy, if not absolution, by being upfront about the downsides of their program. Where costs are calculable, they should take active steps in minimising their impact. Where costs are unavoidable, they should pay more attention to distributing their impact fairly across the population. A failure to do so undermines the claim of the evolutionary liberal order of being a robust real Utopian project that has sufficiently overcome the boogey-man of Social Darwinism.

Conclusion

Evolutionary liberalism is an old doctrine that can be traced back to the Scottish Enlightenment. It reached its arguable heyday in the era of Spencer, Sumner, and Social Darwinism. And it was boosted and reinvented, in the twentieth century, by people like F. A. Hayek. And today it should be reimagined and updated in light of contemporary complexity theory and evolutionary theory, in order to reinvigorate the liberals' *courage to be Utopian* (as Hayek put it)—namely, *real Utopian*. While it is true that classical liberalism has often found itself in the role of the stern admonisher of unrealistic Utopianism (given the importance of the deflationary mode of governance analysis that emphasises the limits of rational social planning), it also has an emancipatory, progressive, imaginative—and, yes, real Utopian—side. Recontextualising and redescribing the emancipatory potential in classical liberal theory in the language of evolutionary theory allows for a more robust form of political economy that combines "non-ideal" social theory with (realistically constrained) "emancipatory" imagination.

We cannot return to nineteenth-century evolutionary triumphalism. Liberal must avoid the pitfalls of Social Darwinism by acknowledging the institutional challenges of evolutionary governance. But they should reject, with equal force, the misguided moral impetus that sees nothing but mischief and trouble in assuming the evolutionary viewpoint. Indeed, Spencer deserves his comeuppance as a herald of social emancipation. Although he was generally too optimistic, he correctly identified evolutionary theory as a radical force for good in the world. In the Spencerian spirit, I have argued that the goals of emancipatory social transformation are best served by *identifying* and *harnessing* concrete institutional structures (both formal and informal) that protect, steer, and guide powerful evolutionary mechanisms in the direction of beneficial social change.

Evolutionary liberalism has a chance to motivate because it gives guidance on turning social emancipation into a robust institutional practice that justifies the courage to be Utopian in the face of seemingly intractable problems. It offers the two main *desiderata* that a good *real Utopian* theory needs: (a) a *plausible normative story* of how and why evolutionary processes matter for the wellbeing of the society, including its most disadvantaged members, and (b) a *plausible causal mechanism* that explains why liberal institutions have an edge over alternative proposals (such as evolutionary socialism) in protecting or facilitating emancipatory evolutionary processes. I have sought to defend both these claims against objections—at least enough to motivate further research.

First, I have argued that evolutionary processes matter greatly for the wellbeing of society, including its least advantaged members, because evolutionary forces have already proven their mettle in achieving miraculous results without the need for wishful thinking—or "miracles." In society, much like in biology, many of the most salient problems are of the sort that require an evolutionary system that is creative enough to produce "miracles without miracles." Evolutionary processes are especially suitable for improving our general problem-solving capacity, i.e., our general capacity for innovation, which is a highly desirable capacity to have, *regardless* of how we prioritise social problems. And they are *especially relevant* if we prioritise the needs of the poor and the downtrodden. They are most in need of radical, qualitative change of the sort that only evolution can provide. *Second*, I have argued that evolutionary liberalism carries the institutional prescription that forms the best starting point for thinking about how evolutionary processes can be facilitated and harnessed in today's world. The institutional framework of the liberal Open Society appears as an appealing evolutionary framework in which diverse experiments (innovations) are allowed to flourish and compete. Of course, this still leaves many of the institutional details unspecified. Finding the right balance between laissez-faire Social Darwinism and corrective social interventionism remains as elusive as ever, and there are no easy panaceas. Within the general framework of the Open Society, many important policy details (including the precise size and scope of government) are properly left for democratic self-governance.

A defence of liberalism as an evolutionary means of social emancipation may not be everyone's cup of tea. It may be too Utopian for many liberals, and too liberal for many Utopians! But let me conclude with an uplifting image. Can there be anything more profound than the articulation of the unified cosmic viewpoint that ties us all together—humans and animals alike—into a seamless web of natural miracles, individuations, and emergent processes? Can there be anything more inspiring than the discovery of our species' nature as evolved *and* still evolving creatures who have discovered evolutionary institutions that are conducive to their own emancipation? If the past is any guide, we are far from tapping into the full potential of powerful evolutionary forces for human betterment. If liberal emancipation means anything, it means *the courage to evolve*—together or apart—as free and equal citizens.

References

Arthur, W. B. (2015). *Complexity and the Economy*. Oxford University Press.

Beinhocker, E. (2006). *The Origin of Wealth: Evolution, Complexity, and the Radical Remaking of Economics*. Harvard Business School Press.

Beinhocker, E. (2011). Evolution as Computation: Integrating Self-organization with Generalized Darwinism. *Journal of Institutional Economics, 7*(3), 393–423.

Beinhocker, E. & Hanauer, N. (2014, September). Redefining Capitalism. *McKinsey Quarterly*. https://www.mckinsey.com/featured-insights/long-term-capitalism/redefining-capitalism

Colander, D., & Kupers, R. (2014). *Complexity and The Art of Public Policy: Solving Society's Problems from the Bottom Up*. Princeton University Press.

Cowen, T. (2018). *Stubborn Attachments: A Vision for a Society of Free, Prosperous, and Responsible Individuals*. Stripe Press.

Cziko, G. (1995). *Without Miracles: Universal Selection Theory and the Second Darwinian Revolution*. MIT Press.

Darwin, C. (1859). *The Origin of Species*. D. Appleton and Co.

Darwin, C. (1871). *The Descent of Man*. Princeton University Press.

Dawkins, R. [1976] (2006). *The Selfish Gene*. Thirtieth Anniversary Edition. Oxford University Press.

Dawkins, R. (2003). The Evolution of Evolvability. In S. Kumar & P. J. Bentley (Eds.), *On Growth, Form and Computers* (pp. 239–255). Elsevier Academic Press.

Ferguson, A. [1767] (2001). *An Essay on the History of Civil Society*. Cambridge, U.K.: Cambridge University Press.

Gaus, G. (2016). *The Tyranny of the Ideal: Justice in a Diverse Society*. Princeton University Press.

Gaus, G. (2021). *The Open Society and Its Complexities*. Oxford University Press.

Hayek, F. A. (1949). The Intellectuals and Socialism. *University of Chicago Law Review, 16*(3), 417–433.

Hayek, F. A. [1960] (2011). *The Constitution of Liberty: The Definitive Edition*. In R. Hamowy (Ed.), *The Collected Works of F. A. Hayek: Volume 17*. University of Chicago Press.

Hayek, F. A. (1967). The Theory of Complex Phenomena. In F. A. Hayek (Ed.), *Studies in Philosophy, Politics and Economics* (pp. 22–42). Routledge & Kegan Paul.

Hayek, F. A. (1982). *Law, Legislation and Liberty*. Routledge & Kegan Paul.

Hayek, F. A. (2002). Competition as a Discovery Procedure. *Quarterly Journal of Austrian Economics, 5*(3), 9–23.

Hodgson, G. M. (2019). *Is Socialism Feasible? Towards an Alternative Future*. Edward Elgar.

Hodgson, G. M., & Knudsen, T. (2010). *Darwin's Conjecture: The Search for General Principles of Social and Economic Evolution*. University of Chicago Press.
Hofstadter, R. [1944] (1992). *Social Darwinism in American Thought*. Beacon Press.
Holland, J. (1995). *Hidden Order: How Adaptation Builds Complexity*. Helix Books.
Hong, L., & Page, S. (2004). Groups of Diverse Problem Solvers can Outperform Groups of High Ability Problem Solvers. *Proceedings of the National Academy of Sciences, 101*(46), 16385–16389.
Hume, D. (1777). *An Enquiry Concerning the Principles of Morals*. http://praxeology.net/enquiry2.htm
Kauffman, S. A. (1993). *The Origins of Order: Self-Organization and Selection in Evolution*. Oxford University Press.
Kauffman, S. A. (2016). *Humanity in a Creative Universe*. Oxford University Press.
Lavoie, D. (1985). *National Economic Planning: What is Left?* Ballinger Publishing Company.
Lehto, O. (2021). Permanent Crisis Management, the Rule of Law, and Universal Basic Income: A Polycentric Approach. *Cosmos+Taxis*, *9*(5+6), 122–136.
Lehto, O., & Meadowcroft, J. (2020). Welfare Without Rent Seeking? Buchanan's Demogrant Proposal and the Possibility of a Constitutional Welfare State. *Constitutional Political Economy, 32*(2), 145–164.
Mill, J. S. [1859] (2003). *On Liberty*. Yale University Press.
Nelson, R., & Winter, S. (1982). *An Evolutionary Theory of Economic Change*. Belknap Press of Harvard University Press.
Ord, T. (2020). *The Precipice: Existential Risk and the Future of Humanity*. Hatchette Books.
Page, S. (2011). *Diversity and Complexity*. Princeton University Press.
Peirce, C. S. (2022). *Philosophical Writings of Peirce*. Dover.
Popper, K. (1966). *The Open Society and its Enemies* (5th ed.). Princeton University Press.
Simon, J. L. (1997). *The Ultimate Resource*. Princeton University Press.
Smith, A. [1776] (2008). *An Inquiry into the Nature and Causes of the Wealth of Nations*. Oxford University Press.
Spencer, H. (1851). *Social Statics: Or, the Conditions Essential to Happiness Specified, and the First of them Developed*. John Chapman.
Spencer, H. (1896). *The Principles of Ethics*. Appleton Press.
Sumner, W. G. (1992). *On Liberty, Society, and Politics: The Essential Essays of William Graham Sumner*. Liberty Fund.

Tebble, A. (2017). Liberty Against Progress. *Social Philosophy and Policy, 34*(2), 237–258.

Thierer, A. (2014). *Permissionless Innovation: The Continuing Case for Comprehensive Technological Freedom.* Mercatus Center at George Mason University.

Tomasi, J. (2012). *Free Market Fairness.* Princeton University Press.

Van Parijs, P. (1995). *Real Freedom for All – What (if anything) can justify capitalism?* Oxford University Press.

Wilson, D. S. (2019). *This View of Life: Completing the Darwinian Evolution.* Pantheon Books.

Wilson, E. O. [1975] (2000). *Sociobiology: The New Synthesis.* Belknap Press of Harvard University Press.

Wright, E. O. (2011). Real Utopias. *Contexts, 10*(2), 36–42.

Wright, E. O. (2013). *Envisioning Real Utopias.* Sage.

Zwolinski, M. (2015). Property Rights, Coercion, and the Welfare State: The Libertarian Case for a Basic Income for all. *Independent Review, 19*(4), 515–529.

CHAPTER 5

Liberal Emancipation as a System of Social Learning

Emily Chamlee-Wright and Mikayla Novak

When we describe a period of emancipatory change, we tend to recall specific moments of political or legal change. This impulse is understandable, given the predominance of governmental activity in contemporary life as well as the state-centric orientation of historical scholarship and commentaries. When an executive order is issued (e.g., the Emancipation Proclamation), when a constitutional amendment is passed (e.g., the 19th Amendment), when landmark policy reform is signed into law (e.g., the Civil Rights Act of 1964), or when a pivotal Supreme Court decision is handed down (e.g., *Obergefell v. Hodges*), change follows. Some of these changes are classed as emancipatory, owing to the effect of certain legal and policy changes in easing restrictions and constraints upon individual liberties and group rights.

That said, emancipation is a complex, usually long process involving a combination of liberal policy reform, market-based entrepreneurship,

E. Chamlee-Wright · M. Novak (✉)
Mercatus Center at George Mason University, Fairfax, VA, USA
e-mail: mnovak@mercatus.gmu.edu

M. Novak (ed.), *Liberal Emancipation*, Mercatus Studies in Political and Social Economy, https://doi.org/10.1007/978-3-031-94406-2_5

paradigm-shifting intellectual work, and liberal social movement advocacy. Emancipation is not limited to the whims and fancies of legislators and other public officials to expand the boundaries of freedom. The complexity of emancipative processes means that pro-liberty reforms are often susceptible to popular backlash dynamics, resistance from influential and privileged figures, and other countervailing forces. This observation implies that the pathway leading to emancipatory change is rarely direct, and never smooth.

This chapter is an attempt to make sense of the emancipative process in its complexity. To do so, we offer a general framework that situates emancipatory change within an overall system of social learning. Social learning is the phenomenon by which society achieves a level of coordination and widespread cooperation that surpasses the ability of individuals, or even a group of individual experts, to do the same (Aligica, 2014; Chamlee-Wright, 2010; Hayek, 1937, 1945; Ostrom, 1993; Ostrom et al., 1992). Liberalism, we argue, works as a system of social learning that aids complex political, economic, and social coordination. And crucially for our purposes here, liberalism fosters social learning that can accommodate and accelerate emancipatory developments that span multiple domains of social life.

Influenced by thinkers within the mainline of political economy—e.g., Adam Smith, F.A. Hayek, Frank Knight, James Buchanan, Elinor and Vincent Ostrom, Vernon Smith, Deirdre McCloskey—we consider ourselves to be participants in the tradition of philosophical liberalism. We are persuaded that, over the course of the last two-and-a-half centuries, liberal institutions (including guarantees of individual freedom, the rule of law, broad enjoyment of civil liberties, and secure property rights), and liberal sensibilities (including a default posture that recognizes the inherent dignity of every person and toleration for differences across ideas, people, and conceptions of a life well-lived) have fostered dramatic improvements in material conditions and human wellbeing. We are persuaded, in other words, that liberalism is the foundation of a good society in which people enjoy the opportunity to live their best lives in an environment of relative peace, abundance, and mutual respect.

This is not to suggest, however, an overly romantic view of liberal societies. Liberal societies have never arrived on the scene fully formed. The American experiment, to name but one prominent example, launched with egregious violations of the liberal principles articulated in its own founding Declaration. Further, we make no claim that liberal societies, once more fully developed, are without serious problems, whether they be fresh challenges or holdovers from an illiberal past. On the contrary, we embrace these facts as the starting point of our inquiry. Given that no society professing liberal values arrives on the scene fully formed, how do they become more consistently liberal? Given that path dependence, private interests, and illiberal attitudes often conspire to oppose emancipatory change, what is the process by which these barriers are overcome?

We begin our inquiry with the understanding that emancipatory change happens in real time, among competent but fallible human beings who possess private interests, moral commitments, and incomplete mental models of how liberal social orders work, all of which can be more or less conducive to emancipatory change. With this as the starting point, we argue that liberal institutional arrangements and cultural norms support a high degree of contestation, which in turn hardwires in a degree of epistemic humility. These properties allow liberalism to work as a system of social learning, through which they can become more consistently liberal over time.

To advance these arguments, in the next section we develop what Chamlee-Wright elsewhere describes as the "four corners of liberalism" (4CL)—political liberalism, economic liberalism, intellectual liberalism, and civic liberalism—into a framework for understanding how each of these primary dimensions is the source of contestation from which emancipatory change can emerge. Further, we explore the dynamics across the four dimensions of the liberal project that can both frustrate and foster emancipatory change. Following this, we situate the 4CL framework within the mainline tradition of political economy, with an emphasis on entrepreneurial action across the four corners of the liberal project that foster social learning favorable to emancipatory change. We then apply the 4CL framework across two modern cases of emancipatory change, highlighting the social learning process involved in each, and the conditions that helped to secure emancipatory change. This chapter then concludes with a summary of key arguments and identification of challenges and new lines of research that may be addressed through the 4CL framework.

The Four Corners of Liberalism Framework

Defining liberalism can be a challenge, in part because its meaning has evolved over the centuries (Merquior, 1991; Smith, 2013). Depending upon their discipline, scholars may speak of liberalism as a political apparatus, a policy framework, or a set of cultural norms. Some emphasize civil liberties as the centerpiece of the liberal tradition. Others emphasize arrangements that support a free and open marketplace. Still others focus on the power of reason to advance scientific discovery and intellectual progress. By some accounts, liberalism is an assemblage of procedural rules, which can (and perhaps should) be explained dispassionately, without reference to moral commitments. By other accounts, liberalism expresses our highest human virtues, and can't be discussed without reference to the moral commitments that define our humanity.

In our view, all these ways of thinking about and talking about liberalism are fair game. But in order to reconcile these differing perspectives, we believe that the best way to understand the liberal project is to see its principal dimensions—political liberalism, economic liberalism, intellectual liberalism, and civic liberalism—as being in dynamic relationship with one another. Figure 5.1 provides a visual representation of these relationships, in which each corner of the liberal project is in a relationship with each of the others, as illustrated by the lines that connect each corner. The double arrow at each end of the connecting lines signifies that each corner of the liberal project can directly support or pull against each of the others, just as the various key parts of a suspension bridge would.

Key Elements of the Four Corners of Liberalism Framework

Political liberalism, arguably the most familiar dimension of the liberal project, emphasizes the importance of institutional rules—rules that constrain government power, check the power of majorities, ensure procedural fairness, and protect individual and minority rights. Rules in the political context may be interpreted expansively to incorporate not only codified constitutional and legislative provisions (in the form of statutes) and administrative orders, but norms and practices concerning the accepted standards of conduct for public governance. In its ideal form, the political corner of the liberal project protects individual rights and

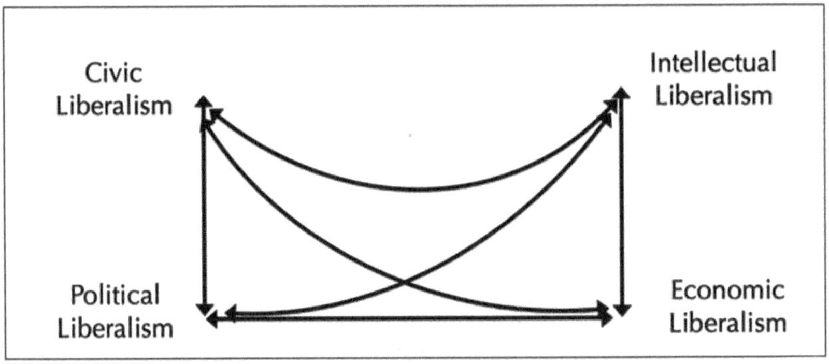

Fig. 5.1 The four corners of liberalism framework

guarantees civil liberties, leaving wide scope for individuals and associations of individuals to pursue their preferences and plans, so long as the rights of others are respected.

At the heart of political liberalism is the notion that government authority is contestable. The thirteenth century's Magna Carta inspired eighteenth-century liberals because it placed limits on the authority of the English monarchy (Fernández-Villaverde, 2016). Contestability features in the works of John Locke, and later in the American Declaration of Independence, which insist that the governing authority is not above the law and that its legitimacy rests upon the consent of the governed (Smith, 2013). Montesquieu's ([1748] 1989), and later, Hamilton's et al. ([1788] 2003) arguments favoring the separation of powers were arguments favoring contestation in the form of dispersed authority, with each sphere checking the power of other spheres. American federalism is itself a system of contestation in which power is divided and dispersed across states and with respect to state and federal jurisdiction (Buchanan, 1995; Ostrom, 1991).

In their ideal form, such arrangements serve as a deliberate check on any single political figure or government entity from abusing its authority. By limiting the authority each branch of government (executive, legislative, judicial) has over the other branches, by limiting the authority the federal government has over states, and by limiting the authority all levels of government have over the individual, contestation is built into the system. Because politically liberal spaces remain open to contestation, a degree of epistemic humility is hardwired in, allowing broad scope for experimentation and the learning that experimentation offers. The epistemological dimensions of key public governance structures, such as federalism (Vihanto, 1992) and democracy (Hayek, [1960] 2011), is a commonly referred insight drawn from modern classical liberal conceptual and analytical scholarship.

Moving from the southwest corner of Fig. 5.1 to the southeast, we consider *economic liberalism*, which affords people the freedom to openly innovate, produce, collaborate, compete, and exchange with others in their commercial lives. In his *Wealth of Nations*, Smith ([1776] 1982: 664) argued against the dirigisme of mercantilist trade ministers in favor of the "liberal plan of equality, liberty, and justice" in which every man is able to "pursue his own interest in his own way." As with political liberalism, contestation and epistemic humility are central features of economic liberalism, especially as it developed in the mainline tradition of political economy. In debates over the workability of socialist economic planning, Hayek (1945), for example, emphasized the cognitive role that the competitive market process plays. Given that the knowledge needed to facilitate coordination in a modern economy is fundamentally dispersed across countless market participants, Hayek asked, how is it possible that such coordination is ever obtained? The short answer is "contestation."

The competitive market process, Hayek explained, is not merely a mechanism for resource allocation. It is a discovery procedure (Hayek, 1945, 1973, [1968] 1978, 1988; Lavoie, 1986). Competitive market prices extend the cognitive reach of market participants beyond what they can know through direct experience and beyond what a bureau of planning experts can know through aggregated economic data. The open and contestable nature of market production and exchange, in other words, renders the market process a system of epistemic humility and social learning, in which a level of complex social coordination is achieved that no individual (or committee of experts) could design.

Moving to the northeast corner of Fig. 5.1, we consider *intellectual liberalism*. Well before the Enlightenment, ancient philosophers had planted seeds of intellectual openness and contestation. See, for example, Plato's (2004) "Apology of Socrates," which emphasized what we would today recognize as liberal intellectual values: curiosity, humility, and the value of unfettered dialogue. By the start of the Early Modern period, Gutenberg's printing press and the print culture it sparked had weakened the grip religious and state authorities had on the transmission and development of ideas. And out of this mix emerged the Scientific Revolution, which showcased the power of evidence-based reasoning, further diminishing the hegemonic influence of church and state authorities on the intellectual life of the age.

By the seventeenth and eighteenth centuries, scientists, philosophers, essayists, inventors, and men of industry had established rich cultures of intellectual openness through correspondence and the sharing of published papers and printed pamphlets. The coffeehouses of Austria and Britain, and the drawing rooms of Parisian Salonnières, were some examples of the physical spaces these communities needed to thrive. And it was in these sites of vibrant intellectual exchange that Enlightenment blossomed (Coser, 1965; Dekker, 2016; Lilti, 2015). Recent studies have referred to these, and other examples (such as university meeting spaces, repeated online interactions, etc.), as "knowledge commons" wherein ideas are produced and refined by subcultural communities of people observing shared rules of discursive engagement and information sharing (Dekker & Kuchař, 2021).

Here too, contestation and epistemic humility are central themes. As John Stuart Mill would famously argue in *On Liberty*, intellectual progress proceeds through an unflinching willingness to expose one's ideas to the scrutiny of intellectual challenge. Intellectual liberalism demands that no individual, no matter their social status, has any special claim to truth. It demands instead that we abide by recognized standards of evidence. It is these demands, and the standards of openness, honesty, and integrity set by intellectual communities that make intellectual liberalism a system of social learning (Polanyi, 1962). It is not only that individual scholars become wiser over time, but society as a whole also accumulates and embodies—through continuous contestation, innovation, and application—whole bodies of knowledge that no single scholar or innovator could ever discover, improve, or apply exclusively through independent effort (Mokyr, 1990, 2016).

The fourth corner, *civic liberalism* affords individuals wide scope to engage in associational life. It is within civil society that we forge commitments—both thick and thin—to families, religious communities, sports clubs, neighborhood playgroups, and countless other ties in which transactional benefits and meaning-rich connections commingle. There is a rich, but arguably underappreciated, history of classical liberal thinking surrounding the nature and consequences of associational life, a dimension of social life that is entangled with but nonetheless distinct from the commercial and political spheres.[1] Civil societal organizations and practices provide support for a diversity of practices (such as care, love, and camaraderie) and values (aesthetic, ideological, religious, etc.) (Cornuelle, [1965] 1993; Ealy, 2018; Garnett Jr. et al., 2015). Further, as thinkers from Alexis de Tocqueville to Vincent Ostrom have observed, the existence of a robust civic liberalism is a necessary condition for the existence of a self-governing ethos within a population (Ostrom, 1997; de Tocqueville, [1835] 2010).

As with intellectual liberalism, civic liberalism involves certain normative commitments, such as a default assumption that each of us is the other's dignified equal, and a default posture of toleration and forbearance in the face of difference. These commitments do not require agreement on normative ends. Rather, they require tacit agreement that a space of associational freedom should be maintained so that individuals and communities can work out what those ends are and how best to achieve them. In other words, civically liberal spaces are also spaces of contestation and humility, in which individuals and groups have the freedom to experiment with different ways of living, without the presumption that any one group should have the authority to impose its ways upon others. It is out of these normative commitments that liberal societies foster an ethos of pluralism, in which people of different cultures, beliefs, and lifestyles peacefully coexist and benefit from each other.

Summing up, contestation within each of the four corners of the liberal project supports a process of social learning. In the economic sphere, the competitive market process allows for a bottom-up process of social coordination and productivity that isn't possible to achieve through top-down design and control. The open contest of ideas in the intellectually liberal sphere springboards innovation, refines good ideas, and corrects errors. Liberal civic spaces provide people the freedom to find and create meaning-rich and socially productive associational life. And though the threat of tyranny is always a concern where political power is exercised, to the extent that liberal constraints divide and limit that power, liberal political orders allow scope for experimentation and learning in the ways we govern. An important implication of our reckoning with the social learning aspects of the 4CL framework is that individuals can exercise ideational, logistical, and organizational creativity, and ingenuity in the use of resources, to activate projects with emancipative purposes and outcomes, even in quite repressive environments, as well as display the requisite flexibility to respond to unforeseen obstacles and challenges when seeking to fulfill their aims for a freer world for evermore people.

Social Learning Dynamics Across the Four Corners

To this point, we have described Fig. 5.1 as if it were a map with four directional reference points. But we might also consider the 4CL framework as having metaphorical properties akin to a suspension bridge. Because it relies upon a system of mutually reinforcing supports and tension across its principal parts, a suspension bridge can withstand a heavy load of traffic and it can adapt to changing conditions without rupturing. Similarly, liberalism works as a system of supports and tensions across each of its principal dimensions that lend properties of functionality, structural integrity, and adaptability. Thus, in addition to the social learning that unfolds within each corner, these cross-corner dynamics also foster social learning. And as we argue below, these cross-corner dynamics can be helpful in fostering social learning that leads to emancipatory change.

For example, a liberal society's neutral enforcement of contracts and property rights—key features of political liberalism—are essential if the benefits of economic liberalism are to take hold, both generally and within communities seeking emancipatory change. Similarly, figures who advance new mental models of emancipatory change within the intellectual liberalism arena—think of W. E. B Du Bois, Ralph Ellison, Richard Wright, and James Baldwin—could not do their work, nor would their ideas have reached so wide an audience, if not for the freedoms of speech and expression found within political liberalism and the specialization and abundance required to support such work, i.e., if not for the fruits of economic liberalism. Further, social networking aimed at emancipatory change that unfolds within the civic sphere relies upon politically liberal rights of association and is fueled by emancipatory paradigms that emerge within the arena of intellectual liberalism.

As with a suspension bridge, tensions also exist across the four corners. In an environment of political and intellectual freedom, for example, those opposing emancipatory change may also find a receptive audience for their views, and there is no guarantee that at any given moment those favoring emancipatory change will win the contest of persuasion in scholarly domains or winning over majoritarian public opinion. That said, such expression can also accelerate emancipatory change and, sometimes, in unanticipated (if not surprising) ways. As Rauch (2013) has argued, First Amendment freedoms exercised by anti-gay rights activists such as Jerry Fallwell and Anita Bryant in the 1980s had the unintended effect of galvanizing the gay liberation movement. Scholarly treatments of these experiences point to the misalignment of the homophobic views of anti-gay rights activism against the increasingly tolerant attitudes toward homosexuality that emerged during the period (Pinker, 2011), and potentially other factors such as incentivization for LGBT rights groups to mobilize against perceived threats posed by religious and other counter-movements (e.g., Clews, 2017).

These examples illustrate the productive potential of cross-corner social learning, and the adaptability necessary for individuals and groups to article pro-liberty rights claims in a world brimming with contestation. But to better understand how, in general, pro-emancipatory social learning unfolds, we situate the 4CL framework within the mainline political economy tradition, to which we turn next.

Situating the 4CL Framework Within Mainline Political Economy

Emancipatory change is a "macro" phenomenon. But such change is not limited to structural effects. The emphasis upon methodological individualism of mainline political economy allows us to recognize that any change is instigated by capable, but fallible, human beings actively seeking opportunities to achieve satisfaction, and realize betterment, in the world in which they live. The mainline approach does not pursue analysis at the expense of the macro-level dimensions of human existence. After all, individuals operate in a particular moment in history, within specific legal, political, and economic conditions, and under the influence of specific moral commitments, beliefs, and mental models of how the world works. Our point is that without an understanding of the activities and roles of individuals, explanation of societal phenomena such as emancipatory economic, political, and social trends would remain incomplete.

In other words, we cannot understand macro-level emancipatory change without reference to individual (micro-level) action in a context of (meso-level) associational life (Wagner, 2020). It is within the mesosphere that institutional rules of the social game, informal norms, and shared mental models emerge and operate, governing micro-level expectations and action. There is no guarantee that at a given moment in time such meso-level phenomena will be consistently aligned with emancipatory outcomes. But so long as contestation is possible, micro-level action has the potential to challenge and change those norms, institutions, and mental models. This micro-meso-macro connection situates emancipatory change within the mainline tradition of political economy (Boettke, 2021).

Mainline political economy is grounded in the recognition that knowledge of a complex social world is fundamentally dispersed and cannot ever be given in totality to a single mind. As such, the benevolence and cognitive reach of the people populating that social order are necessarily limited. Those limitations set up the basic problem of emancipatory change. Extending upon Hayek (1945), if people living within liberally oriented societies were perfectly benevolent, perfectly informed, and perfectly incentivized, the problem of working out emancipatory change would be purely one of logic. But that is emphatically not the problem liberal societies face. The problem, rather, is how, at a given moment in historical time, with all the accompanying restrictions and attitudes that have evolved up to that moment, an inconsistently liberal society becomes more consistently liberal. How does such a society, which has notional ideas of liberal principles, extend a spirit of sympathy and benevolence to those deemed (and who may deem themselves) to be inferior? How are mental models that justify illiberal treatment and undergird illiberal institutional arrangements traded for mental models that demand and institutional arrangements that foster emancipatory change?

These questions call upon two other prominent themes within the mainline tradition of political economy: (1) entrepreneurship as a category of human action, and (2) the socially embedded nature of entrepreneurial action.

Emancipatory change is entrepreneurially driven.[2] We make this claim, in part, in reference to traditional notions of commercial entrepreneurship. As Rojas (2024: 53) explains, "[e]conomically open societies generate additional wealth, which can be applied to activism and social change. As long as resources are 'free' to move where people want, many will choose to use them for social change." Further, commercial enterprises can create social spaces (e.g., gay bars) and intellectual venues (e.g., journals and magazines such as *The Nation* and *The New Leader*) through which emancipatory social movements have gained strength. That said, entrepreneurship is not merely the domain of businesspeople. Within the mainline tradition of political economy, entrepreneurship is a general category of human action, in which we are alert to opportunities that have been overlooked by others. Entrepreneurship, therefore, can take an economic form, but can embrace ideological, social, and political aspects.[3]

This broader view of entrepreneurship helps us to recognize that emancipatory change can be initiated and supported from any corner of the liberal project. Further, it helps us see that emancipatory change is not limited to formal reforms in the political-legal arena, which are often downstream of the social learning that has already unfolded in the intellectual, civic, and economic spheres.

Perhaps most importantly, this broader view helps us to see that emancipatory entrepreneurship can foster social learning through what we might describe as Kirznerian arbitrage or through Schumpeterian innovation (Storr, 2009). Consider, for example the ideological entrepreneurship of American civil rights leaders. Martin Luther King, Jr. engaged in acts of ideological arbitrage when, in his "I Have a Dream" speech, he tied the aims of the Civil Rights Movement to the meanings within and the emotional commitments to the Declaration of Independence. His "Letter from a Birmingham Jail" made a similar arbitrage move by connecting the Movement's aims to the Christian principles of justice and equality. Malcom X, on the other hand, introduced a model of emancipatory change that disrupted the association of emancipatory progress with Christian teachings and collaboration with white allies.

Though emancipatory entrepreneurship is initiated by individuals, mainline political economy also recognizes that such action is socially embedded in at least two ways. First, though emancipatory entrepreneurs may envision a world far different from the status quo, they are nonetheless people of their times and context, influenced by the accumulated lessons, attitudes, and constraints that define that context. Those prior conditions may support liberal reform if, for example, prior periods of emancipatory change offer transferable lessons for overcoming contemporary impediments. On the other hand, those prior conditions can also be the source of illiberal path dependence, making it difficult for emancipatory entrepreneurs or those around them to imagine how a wider application of liberal freedoms might work out. Entrenched interests that have developed within the status quo can make that path dependence all the stickier.

The second way in which entrepreneurial action is socially embedded is that the success of micro-level entrepreneurial action usually depends upon the cooperation of other people. Acts of emancipatory entrepreneurship will not succeed if they are merely micro-level exploits by an adventurous, or charismatic, individual operating on their own. Meso-level social entrepreneurship—e.g., the formation of associations, networks, and organizations—reduce coordination costs, channel specialized talent according to comparative advantage, propagate emancipative ideas and tactics, and create collective focal points of attention for emancipative causes. Further, new mental models favoring emancipatory change have greater likelihood of taking hold in group settings, where intersubjective processes of meaning, sensemaking, and understanding can unfold. And it is within meso-level associational life, often among rival social groups, where emancipatory proposals are negotiated, refined, and not infrequently, stalled, and rejected.

Implicated in the foregoing discussion is one further mainline political economy theme: the relevance of time. Social learning dynamics that propagate emancipative ideas, sentiments, and practices unfold through the forward arrows of time. In an initial time period 1, liberal political freedoms may be narrowly and inconsistently applied, constraining what should be the emancipating effects of the liberal order. Despite their limited scope, however, the political freedoms that do exist create space in the intellectual and civic corners of the liberal project, or at least enable toleration for intellectual and civic creativity to proceed. It may be in these corners that emancipatory movements gain momentum, and so during period 2, a more radical commitment to emancipatory freedom might be imagined, articulated, shared, and debated. Shifting sentiments and mental models may eventually support more consistently liberal political change. The temporal sequence stated here is one possibility among many that may proceed as pro-emancipation individuals and group representatives imagine liberatory alternatives to the oppressive or marginalized situations they face, and then organize themselves and others to activate a range of strategic and logistical projects with the attempted effect of expanding the boundaries of freedom. As time unfolds, people may not only discover opportunities to relax constraints upon freedom but encounter a variety of hurdles and obstacles with cultural, economic, social, and political characteristics.

In brief, through a process of contestation, socially embedded entrepreneurs drive a dynamic process of social learning across the four corners of the liberal project. While these dynamics can be the source of emancipatory change, such outcomes are never guaranteed. The achievement of emancipatory outcomes may be realizable under certain conditions and not others, all of which become the subject of conceptual, analytical, and empirical interest. In the case studies that follow, we will identify some of those conditions.

Applying the Four Corners of Liberalism Framework to Selective Emancipative Episodes

Having explained the 4CL framework of liberal emancipation and situating that framework within the mainline tradition of political economy, our task is to now demonstrate the utility of the model with reference to two case studies. In what follows, we shall focus upon the historical and contemporary trajectories of emancipation including the social learnings involved in realizing liberties and rights for racial minorities, and for people with diverse sexual orientations and gender identities.

Racial Equality

One of the more regrettable aspects of the human experience has been the persistence of relations of domination and subjection along racialist criteria. While the illiberal deprivations of slavery were experienced in numerous regions of the world since ancient times, modern history has until recent decades been marked by extensive systems of slave trading occurring in the continent of Africa. Discrimination and prejudice on racial lines was not limited to the forcible trade in human beings, with a combination of social norms and political institutions enshrining race-based differences in respect to individual and group capacities to access an array of private and public goods (including basic civil and economic rights). The normative aspiration to enshrine racial equality remains a focus of contemporary social and political concern, with a range of studies indicating that the historical lack of racial equality has yielded persistent effects regarding employment outcomes, education and health status, and other key quality of life indicators (e.g., Chetty et al., 2020).

Much of the focus of racial equality has focused upon, but is not limited to, the structurally divergent circumstances faced by descendants of African slaves in the U.S., and by other racial minority groups. African Americans struggled for emancipation from slavery in the American South during the nineteenth century, with coalitions of leading African American figures (such as Frederick Douglass, Booker T. Washington, and Ida B. Wells) with white sympathizers (including from the first-wave feminist movement) seeking emancipatory changes as animated by classical liberal concerns for racial equality (Powell, 2000). The defeat of the segregationist Southern jurisdictions during the American Civil War of the 1860s, and a wave of abolitionist and pro-equality constitutional amendments introduced at the federal level, promised the cessation of racial discrimination at all levels of U.S. public administration. Such aspirations proved to be premature as a lack of constitutional enforcement facilitated the institutionalization of so-called "Jim Crow" state-local segregationist provisions affecting access to public facilities, education, and transportation, as well as racial discrimination in terms of voting rights.

The distance between the liberal spirit animating constitutional design, and racial equality amendments, in the U.S., and the discriminatory practices that African Americans endured for generations, attracted significant criticism by those dedicated to the precepts of equality between the races. Classical liberal figures such as Knight (1960) and Hutt (1966) articulated penetrating critiques as to how racism illustrated the liberal incompleteness of the American political project, while scholars such as Milton Friedman and Warren Nutter proposed school education voucher funding reforms as a mechanism to racially desegregate public schools in the South (Magness et al., 2019). Critics of liberalism, both in the U.S. and internationally, also pointed to the application of racial economic and political discriminations in the American South as undermining theoretical arguments concerning institutional federalism's capacity to undermine group exploitation at the local level (Levy, 2015).

One of the consistent claims of activists and supporters of civil rights campaigning surrounded the effect of anti-black racism upon equality of economic opportunity. Racial discrimination and prejudice were manifested in the form of insecurity of property rights for African Americans, an argument reinforced by traumatic experiences such as the 1921 Tulsa, Oklahoma, race massacre wherein prosperous black neighborhoods were destroyed by vigilante white mobs (Ellsworth, 1982). These arguments were invariably combined with assertions to the effect that an inability to vote under Jim Crow provisions compromised the democratic ability of racial minorities to effectively demand better quality provision of public sector services, effectively representing a diminution in the effectiveness of the "voice" mechanism to ensure a responsiveness of the state to its citizens (Hirschman, 1970).

As the experience of the U.S. Civil Rights movement of the mid-twentieth century attested, racial minorities refused to maintain a position of acquiescence and passivity in response to the discriminatory and prejudicial experiences they endured. The mobilization by African Americans, and their supporters of all other races, demonstrates the applicability of the four-corners framework embraced in this chapter in describing the struggles for racial equality in the U.S. case. Recalling Rojas (2024), a somewhat underappreciated, but undoubtedly crucial, means to apply socio-political pressure for racial emancipation is the accumulation and disposition of economic resources purposefully dedicated to pro-racial equality collective action projects. The classic economic argument is that money is fungible insofar as proceeds can be used for multiple purposes, including anti-racist mobilizations, and even certain heterogeneous products may be repurposed to campaign for racial equality between blacks and whites.[4]

Historical evidence attests to the gradually, albeit unevenly applied, improvement in economic status of African Americans during the first half of the twentieth century and beyond (Higgs, 1977; Smith & Welch, 1989). With rising labor market participation and improving employability providing gradually rising disposable incomes on average over time, African Americans and their families enjoyed growing opportunities to use their earnings to support anti-racism collective actions in the South and elsewhere. Organizations such as the National Association for the Advancement of Colored People (NAACP) were joined by a growing cohort of interest organizations and associations that invested resources to overcome racial inequalities (Andrews, 2004; Chong, 1991). The generation of campaign funds through black churches, and the emergence of bail funds for jailed protestors, are arguably additional examples of how economic liberalism enabled the amelioration of racial discrimination and prejudice (Morris, 1984). Of note is that the key figures and organizations of the budding Civil Rights movements also secured financial and other supports from anti-racism activists throughout the U.S. (Chappell, 1994; Korstad & Lichtenstein, 1988).

Associated with the application of expanding economic opportunities and freedoms to press the case for racial equality, African Americans actively pursued strategies to extend cultural liberalism in the shape of dignification of people irrespective of racial background. Numerous accounts of the Civil Rights movement have indicated how freedom of association, including through religious organizations, social movement organizations, and other establishments, enabled black Americans to organize for reform (e.g., Novak, 2021). Similarly, black communities benefited from their ability to exercise freedom of speech. This allowed individuals and groups to produce publications, and use other communicative strategies (e.g., appearances on radio and, eventually, television) to disseminate messages oriented to the imperatives of anti-racism and emancipatory socio-political changes (Roberts & Klibanoff, 2007).[5]

The civic liberalism dimension of the four-corners approach is in dynamic relationship with intellectual liberalism. For the Civil Rights movement to effectuate positive changes for racial minorities, African Americans needed to gain a shared awareness and consciousness of their struggles against informal and formal dimensions of racism. Charismatic ideological entrepreneurs such as Martin Luther King and Malcolm X would rely upon a range of argumentative frames—including reference to liberal precepts of equality and justice, and the need to engage in concerted effort against the coercive effects of structural racism—to bring about cognitive consilience among African Americans (e.g., Selby, 2008). Efforts by these individuals and other activists were supported by the epistemic prerequisites of collective action and anti-hegemonic organizational capacity. These epistemic prerequisites often came in the form of collective narratives and stories shared among groups, and subsequently spread through communication and interaction,[6] all of which diagnosed the nature and ill-effects of racism and offered a hypothesis of a connection between activism and achievement of a future of equality between the races.

The interconnective nature of the 4CL framework incorporates political liberalism as a central element. The political dimension of the Civil Rights movement was by no means restricted to an understanding that social pressure through anti-hegemonic collective action was an essential ingredient to drive out racism against black minorities. Given the harsh lessons of the Jim Crow era that codification of racial equality could not be achieved in the absence of rights enforcement, civil rights activists actively sought to gain a range of legislative, if not constitutional, political concessions that would significantly raise the costs of racial discrimination and prejudice. The ultimate success of the Civil Rights movement as a liberal project may be traced to the iterative gains made by micro-level action and meso-level organizations and social networks in areas such as education, housing, and public accommodations during the 1950s and 1960s, if not earlier, which eventually culminated in the *Civil Rights Act* of 1964 which was followed a year later by the *Voting Rights Act* of 1965. Of note here was that the intransigence of U.S. state and county governments to unwind Jim Crow provisions, even in the face of growing protests, led Civil Rights movement campaigners to turn their attentions to national-level public authorities (including the Presidency, Congress, and the Supreme Court) in order to override local discrimination and enshrine formal racial equality.

While improvements in the economic, political, and social status of African Americans may be discerned from empirical evidence, there is more to do to realize the liberal normative project of equality between the races. Recent studies in the field of stratification economics indicates continuing economic disparities between black and white Americans (Stewart, 2018). There also remains a degree of racial tension in the U.S., especially considering issues such as police brutality, incarceration rates, and related criminal justice issues (Davis, 2024). With the legislative victories at hand, and arguably in the face of pressure from the radical flanks of the Black Liberation movement, King later sought—unsuccessfully—to translate the formal racial equality agenda into an economic program involving greater access to education, employment, and health care for African Americans (e.g., Honey, 2018; Jackson, 2007). While the preferred pace of racial emancipation is presumed to differ among some, the four-corners framework of liberalism retains its efficacy as a model of the interdependent attributes of emancipation that align reasonably well with American experience of the generally improving positionality of African American communities since the achievement of Civil Rights reforms.

LGBT Rights

Another discernible trend in the evolution of modern liberalism has been the improvement in status afforded to lesbian, gay, bisexual, and transgender (LGBT) people in North America, Europe, and Australasia, and, increasingly, in various regions of the Global South. This improvement over recent decades have emanated against the backdrop of severe discrimination and prejudice, both of an informal and formal (or legal) nature, exhibited toward the expression of non-conventional sexual orientations and gender identities. These experiences have been manifested in the form of imprisonment of queer persons, conversion therapies that attempt to reinforce heteronormative attitudes, disproportionately high assault and homicide rates, employment discrimination, a lack of access to goods and services (such as education, healthcare, and housing), and so on. From this historical position of extreme deprivation in terms of rights and liberties, it is important to comprehend the processes through which LGBT communities have experienced liberal emancipation especially during the latter half of the twentieth century.

For the purposes of our arguments, we will focus upon the emancipatory experiences of gays and lesbians in the San Francisco area of the U.S. from the early 1960s.[7] Prior to the period of queer cultural and political mainstreaming, same sex attracted, and gender diverse, individuals congregated in small-scale settings such as bars, clubs, and restaurants, mainly in the Tenderloin district of San Francisco, or otherwise associated with one another through gatherings at private residences. However, the bar scene tended to operate clandestinely and was susceptible to police harassment (DellaPosta et al., 2016). While individual gays and lesbians enjoyed some capacity to work, especially insofar as their identities remain largely publicly undisclosed, transgender individuals sometimes found themselves relying upon illicit activities, such as prostitution, for their economic subsistence (Sides, 2009). While there is little doubt that engagement of the LGBT community in the formal economy rapidly expanded from the late 1970s, as did commercial interest in LGBT individuals as potentially lucrative consumer market segments, it may be argued that non-economic factors were more influential in instigating the expansion of the four corners of liberalism for these minorities.

An important development in expansive cultural liberalism in the LGBT community was the post-war development of several gay and lesbian advocacy organizations in California and in other U.S. states. The Mattachine Society initially established in Los Angeles, and eventually headquartered in San Francisco from 1956, and it sought to not only facilitate association among otherwise isolated gay men but to advance a normative project of achieving equal respect and rights for homosexuals as American citizens. Another important cultural group that formed in San Francisco during this period was the lesbian group Daughters of Bilitis, which sought to provide an alternative social space for women outside of bars and clubs (Ness, 2004). During the ensuing decade a few groups developed in the area—including the Council on Religion and the Homosexual, and the Society for Individual Rights—most of which shared the generic aim of normalizing same sex relationships and petitioning for reforms such as eliminating police harassment and the legal decriminalization of sodomy.

The development of queer societies had important, yet arguably unintended consequences, along the epistemic dimension of emancipatory liberalism. Individual members of the gay and lesbian rights groups actively negotiated the meaning of their sexual and gender differences to that of conventional society, contributing toward an evolving sense of shared interests (and, later, a community) whose sentiments spread to bargoers as well as relatively isolated individuals within the LGBT community. However, queer scholars have indicated that especially during the 1960s and early 1970s tensions emerged with respect to subscriptions to an "assimilative" model of queer life that sought public normalization of LGBT identities versus a "difference" model that elevated the norms of self and community pride in the distinctive attributes and contributions of the LGBT community to American social life (Stein, 2005; c.f., Ormsbee, 2010). As attested by the exuberant growth of "pride" festivals—and events and opportunities facilitating the public disclosure (or "outing") of individuals as members of sexual and gender minorities—it may be argued that the epistemological variant of freedom for LGBT individuals gravitated toward socio-political projects advancing not only freedom of association for members of queer communities, but broader public recognition and respect for difference. To use the suspension bridge metaphor when describing our 4CL framework once more, a swaying (but not collapse) of the bridge of queer liberalism historically unfolded as queer communities contended with, and negotiated, the meaning and appropriateness of emancipation as cultural, economic, political, and social projects.

It was evident even to the early community organizers in San Francisco, and in other major cities across the U.S., that a political dimension of queer activism coexisted with the desire to develop a safe and respectable sense of community life for LGBT individuals. Part of the development of a shared consciousness among coalitions of sexual and gender minorities during the 1950s and 1960s rested in the recognition of problems stemming from routine police harassment, and the link between criminalization of intimate and other activities undertaken by LGBT community members and lack of economic and social participation. These understandings were reinforced by events such as the 1965 New Year's Day raid on a costume ball hosted by the Council on Religion and the Homosexual in San Francisco's California Hall, noted by some scholars as a turning point in the political consciousness of the local LGBT community and a galvanizer of mutual interests between the likes of bargoers and homophile organizations (e.g., Boyd, 2003). Police harassment and broader economic and social discrimination opened opportunities for LGBT activists to petition politicians for legal reforms, and soon paved the way for notable queer community figures such as Harvey Milk to stand for public offices on anti-harassment platforms (Milk, 2013).

Reflecting broader trends in economic prosperity during the post-war period, individual members of the LGBT community were increasingly able to attain employment across a diverse range of industries and occupations. With the benefit of rising disposable incomes, certain people dedicated some of their growing economic resources toward queer emancipation projects. For example, Harvey Milk was involved in establishing the Castro Village Merchants Association in response to the exclusion of gay-operated businesses by the then-existing Eureka Valley Merchants Association (Alan, 2023; Harry & DeVall, 1978). Prior to this, a coalition of gay bar owners and liquor wholesalers established the Tavern Guild to, in part, protect members from the economic and financial instabilities resulting from regular bar raids by law enforcement personnel in San Francisco. This objective had a clear political dimension which is, in turn, suggestive of the deeply entangled character of LGBT intermediary activities during this period. It has been noted that "[t]he Tavern Guild used queer economic resources in the 1960s to achieve limited political alliances and expanded civil rights without relying on a politic of mainstream visibility" (Boyd, 1988: 1362–1363).

The application of economic liberalism to help develop San Francisco's LGBT community was not without its tensions. Certain members of the community expressed a concern that queer commercialism and LGBT economic mainstream could threaten the community infrastructures that had been painstakingly built over previous decades. While such concerns persist, it is notable that community members creatively adapted economic resources to build up health care centers and social work regimes that proved effective in addressing challenges, such as the HIV-AIDS epistemic during the 1980s and 1990s. To some extent the communitarian-style critique that capitalism would potentially corrode queer community life overshadowed the practical interdependencies between economic and social interactions. For example, bars, hotels, nightclubs, and restaurants hosted club and community meetings for LGBTQ groups. Additionally, such commercial enterprises provided donations, sponsorship money, and goods in-kind to support social activities for gay, lesbian, bisexual, transgender, and queer groups. San Francisco's gay bars donated food and drinks for Society for Individual Rights parties in the mid-1960s (D'Emilio, 1983), while bars and other commercial premises in this area and elsewhere funded gay and lesbian sporting activities (Harry & DeVall, 1978).

Interdependent processes governing liberal emancipation, as indicated by the four-corners framework, attest that life for LGBT communities in the early decades of the twenty-first century was a far cry from that experienced by their generational forebears. The degree of public acceptability of diversity in sexual orientation and gender diversity is arguably greater than at any time in America's past, with survey data now consistently indicating majoritarian tolerance of LGBT community members (Gallup, 2024). While it is certainly true that contentiousness surrounding certain elements of queer life—especially surrounding transgenderism and gender nonconformity—have appeared in political debates, the four-corners framework of liberal emancipation provides analytical rigor toward an understanding as to how a closeted and marginalized community managed to achieve much improved economic, political, and social outcomes during the post-war period.

Conclusion

In this chapter, we explored the ways in which liberalism works as a system of social learning through which emancipatory change is accommodated and accelerated. We advance a framework—what we call the "four corners of liberalism" framework—to better understand the epistemic features of the liberal order. Essentially, this chapter provides an account as to how the four principal dimensions of the liberal project (political, economic, intellectual, and civic) work together to accommodate and support emancipatory change, while maintaining the integrity of the social order itself. We then applied that framework to better understand certain specific instances of emancipatory development both in historical times and in modern contexts.

The 4CL presents a realist orientation with respect to the possibilities of liberal emancipation. The expansive set of recognition and practice of freedoms under liberalism does not arrive on the scene fully formed. Nor does the framework we articulate promise there will be no problems or constraints in the actualization of emancipation. On the contrary, what liberalism offers are open spaces in which people are free to examine, experiment, and discover. What liberalism promises is a society that is capable of learning, identifying better solutions, and adapting to change. Disruption, in other words, is not a bug, it is a feature of a dynamic society that can adapt to new circumstances. This capacity for social learning affords liberal societies a particular advantage in broadening and accelerating emancipatory outcomes, an observation that we regard as being affirmed considering historical and contemporary experiences.

There are opportunities to build upon the insights illuminated in this chapter. In general, the 4CL framework may be further explored including in connection with modern literature concerning the connections between economic, political, and social freedom (e.g., Lawson & Clark, 2010). Another potential theoretical development is to integrate the 4CL framework with complex systems models. In an empirical vein the 4CL framework may be applied to interpret the past and present of emancipative episodes not only in Western countries, but in the Global South, and draw upon additional case studies in emancipation. Finally, instances of emancipative backsliding could be further explored as imbalances between the affirmation of liberalism and of authority, with the latter having the effect of reducing the scope of political, economic, intellectual, and civic freedoms.

Notes

1. It is owing to the distinctive position that contrasts market and political modes of operation and organization that civil society is often (mis)characterized as the "third sector" of society, or is viewed as being synonymous with not-for-profit organizational forms. Authors, such as Aligica and Wagner (2020), Auteri and Wagner (2007), and Novak (2018), have indicated that civil societal entities are practically entangled with commercial and political enterprises, rather than being straightforwardly separable.
2. Recent scholarship has identified an emancipatory function of entrepreneurship (e.g., Rindova et al., 2009) which entail efforts to realize greater autonomy for oneself, and, consistent with this, achieve improving conditions for others in respect to economic,

political, and social status. This emancipatory function can be interpreted as complementing certain entrepreneurial attributes already identified in literature, including opportunity identification and the use of judgment, and could also provide activities to reduce stigma attaced to certain individuals and groups (Bacq et al., 2018).

3. See Schumpeter (1934) and Kirzner (1979) on economic entrepreneurship, North (2005) and Storr (2009) on ideological entrepreneurship, Swedberg (2006) on social entrepreneurship, and Shockley et al. (2006) on political entrepreneurship.
4. To take a simple example, a slogan may be emblazoned upon a piece of white cardboard for use in a public rally or protest, or that same cardboard could be used to sketch out plans and tactics in a meeting of social movement activists.
5. For an examination of the effects of music and song in facilitating cultural coherent among Civil Rights activists, see Reed (2015).
6. This statement alludes to Korzybski's (1950) remark that "the map is not the territory."
7. It may be argued that reasonably similar emancipative trajectories were realized in roughly similar ways to the benefit of LGBT individuals and groupings in other major Western cities during the same period.

Acknowledgements We thank an anonymous reviewer for their comments on a draft version of this chapter. The usual disclaimers apply.

References

Alan, T. (2023, April 19). Harvey, the Merchants, and the Theater. *Bay Area Reporter*. https://www.ebar.com/story.php?ch=news&sc=news&id=324657

Aligica, P. D. (2014). *Institutional Diversity and Political Economy: The Ostroms and Beyond*. Oxford University Press.

Aligica, P. D., & Wagner, R. E. (2020). Economic Coordination in Environments with Incomplete Pricing. *Review of Austrian Economics, 33*(3), 315–329.

Andrews, K. T. (2004). *Freedom Is a Constant Struggle: The Mississippi Civil Rights Movement and Its Legacy*. University of Chicago Press.

Auteri, M., & Wagner, R. E. (2007). The Organizational Architecture of Nonprofit Governance: Economic Calculation Within an Ecology of Enterprises. *Public Organization Review, 7*(1), 57–68.

Bacq, S., Toubiana, M., Ajunwa, I., Ormiston, J., & Ruebottom, T. (2018). Stigma Entrepreneurship: Exploring Stigma as a Source of Entrepreneurial Motivations. In *Frontiers of Entrepreneurship Research 2018: Proceedings of the Thirty-Eighth Annual Babson College Entrepreneurial Research Conference* (pp. 139–144).

Boettke, P. J. (2021). *The Struggle for a Better World*. Mercatus Center at George Mason University.

Boyd, N. A. (1988). Shopping for Rights: Gays, Lesbians, and Visibility Politics. *Denver University Law Review, 75*(4), 1361–1374.

Boyd, N. A. (2003). *Wide Open Town: A History of Queer San Francisco to 1965*. University of California Press.

Buchanan, J. M. (1995). Federalism as an Ideal Political Order and an Objective for Constitutional Reform. *Publius: The Journal of Federalism, 25*(2), 19–28.

Chamlee-Wright, E. (2010). *The Cultural and Political Economy of Recovery: Social Learning in a Post-Disaster Environment*. Routledge.

Chamlee-Wright, E. (2015). *Liberal Learning and the Art of Self-governance*. Routledge.

Chappell, D. L. (1994). *Inside Agitators: White Southerners in the Civil Rights Movement*. Johns Hopkins University Press.

Chetty, R., Hendren, N., Jones, M. R., & Porter, S. R. (2020). Race and Economic Opportunity in the United States: An Intergenerational Perspective. *Quarterly Journal of Economics, 135*(2), 711–783.

Chong, D. (1991). *Collective Action and the Civil Rights Movement*. University of Chicago Press.

Clews, C. (2017). *Gay in the 80s: From Fighting For Our Rights to Fighting For Our Lives*. Troubadour Publishing.

Cornuelle, R. B. [1965] (1993). *Reclaiming the American Dream: The Role of Private Individuals and Voluntary Associations*. Routledge.

Coser, L. A. (1965). *Men of Ideas: A Sociologist's View*. Free Press.

Davis, B. R. (2024). The Predatory States of America. In F. Rojas & C. Stern (Eds.), *Sociology and Classical Liberalism in Dialogue: Freedom is Something We Do Together* (pp. 67–88). Rowman & Littlefield.

Dekker, E. (2016). *The Viennese Students of Civilization: The Meaning and Context of Austrian Economics Reconsidered*. Cambridge University Press.

Dekker, E., & Kuchař, P. (2021). *Governing Markets as Knowledge Commons*. Cambridge University Press.

DellaPosta, D., Nee, V., & Opper, S. (2016). Endogenous Dynamics of Institutional Change. *Rationality and Society, 29*(1), 5–48.

D'Emilio, J. (1983). *Sexual Politics, Sexual Communities: The Making of a Homosexual Minority in the United States, 1940–1970*. University of Chicago Press.

de Montesquieu, C. L. S. [1748] (1989). *The Spirit of the Laws*. Cambridge University Press.

de Tocqueville, A. [1835] (2010). *Democracy in America*. Liberty Fund.

Ealy, L. T. (2018). Lost in Methodenstreit: Reflections on Theory, History, and the Quest for a Science of Association. In M. J. Douma & P. W. Magness (Eds.), *What is Classical Liberal History?* (pp. 59–94). Lexington Books.

Ellsworth, S. (1982). *Death in a Promised Land: The Tulsa Race Riot of 1921*. Louisiana State University Press.

Fernández-Villaverde, J. (2016). Magna Carta, the Rule of Law, and the Limits on Government. *International Review of Law and Economics, 47*, 22–28.

Gallup. (2024). LGBTQ+ Rights. https://news.gallup.com/poll/1651/gay-lesbian-rights.aspx

Garnett, R., Jr., Lewis, P., & Ealy, L. T. (2015). *Commerce and Community: Ecologies of Social Cooperation*. Routledge.

Hamilton, A., Madison, J., & Jay, J. [1788] (2003). *The Federalist Papers*. Cambridge University Press.

Harry, J., & DeVall, W. B. (1978). *The Social Organization of Gay Males*. Praeger.

Hayek, F. A. (1937). Economics and Knowledge. *Economica, 4*(13), 33–54.

Hayek, F. A. (1945). The Use of Knowledge in Society. *American Economic Review, 4*(35), 519–530.

Hayek, F. A. [1960] (2011). *The Constitution of Liberty: The Definitive Edition*. In R. Hamowy (Ed.), *The Collected Works of F. A. Hayek: Volume 17*. University of Chicago Press.

Hayek, F. A. [1968] (1978). Competition as a Discovery Procedure. In F. A. Hayek (Ed.), *New Studies in Philosophy, Politics, and Economics and the History of Ideas* (pp. 179–190). University of Chicago Press.

Hayek, F. A. (1973). Cosmos and Taxis. In L. Law (Ed.), *And Liberty: Volume I, Rules and Order* (pp. 35–54). University of Chicago Press.

Hayek, F. A. (1988). *The Fatal Conceit: The Errors of Socialism*. University of Chicago Press.

Higgs, R. (1977). *Competition and Coercion: Blacks in the American Economy, 1865–1914*. University of Chicago Press.

Hirschman, A. O. (1970). *Exit, Voice, and Loyalty: Responses to Decline in Firms, Organizations, and States*. Harvard University Press.

Honey, M. K. (2018). *To The Promised Land: Martin Luther King and the Fight for Economic Justice*. W. W. Norton & Company.

Hutt, W. H. (1966). Civil Rights and Young "Conservatives." *Modern Age, 10*(3), 231–238.

Jackson, T. F. (2007). *From Civil Rights to Human Rights: Martin Luther King, Jr., and the Struggle for Economic Justice*. University of Philadelphia Press.

Kirzner, I. M. (1979). *Perception, Opportunity, and Profit: Studies in the Theory of Entrepreneurship*. University of Chicago Press.
Knight, F. H. (1960). *Intelligence and Democratic Action*. Harvard University Press.
Korstad, R., & Lichtenstein, N. (1988). Opportunities Found and Lost: Labor, Radicals, and the Early Civil Rights Movement. *Journal of American History, 75*(3), 786–811.
Korzybski, A. (1950). *Science and Sanity: An Introduction to Neo-Aristotelian Systems and General Semantics*. International Non-Aristotelian Library Publishing Company.
Lavoie, D. (1986). The Market as a Procedure for Discovery and the Conveyance of Inarticulate Knowledge. *Comparative Economic Systems, 28*(1), 1–19.
Lawson, R. A., & Clark, J. R. (2010). Examining the Hayek-Friedman Hypothesis on Economic and Political Freedom. *Journal of Economic Behavior & Organization, 74*(3), 230–239.
Levy, J. T. (2015). *Rationalism, Pluralism, and Freedom*. Oxford University Press.
Lilti, A. (2015). *The World of the Salons: Sociability and Worldliness in Eighteenth-Century Paris*. Oxford University Press.
Magness, P. W., Carden, A., & Geloso, V. (2019). James M. Buchanan and the Political Economy of Desegregation. *Southern Economic Journal*, *85*(3), 715–741.
Merquior, J. G. (1991). *Liberalism, Old and New*. Twayne Publishers.
Milk, H. (2013). *An Archive of Hope: Harvey Milk's Speeches and Writings*. University of California Press.
Mokyr, J. (1990). *The Lever of Riches: Technological Creativity and Economic Progress*. Oxford University Press.
Mokyr, J. (2016). *A Culture of Growth: Origins of the Modern Economy*. Princeton University Press.
Morris, A. (1984). *The Origins of the Civil Rights Movement: Black Communities Organizing for Change*. Free Press.
Ness, I. (2004). *Encyclopedia of American Social Movements*. Sharpe Reference.
North, D. C. (2005). *Understanding the Process of Economic Change*. Princeton University Press.
Novak, M. (2018). *Inequality: An Entangled Political Economy Perspective*. Palgrave Macmillan.
Novak, M. (2021). *Freedom in Contention: Social Movements and Liberal Political Economy*. Lexington Books.
Ormsbee, J. T. (2010). *The Meaning of Gay: Interaction, Publicity, and Community among Homosexual Men in 1960s San Francisco*. Lexington Books.

Ostrom, E., Walker, J., & Gardner, R. (1992). Covenants With and Without A Sword: Self-Governance is Possible. *American Political Science Review, 86*(2), 404–417.
Ostrom, V. (1991). *The Meaning of American Federalism: Constituting a Self-Governing Society*. ICS Press.
Ostrom, V. (1993). Epistemic Choice and Public Choice. *Public Choice, 77*(1), 163–176.
Ostrom, V. (1997). *The Meaning of Democracy and the Vulnerability of Democracies: A Response to Tocqueville's Challenge*. University of Michigan Press.
Pinker, S. (2011). *The Better Angels of Our Nature: Why Violence Has Declined*. Viking Books.
Plato. (2004). *Apology, Crito, and Phaedo of Socrates*. https://www.gutenberg.org/files/13726/13726-h/13726-h.htm
Polanyi, M. (1962). The Republic of Science: Its Political and Economic Theory. *Minerva, 1*(1), 54–73.
Powell, J. (2000). *The Triumph of Liberty: A 2,000 Year History Told Through the Lives of Freedom's Greatest Champions*. Free Press.
Rauch, J. (2013). *Kindly Inquisitors: The New Attacks on Free Thought*. Expanded Edition. Cato Institute.
Reed, T. V. (2015). *The Art of Protest: Culture and Activism from the Civil Rights Movement to the Streets of Seattle*. University of Minnesota Press.
Rindova, V., Barry, D., & Ketchen, D. J., Jr. (2009). Entrepreneuring as Emancipation. *Academy of Management Review, 34*(3), 477–491.
Roberts, G., & Klibanoff, H. (2007). *The Race Beat: The Press, the Civil Rights Struggle, and the Awakening of a Nation*. Vintage.
Rojas, F. (2024). Race, Freedom, and Social Change. In F. Rojas & C. Stern (Eds.), *Sociology and Classical Liberalism in Dialogue: Freedom is Something We Do Together* (pp. 45–64). Rowman & Littlefield.
Selby, G. S. (2008). *Martin Luther King and the Rhetoric of Freedom: The Exodus Narrative in America's Struggle for Civil Rights*. Baylor University Press.
Schumpeter, J. A. (1934). *Theory of Economic Development: An Inquiry into Profits, Capital, Credit, Interest, and the Business Cycle*. Harvard University Press.
Shockley, G., Stough, R., Haynes, K., & Frank, P. (2006). Toward a Theory of Public Sector Entrepreneurship. *International Journal of Entrepreneurship and Innovation Management, 6*(3), 205–223.
Sides, J. (2009). *Erotic City: Sexual Revolutions and the Making of Modern San Francisco*. Oxford University Press.
Smith, A. [1776] (1982). *An Inquiry into the Nature and Causes of the Wealth of Nations*. Liberty Fund.
Smith, G. H. (2013). *The System of Liberty: Themes in the History of Classical Liberalism*. Cambridge University Press.

Smith, J. P., & Welch, F. R. (1989). Black Economic Progress After Myrdal. *Journal of Economic Literature, 27*(2), 519–564.
Stein, M. (2005). Theoretical Politics, Local Communities: The Making of U.S. LGBT Historiography. *GLQ: A Journal of Lesbian and Gay Studies*, *11*(4), 605–625.
Stewart, J. B. (2018). Insights Regarding Black-White Economic Inequality from Stratification Economics. In J. L. Conyers (Ed.), *Africana Social Stratification* (pp. 71–86). Lexington Books.
Storr, V. (2009). North's Underdeveloped Ideological Entrepreneur. *Annual Proceedings of the Wealth and Well-Being of Nations, 1*, 99–115.
Swedberg, R. (2006). Social Entrepreneurship: The View of the Young Schumpeter. In D. Hjorth & C. Steyaert (Eds.), *Entrepreneurship and Social Change* (pp. 21–34). Edward Elgar.
Vihanto, M. (1992). Competition Between Local Governments as a Discovery Procedure. *Journal of Institutional and Theoretical Economics, 148*(3), 411–436.
Wagner, R. E. (2020). *Macroeconomics as Systems Theory: Transcending the Micro-Macro Dichotomy*. Palgrave Macmillan.

CHAPTER 6

Ostromian Self-governance: Emancipation or Simply Changing the Locus of Servitude?

Roberta Herzberg

In a robust collective choice process, it is essential not only for individuals to have the formal right to participate in governance but also for them to exercise this right meaningfully. This requirement presents a core challenge within modern democratic systems, where active citizen participation is crucial to realizing democratic ideals. Elinor and Vincent Ostrom dedicated much of their scholarly work to demonstrating the value of self-governance—both as a reflection of citizen interests and as a framework for collective decision-making (Aligica & Boettke, 2009: 159; Aligica, 2019). Through their analyses of federalism, metropolitan service delivery, and common-pool resource management, the Ostroms illustrated that engaging citizens directly in governance yields more effective outcomes, particularly when the good or service in question requires coproduction between government and the public (Ostrom, 1997, 2010). Vincent Ostrom's theoretical foundation, rooted in the ideas of the American Federalists (especially Madison and Hamilton) and

R. Herzberg (✉)
Mercatus Center at George Mason University, Fairfax, VA, USA
e-mail: bherzberg@mercatus.gmu.edu

M. Novak (ed.), *Liberal Emancipation*, Mercatus Studies in Political and Social Economy, https://doi.org/10.1007/978-3-031-94406-2_6

Alexis de Tocqueville's *Democracy in America*, is elaborated most fully in his last important book, *The Meaning of Democracy and Vulnerabilities of Democracies* (Ostrom, 1997). These themes are similarly reflected in Elinor Ostrom's extensive studies on the role of institutions2005 in enabling citizens to resolve social dilemmas within diverse political systems (Ostrom, 1990, 2010).

In considering the importance of emancipation within this theoretical context, the responsibilities of enfranchised individuals become as critical as their formal rights in determining the extent to which individual and group interests are effectively translated into social outcomes. As V. Ostrom observes, "An exercise of power with others implies both responsibility and a willingness to take account of the interests of others in what can be called 'patterns of social accountability'" (Ostrom, 1997: 287). Citizens have a responsibility to work together within a system of "power with others" to achieve democratic outcomes. The duty of citizens to act as a check on potential manipulations by those in power is fundamental to realizing democracy's benefits within self-governing systems but this requires significant work when one considers the many layers of governing authority within a system such as U.S. federalism. Individuals may be willing to work together with neighbors and friends to achieve common goals but are they willing to do this at all levels of decision-making including those quite distant from them. How can such a system accommodate the broader more complex issues that arise especially in modern society? This tension within the system of self-governance suggests that a hybrid governing approach is needed—a system of polycentricity.

The Ostromian perspective underscores the significance of suffrage and emancipation in a complex system of self-government. For government to reflect the values and interests of its members, citizens must not only possess a seat at the table, but they must actively claim it, along with the associated responsibilities. When citizens delegate this power to experts or distant policymakers, they relinquish essential benefits of their emancipation; hence, for the Ostroms, active self-governance is indispensable both in governing and in maintaining meaningful emancipation for citizens. Within communities, when individuals are free to organize and act to serve collective interests, diverse institutional arrangements, and social outcomes emerge, reflecting the heterogeneity of broader society. However, this diversity raises questions about coordination and conflict resolution at larger societal levels. If communities pursue interests not shared by others, what mechanisms can ensure that these pursuits do not infringe on the rights or well-being of those outside the community? This necessitates examining governance structures that can address common concerns across various community types.

One solution the Ostroms propose is the adoption of polycentric institutions, which support the formation of diverse communities within a complex network of overlapping, nested groups capable of addressing specific problems at appropriate levels of generality. For instance, an air pollution issue may require regional, national, or even international coordination among various affected communities (Lofthouse & Herzberg, 2023), whereas excess litter in a neighborhood might be managed locally by a municipality or even a small group of residents. Polycentric governance allows for flexible, efficient problem-solving, enabling different groups to operate at the scale most suitable to the issue at hand.

Since polycentric governing systems operate in many overlapping and nested decision arenas, citizens maintain their democratic influence by participating either directly or through representatives in multiple levels simultaneously depending on the problem they face. As a result, these provide the ties that bind smaller communities and interests/associations with broader governing communities (Ostrom, 1999a). Of course, the degree to which people maintain a bond depends on the ways in which and how actively individuals participate in these multiple levels to maintain accountability. This theory of polycentricity is at the heart of Ostrom's self-governing logic.

Consequently, polycentric governance accommodates a range of social goals, enabling overlapping groups of individuals to work at levels best suited to the specific issue. An individual may simultaneously belong to multiple governance communities, each with distinct obligations and opportunities. However, the complexity and sheer number of these affiliations can strain individual capacity for self-governance, leading citizens to defer authority to those who step in to "solve" their problems. This situation can, as F.A. Hayek warns in "Why the Worst Get on Top" (Hayek, 2007, ch. 10), create conditions where those who promise the most while expecting the least succeed, replacing those who honestly suggest the need for citizens to step up.

This chapter explores the Ostromian approach to self-governance, assessing the extent to which it promotes equal access to meaningful participation. Citizens must have decision-making access at multiple levels to harness the advantages of polycentric systems. However, factors that foster local community formation within polycentric systems can also impede collaboration at broader levels. For instance, while trust within communities facilitates social cohesion and action, it often depends on distinctions between community members and outsiders, reinforcing a "brotherhood *versus* otherhood" dynamic (Hardin, 2006). Such dynamics may limit the extent to which polycentric systems can fully realize their emancipatory potential of giving citizens effective access to multiple competing levels of policy control.

Polycentrism serves to facilitate citizen input in a democratic process to emancipate the populus at large. But, with this greater potential for democratic involvement comes an expanded responsibility on citizens. The obligations imposed by such a complex and interconnected system in terms of citizen participation may act to discourage universal participation and enhance elite influence. Together, Elinor and Vincent Ostrom's work illustrates that while polycentric systems offer significant potential for self-governance, their success depends on active citizen participation, robust institutional frameworks, and a shared commitment to mutual accountability.

To explore these issues in greater detail, the chapter is organized as follows. In the next section, I outline the logic of the Ostromian self-governance system which is essential to achieving polycentric structures' emancipatory potential. Next, I examine how distinct individual communities integrate within a broader polycentric framework and I situate this approach within other major theories of democratic participation. I consider the extent to which this polycentric form and the myriads of communities within which individuals must participate place an excessive burden on citizens. This is followed by an analysis of the role of exit and sorting in Ostromian self-governance to consider how exit and entry rules influence trust within and between communities and the implications for the sustainability of this institutional arrangement. A conclusion follows.

Ostromian Self-governance

The literature on polycentric governance highlights its potential as an emancipatory framework that enables communities to self-organize based on their distinct needs and values. Such arrangements, especially federal systems, empower individuals to shape policies within their communities while engaging in broader regional or national coalitions when appropriate. Elinor and Vincent Ostrom have analyzed this structure across diverse local governance units—such as cities, towns, and counties—within federal systems. Their work demonstrates how decentralized policymaking accommodates various interests and fosters coherence across governance levels. Rather than rely on uniform consensus, policy alignment across these arenas emerges from adaptable coalitions that reflect the range of support across different communities.

The Ostroms argue that local decision-making is fundamental to self-governance and emphasize the importance of retaining as much policy authority as possible within communities. When decisions are shifted to state, national, or international levels, the influence of local communities is diminished, weakening the efficacy and legitimacy of self-governance. Centralized decisions often undermine the personal agency, legitimacy, and access to local knowledge intrinsic to localized governance. In their work on local public economies in metropolitan areas, the Ostroms and their research partners document the diversity in citizen preferences over local public services and how they are delivered (McGinnis, 1999). They identified the unseen challenges posed by reforms that moved policy decisions to larger and more expert administrative bureaucracies and suggested that the seemingly chaotic patchwork of more localized delivery approaches better served the citizens expressed preferences. Ostrom documents successful self-governance examples within metropolitan service deliveries such as education and police services to suggest the potential of communities to resolve their own policy problems.

Likewise, Elinor Ostrom's foundational work on common-pool resources (CPRs), *Governing theCommons*, challenges the assumption that state intervention is essential to prevent resource depletion. In her 1990 study, Ostrom identifies conditions enabling communities to self-manage shared resources effectively, proposing six design principles found in successful self-governing systems. However, such governance is often limited to small, isolated communities. Throughout her career, she demonstrates empirically that, across many settings, polycentric systems can better address a wide array of policy needs by recognizing and adapting to the diverse preferences expressed by citizens (Ostrom, 2010). This placed the Ostrom's work squarely at odds with those arguing for more centralized expert solutions. Citizens, though not expert, often understand the policies they prefer and seek representational systems that can deliver these to them. For the Ostroms, that system was polycentric.

Ostrom's findings suggest that while self-governance closer to citizens is feasible, it does require both a shared commitment among participants and specific institutional conditions to be realized. Vincent Ostrom expands on this perspective in *The Meaning of Democracy and the Vulnerability of Democracies* (1997), stressing that the resilience of democratic systems relies on citizens who are actively engaged and mindful of their role in shaping collective relations. According to Vincent Ostrom, sustainable democratic systems necessitate that citizens take responsibility and exercise an ethic of "power with" rather than "power over," underscoring that democracy depends on a significant commitment to self-governance.

Without active citizen involvement, Vincent Ostrom warns, democratic systems risk capture by elites or domination by tyrannical majorities. This threat becomes more pronounced as societies expand, with citizens increasingly "shirking" their civic responsibilities—either by assuming others will take up the necessary civic work or by believing their own individual impact is too limited to matter. As decision-making groups grow, so do the costs of staying informed, due to factors such as (1) the growing distance from decision centers, (2) reduced knowledge of others' interests or of elite positions, and (3) the complexity of issues in larger settings. But the shirking comes at a cost to citizens.

Vincent Ostrom articulates the implications of disagreement:

> … If people are to rule, members of society should know how to govern themselves. Democratic societies are vulnerable to an unlimited pursuit of strategic opportunism when people are spared the cares of thinking and the troubles of living (Ostrom, 1997: 271).

In expanding societies, the dilution of local knowledge and increased complexity often lead individuals to delegate their responsibilities to elites, relying on others such as political parties or interest groups to hold these elites accountable. Nonetheless, Elinor and Vincent Ostrom assert that self-governance remains viable even in such contexts if structured within a polycentric system. Polycentric institutions preserve the advantages of localized decision-making while introducing checks on potential abuses through overlapping jurisdictions (Aligica & Tarko, 2013). This structure enables individuals to address grievances in alternative venues, thus containing possible misuses of power. Successful polycentric governance requires clearly defined authorities within decision centers, each tasked with addressing specific issues. This helps keep decision-making as close to the community level as practical.

The Emancipating Forces of Ostromian Self-governance

In examining the relationship between emancipation and liberalism, a key question is how best to facilitate the often-competing values involved. A fundamental assumption here is that individuals within a democratic system wish to influence the collective decisions that shape their governance. However, as Buchanan and Tullock [1962] (1999) explain, guaranteeing a say in every decision for each individual (via unanimity) incurs high costs, making consensus challenging, if not impossible. The limitations of individual capacity to address diverse issues in a pluralistic society necessitate organized frameworks to make self-governance more practical and reduce decision-making costs (both bargaining and transaction). Thus, institutional design must strike a balance, ensuring meaningful participation while accommodating shared social concerns. In more diverse societies, this balance requires transparent, reliable processes that can earn public trust and achieve stability across varied value communities.

E. Ostrom (1990, 2005, 2010) and V. Ostrom (1991, 1999a, 1999b) argue that a polycentric governance model is best in striking this balance. Polycentricity allows smaller groups to self-govern within defined domains while accessing broader decision-making structures when issues extend beyond their purview. As E. Ostrom defines:

> ... By polycentric, I mean a system where citizens are able to organize not just one but multiple governing authorities at differing scales. ... Each unit exercises considerable independence to make and enforce rules within a circumscribed domain of authority for a specified geographical area (Ostrom, 2005: 283).

Through polycentric structures, individuals participate at multiple levels, achieving full emancipation across the decision-making landscape, even if their influence varies across these different arenas. V. Ostrom argues that polycentric systems, as exemplified by U.S. federalism, enable local autonomy while providing checks on centralized power within larger, more diverse contexts such as the U.S. (Ostrom, 1991).

Citizens with authority at local, intermediate, and national levels can restrain actions at each level, preventing decisions at one level from disrupting the overall balance (Ostrom & Parks, [1987] 1999). Over time, citizens develop institutional rules that formalize the personal bonds initially forged within smaller communities, thus preserving these communities as they grow (Cook et al., 2005).

As Lofthouse and Herzberg (2023) discuss, polycentric systems offer several advantages in citizen informed policymaking over their monocentric counterparts:

1. Competition—among decision-makers enhances outcomes as communities strive to retain members and gain broader recognition.
2. Cooperation—across levels allows communities to pursue broader goals that individual efforts may not achieve.
3. Enhanced legitimacy—for locally driven decisions facilitates the success of co-produced public goods like education and health.
4. Mutual learning—enables communities to observe and adapt based on others' successes or failures.
5. Institutional resilience—grows as successful practices spread, while failures remain localized.
6. Emergent orders—foster better social outcomes, developing organically rather than by central design.

Likewise, competition and collective learning in a polycentric structure play crucial roles in expanding political participation and empowering marginalized groups (Coyne et al., 2007; Lemke, 2016).

Polycentric systems also may incorporate decision points outside of traditional political institutions. Any given policy process can span political jurisdictions and voluntary associations and corporations, with governance adapted to the issue at hand. For example, global climate change, as discussed by Ostrom (2012) and Lofthouse and Herzberg (2023), demands responses beyond any single public or private jurisdiction. While global consensus is unlikely, progress can be achieved through cumulative local and regional efforts, each addressing aspects of the issue that reflect community-specific interests. This flexibility enables collaboration among groups with shared goals while allowing others to pursue divergent paths. Consequently, polycentric governance promotes diversity in values and policy, providing an avenue for minorities to pursue goals independent of majority sentiment (Goodman, 2023; Lemke, 2020; Novak, 2021). These authors argue that polycentricity permits dissent within a framework, allowing marginalized voices to challenge dominant coalitions within structures like federalism through market, social, and political pressures that might not be effective across a more centralized system.

At its core, polycentric self-governance is about emancipation. It embodies a system where individuals are fully involved in their own governance and accountable for the outcomes they help create. Theoretically, this form of liberty aligns with Buchanan and Tullock's [1962] (1999) notion of unanimity in *The Calculus of Consent*—yet absolute consent is rarely possible, as individuals are born into pre-existing societies where consent is contextual (Lemke, 2020).

Three major challenges pose risks to polycentric systems:

1. Internal autonomy within smaller centers: How much internal control should communities exercise? For instance, should religious or cultural groups within liberal societies be permitted to impose restrictive policies on members who disagree? This question is crucial in contexts where minority rights might be curtailed by majority preferences within local communities.
2. Inter-community tolerance: To what extent should smaller communities respect others in a diverse system? This is particularly problematic when a community's values hinder its ability to cooperate on broader issues, like environmental policy, which require collective action (Martin, 2019). When community cohesion is built on contrasting with outsiders, inter-community hostility can impede effective responses to shared problems and solidify divisions (Hardin, 2006).
3. Rules of entry and exit: Polycentric systems rely on individuals' ability to "vote with their feet" by moving between communities. Rules that overly restrict entry or exit are inconsistent with the freedom that liberal emancipation promises. For instance, relocation offers a feasible alternative to internal reform only when viable movement options exist, making entry and exit regulations critical to the system's success.

Polycentric Structure in an Ostromian System of Self-governance

To enhance freedom, community members must be free to organize themselves as they see fit and pursue those policies that they deem in their social interest within the broad limits of individual rights. These individuals' rights to self-organize are maintained best through clear and fair rules of democratic engagement and reasonable rights of exit out of and entry into communities of interest or geographic jurisdictions. Such mechanisms permit both community distinction and individual freedom or empowerment. The logic of polycentricity operates around this core value/concern, but it cannot operate without some essential decision rules that define the boundaries of authority for each group/jurisdiction as well as the mechanism and rules for moving across those jurisdictions. The U.S. federalist system is a common example for evaluating how a polycentric order can operate, but it is not the only form this can take, and every polycentric rule system must be evaluated along both these social and individual dimensions. The opportunity to choose a preferred jurisdiction or community that is more consistent with your values is liberating and the potential for self-governance within that community enhances the prospect for maintaining those values going forward.

Permitting different social communities to organize and pursue their distinct preferences is liberty enhancing, but it leaves the issue of how to facilitate movement into and out of the community and the degree to which such groups are free to pursue policies that are inconsistent with human liberty. For example, should an Amish group be free to exclude women from pursuing certain jobs or positions within their community? Should they be able to enforce certain rules with strict corporal punishment if the broader state policies would deny it? Should they be able to prevent external authorities enforcing such rules upon members of their community?

These questions suggest the need for some level of agreement on the limits within which a community may construct its own rules and a mechanism—for example, a court challenge—by which such limits may be applied. As long as no one complains (all agree within the community), then even very restrictive or limiting behaviors may continue voluntarily. As communities broaden and become more diverse, it is far less likely that they will be able to maintain strict restrictions without interference. At this point, it becomes necessary to have access to some mechanism to resolve differences over acceptable limits on individual behaviors within the community. In E. Ostrom's *Governing the Commons* (1990) she suggests the importance of having access to an independent mechanism to hold oneself and others accountable to the agreements reached together. This is government in the broadest sense, but for Ostrom, individuals were free to broaden beyond narrow institutional definitions of government. As she notes:

> ... the problem of achieving a good society is *not to move outside of government but rather to broaden our conception of what government means*. If we adopt the idea that covenants are the foundation for a self-governing society, then institutional arrangements for governance exist in many forms at many levels. By covenants, I mean the willingness of individuals to come to basic agreements about how they will achieve future tasks, to keep to these agreements, and to monitor one another so that temptations to break agreements do not threaten the viability of the agreements (Ostrom, 1993: 7; emphasis added).

Usually, such an approach would operate within a formal governing structure, but there is no explicit requirement in their analysis that would require that in a polycentric system.

How Self-governing Communities Fit into a Polycentric System

Several have considered how such systems might provide meaningful participation for individuals, especially those who may find themselves in a minority relative to societal values and customs. (see, for example, John Stuart Mill, John Rawls, Isaiah Berlin, Chandran Kukathas, Paul Aligica, Jamie Lemke, Mikayla Novak, and Nathan Goodman). Liberalism often involves balancing individual rights with the collective good. While individual freedom is key, liberalism recognizes that certain regulations or restrictions might be necessary to ensure the well-being of the larger community/nation.

Liberal theories provide a framework for balancing individual rights with social order. Central to this discussion is John Stuart Mill's harm principle, which advocates for individual freedom unless one's actions harm others, underscoring the necessity of democratic processes to set limits fairly (Mill, 1977). Isaiah Berlin's concepts of negative and positive liberty further underscore the importance of both freedom from interference and the ability to pursue meaningful goals, promoting tolerance of diverse lifestyles (Berlin, 1969). John Rawls, in his *Theory of Justice* (1999), uses two principles of justice and the "veil of ignorance," to develop a societal structure where basic liberties are equal and social inequalities are justified only if they benefit everyone, focusing on an inclusive and fair perspective.

Kukathas (2003) suggests that liberal societies should function as loosely connected communities, each with significant autonomy to determine how citizens wish to live. Ostrom's polycentric model, paralleling U.S. federalism, proposes local autonomy combined with checks from broader institutions to balance power and promote diverse viewpoints within a unified structure. However, Aligica (2019) highlights the challenges in such a system, advocating for a "modus vivendi" or mutual tolerance to sustain stability and prevent conflicts among competing value communities, suggesting that "live and let live" principles can support governance that respects local values while maintaining unity. If individuals are willing to enter a bargain that permits others to follow different value systems as long as they are free to follow their own preferred value system, then this polycentric structure can generate stable governance around a shared commitment to tolerance. Such an approach protects minority communities within diverse societies and adapts to social changes over time. For example, recent debates over drug policy in the U.S. illustrate this flexibility. While some states resisted marijuana legalization, others like Colorado moved forward based on local preferences. Observing Colorado's experience, other states have gradually followed suit, allowing for diverse views on costs and benefits to guide decision-making. Without a rigid national consensus, this gradual evolution fosters less conflict than a top-down imposition.

Ultimately, this approach of distinct communities that differ on values and policy differences enables community members to self-select based on values, reducing friction among those with strongly held beliefs. Individuals favoring liberal policies can relocate to communities that reflect their values, while those preferring more regulation can remain in like-minded areas. This diversity of values allows society to achieve stability even amid moral disagreements. Aligica argues that a liberal society committed to individual freedom can support polycentric arrangements by allowing communities to restrict their behaviors if they tolerate others making different trade-offs.

The competition and learning fostered by polycentric structures offer an effective path to individual empowerment within large, diverse societies, enabling self-governance from the bottom up. U.S. history provides numerous examples of how such competition has expanded minority freedoms. Early civil rights advances in New York eventually became models for broader reforms. Similarly, marriage equality began in Massachusetts, Connecticut, and Iowa before national legalization, showing how incremental, community-driven changes can minimize social disruption. This dynamic has also influenced policies on healthcare (e.g., Massachusetts's precursor to the *Affordable Care Act*), education (e.g., Arizona's school vouchers), and labor (e.g., right-to-work laws in states like Arizona and North Carolina in the 1940s and more recently in Wisconsin and Indiana). These examples demonstrate that polycentric systems promote effective policy by encouraging local experimentation and limiting the risks of centralized failures.

State-level competition drives progress in individual rights, facilitating policy innovation, creating models for successful reforms, and exerting pressure on other states to adopt similar measures. This dynamic federalism fosters a governance structure that is responsive, adaptive, and ultimately supportive of individual freedoms across the nation. One of the key mechanisms in driving such change is the degree to which communities establish within group trust to pursue more innovative policy strategies. Being a first mover can generate potential for future growth and policy vibrancy within a community, but a misstep could isolate this community and instead of attracting new community members, may incentivize existing members to exit. This may explain why many of these changes occur in communities where there is high consensus around the innovation in question. Members share trust that permits a less incremental response.

When individuals consider joining or remaining in a group or political jurisdiction within a self-governing system, trust is a crucial factor. Where people can align with others who share their values, interests, and preferences, greater within-group consensus can facilitate social decisions, often reducing the need for authoritative state intervention. In these settings, social actions rely more on voluntary compliance, and within-group trust is high because members anticipate that collective decisions will align with their own interests. This arrangement fosters confidence in social authority and decisions. However, these benefits hinge on high consensus, which may limit the jurisdiction's size relative to the broader society.

Since many social issues extend beyond such boundaries, it is essential to consider how governments and groups can act when personal trust is weak and how they can address cross-group policies and larger community problems.

Hardin (2006) argues that trust is fundamental to well-functioning markets and societies, but the type of trust matters. While personalized trust builds through interactions within a community, system trust depends on institutional structures. In closely knit communities, where values are aligned, trust grows through direct relationships and monitoring of others' actions. However, as communities expand and become more diverse in experiences and values, personalized trust may be insufficient for guiding social actions. Hardin posits that when personalized trust falters, institutional rules can serve as substitutes to support social cohesion. Cook et al. (2005) suggest that clearly defined property rights, contract law, strong rule of law, effective leadership, and open communication are crucial in building trust, particularly among strangers. As societies grow and diversify, these elements become even more critical. Institutions substitute for the bonds of personal trust that operate in the smaller, more cohesive community. Trust in institutions substitutes for trust in one's neighbors or leaders.

Adam Smith recognized that trading with strangers required shared values and mechanisms to reduce risks. While these may be internalized, they ultimately rely on institutions that uphold expectations, promoting trust even in broader exchanges. Alesina and Ferrara (2005) argue that trust—specifically, confidence in others to act predictably and beneficially—is vital for economic transactions, social interactions, and institutional success. Higher trust levels correlate with better economic performance, including GDP growth, investment, and financial development, by lowering transaction costs, facilitating cooperation, and enhancing efficiency. However, ethnic, racial, and linguistic diversity tends to reduce generalized trust within a society, as individuals often exhibit lower levels of trust toward those from different backgrounds. Yet, the potential benefits of diversity, such as innovation, creativity, and economic dynamism, can offset the trust deficits associated with diverse communities, especially when supported by institutional and educational policies that promote positive intergroup interactions.

These dynamics highlight competing effects of trust within society. While strong group identity can boost political engagement and efficacy within groups, it may also intensify divisions with those outside the group.

Scholars define these dynamics as consolidating trust versus extending trust (Hardin, 2006). Consolidating trust within a group can be challenging when consistent behavior is interpreted differently across value systems. Consequently, groups may hesitate to extend trust to those with different values, perceiving risks and uncertainties in their interactions.

Although repeated interactions can help overcome initial distrust, institutional and policy measures can also improve cross-group relations. Clear, open communication about expectations and values aligns understanding, consolidating trust across value communities. Well-specified contracts, transparent rules, and consistent law enforcement further reduce perceived risks and promote fairness across different groups (Cook et al., 2005).

Public choice theory highlights that when institutional rules favor specific interests, excluded groups have little reason to trust the system. Conversely, if institutions act as neutral facilitators for diverse interests, they can reduce conflict and foster trust. By addressing the balance between extending and consolidating trust when group values diverge, institutions can help organizations navigate diversity more effectively, leading to stronger, more cohesive relationships.

Elinor and Vincent Ostrom emphasized that self-governance is essential to building trust in institutions that shape social interactions. Individuals involved in the rules that govern them, both in shaping and enforcing those rules, find those restrictions more legitimate even when they disagree with the outcomes. However, as societal decisions grow in number and complexity, the demands on citizens to remain fully informed, engage in negotiations, and participate meaningfully in self-governance become challenging to meet. Consequently, individuals increasingly rely on interest groups and community representatives to represent their interests in the political sphere. As some of these actors become more professionalized and distant, citizen oversight is crucial to ensuring alignment between leaders' and members' interests. This underscores the importance of transparent processes and whether these rules of engagement are consistent across groups and jurisdictions.

The High Costs of Polycentrism's Obligations

The question remains: how does polycentrism function in real-world settings, and does the self-governance required in polycentric systems demand too high a price of citizens as society grows large? Polycentric systems rely on individuals across various governance arenas to actively participate, serve as checks on other levels, and coordinate actions to achieve broader interests. The more arenas an individual perceives as relevant to their interests, the greater the demands on their time and attention to achieve these outcomes. As Buchanan and Tullock [1962] (1999) noted, expanding access to multiple communities with diverse preferences is not cost-free; higher decision-making costs arise from working through differences and finding sufficient consensus for action.

In the U.S. today, individuals are simultaneously members of numerous governance levels: local communities, states, the nation, and, by representation, various international organizations. They also belong to a multitude of local jurisdictions—such as school districts, counties, and service districts—not to mention professional, social, and religious communities, which may even include compulsory membership in unions or licensing associations. These affiliations easily number in the dozens, if not hundreds, making it unrealistic to be fully informed and engaged in each. Consequently, a central challenge for self-governance is defining the optimal level of citizen participation necessary to achieve meaningful control.

Representation by individuals with shared interests within subcommunities of polycentric orders can alleviate individual demands, yet it introduces principal-agent issues. In small, homogeneous communities, members may feel well-represented by a community leader, but as decisions shift to broader, more diverse arenas, representatives face challenges in balancing competing views across constituents. Martin (2019) notes that while competition among levels in a polycentric system is meant to safeguard against majority tyranny, policies that ascend to higher levels often encounter a "ratchet effect," making it difficult to return decision-making to more localized processes. This centralizing tendency diminishes polycentrism's effectiveness in protecting minority interests. As a result, individuals seeking redress may find it more advantageous to approach broader jurisdictions within a polycentric system. Once a policy is adopted at this broad level, it applies universally, incentivizing further centralization and limiting the capacity for minority perspectives to achieve local satisfaction through sorting.

The extent of differences between communities also depends on the stability of these communities. If individuals are free to enter and exit easily, representation might improve as individuals sort by shared values.

However, frequent sorting may create greater instability across jurisdictions, widening inter-community differences and complicating interactions within the broader system. Alternatively, unrestricted entry and exit could dilute the cultural distinctiveness of communities, reducing their ability to distinguish themselves from one another (a subject considered in greater detail below).

The Role of Exit and Entry in Political Competition

The effectiveness of market-based political competition fundamentally depends on individuals' ability to exercise their rights of exit and entry—specifically—their capacity to choose among different social contracts and "vote with their feet." This freedom of movement and choice stands as a cornerstone of democratic self-governance, both within and beyond formal political institutions.

Hirschman's seminal work on *Exit, Voice, and Loyalty* (1970; also Hirschman, 1980) establishes a framework for understanding how competitive environments foster responsiveness and accountability. Hirschman identifies three primary responses available to individuals: expressing dissent (voice), maintaining allegiance (loyalty), or departing (exit). This framework enables individuals to weigh costs and benefits while allowing organizations or individuals to respond to market signals for membership. This concept aligns with Tiebout's (1956) model, later expanded by Ostrom et al. (1961), which explains how residential choices reflect preferences for public services and taxation levels in metropolitan areas. The model demonstrates how inter-jurisdictional competition compels communities to offer optimal service-cost combinations, thereby creating a competitive marketplace for governance.

While voting with your feet is a core aspect of Elinor and Vincent Ostrom's work on metropolitan governance, Elinor Ostrom (1990) provides a somewhat contrasting perspective for why limiting entry can enhance community success in her analysis of common-pool resource management. She argues that successful self-governance requires communities to establish rules regulating entry and exit to maintain trust and enforce accountability within the community. Open boundaries, while promoting mobility, can potentially undermine long-term resource management by risking overuse and diminishing community cohesion.

Robert Nozick's (2013) *Anarchy, State, and Utopia* advocates for voluntary communities in which individuals freely associate based on preferences. However, he recognizes that societal power dynamics often constrain the realization of such communities, as public choice pressures and entrenched interests resist reductions in state intervention. Thus, while citizens may ask for smaller state action, policy dynamics that operate with a ratchet effect dampen government responsiveness to these individual interests and lead to greater reliance on authority or coercion.

Recent scholarship has expanded these foundational theories to consider a variety of applications. Lemke (2020), for example, emphasizes the importance of implied consent through continued community membership, arguing that exit rights are essential for constitutional legitimacy, particularly for historically marginalized groups. The historic absence of choice reduces any meaning that may be implied from such agreements to remain within a community. Goodman (2023) demonstrates how market mechanisms and civil society have expanded opportunities for minorities, especially women, by enabling coalition-building and information sharing outside traditional political institutions. Novak (2021) highlights how exit rights empower individuals within voluntary associations by providing control over affiliations without requiring institutional reform. Organizing outside the traditional political institutions can satisfy the desire for representation and voice. Likewise boycotts and protest are frequent methods to express interests when formal political representation is unavailable.

Reactions to the COVID-19 pandemic illustrated the practical implications of exit rights in exercising choice over social policy and values, as millions of individuals and businesses relocated from jurisdictions with restrictive policies to those with fewer constraints and vice versa. This movement between U.S. states demonstrated how the ability to exit can influence policy decisions and governance approaches. It also suggests the degree to which voting with your feet may reduce conflict within any community especially when individuals feel deeply about the issue under consideration.

However, the effectiveness of exit rights depends critically on the availability of alternatives and the absence of entry barriers to those alternatives. While the U.S. generally permits unrestricted interstate migration that extends a wide range of choice to those seeking a community that provides a better fit with their values and preferences, other nations may offer fewer choices for social mobility. During Covid, for example, several nations implemented stringent movement controls during the pandemic, exemplified by Australia's limitations on both citizen and non-citizen movement. These restrictions, while supported by many, caused deep rifts among some groups ill-served by the restrictive lockdowns but unable to exercise a right to find an alternate community to enter.

Immigration and customs laws, more generally, often act as a barrier to individuals freely pursuing their preferred residency. While liberalism would argue in favor of the most open processes of immigration, travel, and free trade that can be facilitated, often community members who value their current community makeup and population density oppose those who wish to join them. In addition to immigration restrictions, the rise of restrictive zoning laws and homeowners' associations with restrictive covenants suggest that the desire to control one's community remains a meaningful barrier to exclusively relying on the mechanism of voting with your feet to enhance individual freedom.

The scholarly discourse on exit and entry rights reveals their crucial role in fostering responsive governance and individual autonomy. These rights function as competitive checks on authority, while their exercise creates a marketplace for jurisdiction shopping that can promote diversity and innovation. However, the equitable application of these rights across groups and jurisdictions remains a critical consideration for their effectiveness in promoting democratic self-governance (Orgad, 2010). Throughout history, some officials have used such rights of entry and exit to favor some groups at the expense of others. Without access to equal opportunity to exercise such rights, the emancipating benefits suggested here fall short.

This concern is often raised regarding open immigration policies as there can be disruption for both the immigrant moving and for community members receiving them. While open boundaries are inherently liberal, they may compromise effective representation of unique minority interests, especially for communities with values that are less liberal or emphasize specific moral regulations. If all communities begin to look alike, they may lose their effectiveness in representing a diverse array of policy and value options emerging from these majority processes. This can limit the sorting options available to individuals. Some argue that communities should have the freedom to be "unfree" with respect to their core values to provide authentic representation of all perspectives, ensuring that members feel their core interests are genuinely reflected (for example, Berlin (1969) on negative freedom). This logic is associated with a logic of negative liberty in which we choose to not interfere with the unfree practices of another made by their own choice. This usually involves the desire to maintain a set of unfree cultural practices or religious beliefs.

Of course, such restrictions create potential problems for a free society in knowing whether all members of that society freely choose these restrictions. As noted earlier we cannot always assume that continuing to stay in a community is an indication of consent for the practices and culture of that community, especially when we are considering vulnerable members of the community such as women and children (Lemke, 2020). Prominent examples such as the polygamous families of the Fundamentalist Church of Jesus Christ of Latter Day Saints in Colorado City, Arizona, and Hildale, Utah with their practices of "marrying" underage brides suggest the difficulty of assuming away individual rights as a consensual choice by all involved (AZFamily Digital News, 2024). While these behaviors were tolerated within the legal rules as applied in their community, they failed to comply with the rights and legal protections afforded their citizens within the broader state and federal jurisdictions. Eventually, access to these broader protections provided some check on the tyrannical and abusive actions of localized elites and majorities.

Conclusion

It is important to understand the potential of polycentric governance as an emancipatory framework within democratic systems as outlined in the work of Elinor and Vincent Ostrom. In this structure, citizen participation becomes an essential ingredient in achieving democratic ideals. Polycentric systems empower individuals and communities to participate meaningfully in governance, as evidenced in the Ostroms' careful theoretical and empirical work on federalism, common-pool resources, and metropolitan governance. They argue that for governance to reflect the values of its citizens, individuals must actively engage in decision-making. Such engagement enhances legitimacy, builds trust, and provides citizens with agency. Moreover, disengagement risks the capture of democratic systems by elites or tyrannical majorities. Polycentric structures adapt in each of these contexts in response to diverse policy challenges and empower individuals and communities to participate meaningfully in the governance of their communities.

Polycentric systems further allow governance to occur across multiple overlapping jurisdictions, enabling individuals to influence decisions and seek protection at various levels in ways that would be less likely in a centralized system. This structure is particularly effective in accommodating diverse preferences while addressing complex societal issues. For example, local communities may focus on neighborhood issues, while regional or national authorities address broader concerns like environmental pollution that crosses jurisdictional boundaries. But all levels may be engaged in any policy area addressing those aspects most linked to that locality.

Trust is an essential feature of maintaining self-governing systems and facilitating effective governance, especially within polycentric systems. In order to ensure the best results, personalized trust within communities must be supplemented by institutional trust as decisions move to broader contexts. Mechanisms such as clear property rights, transparent rules, and strong legal frameworks help build this trust. Polycentric governance also relies on individuals' ability to "vote with their feet," choosing communities that align with their values. This mechanism fosters competition and accountability among jurisdictions that leads to stronger policy outcomes that reflect community interest. Barriers to entry and exit, such as immigration restrictions or zoning laws, can limit the emancipatory potential of polycentric systems and so these must be an important concern when designing these systems.

Despite these many benefits of self-governance within a polycentric system there are a number of challenges as well. For example, participation in polycentric governance requires substantial effort from citizens which creates significant demands on time, attention, and resources. Moreover, there is a tendency for power to centralize unless those citizens are actively involved in checking these centralizing actions. This tendency diminishes the autonomy of local communities and undermines the system's protective role for minority perspectives. Finally, tensions emerge between local governance and broader concerns. While polycentric systems encourage local self-governance, they must also address cross-community issues that require coordination at higher levels and the need for protecting individual rights. Balancing local autonomy with the need for broader collaboration is critical to achieving equitable and effective governance.

Polycentric governance offers a promising model for enhancing democratic participation and individual autonomy. However, its success depends on active citizen engagement, robust institutional design, and mechanisms that ensure equitable access to governance. By accommodating diverse interests and fostering innovation, polycentric systems can empower communities while preserving broader social cohesion.

References

Alesina, A., & La Ferrara, E. (2005). Ethnic Diversity and Economic Performance. *Journal of Economic Literature, 43*(3), 762–800.

Aligica, P. D. (2019). *Public Entrepreneurship, Citizenship, and Self-governance.* Cambridge University Press.

Aligica, P. D., & Boettke, P. J. (2009). *Challenging Institutional Analysis and Development: The Bloomington School.* Routledge.

Aligica, P. D., & Tarko, V. (2013). Co-Production, Polycentricity, and Value Heterogeneity: The Ostroms' Public Choice Institutionalism Revisited. *American Political Science Review, 107*(4), 726–741.

AZFamily Digital News. (2024). Arizona Jury Convicts 2 Brothers of Aiding FLDS Prophet's 'Child Brides' Scheme. Retrieved October 2, 2024, from https://www.azfamily.com/2024/10/03/arizona-jury-convicts-2-brothers-aiding-flds-sect-leaders-child-brides-scheme

Berlin, I. (1969). Two Concepts of Liberty. In I. Berlin (Ed.), *Four Essays on Liberty* (pp. 118–172). Oxford University Press.

Buchanan, J. M., & Tullock, G. [1962] (1999). *The Calculus of Consent: Logical Foundations of Constitutional Democracy.* In G. Brennan, H. Kliemt & R. D. Tollison (Eds.), *The Collected Works of James M. Buchanan: Volume 3.* Liberty Fund.

Cook, K. S., Hardin, R., & Levi, M. (2005). *Cooperation Without Trust?* Russell Sage Foundation.

Coyne, C. J., Isaacs, J., & Schwartz, J. (2007). Put Me in Coach, I'm Ready to Play. *Review of Austrian Economics, 20*(4), 237–246.

Goodman, N. P. (2023). Commerce, Spontaneous Order, and Gender Freedom Movements. *Cosmos+Taxis, 11*(11+12), 24–36.

Hardin, R. (2006). *Trust.* Polity Press.

Hirschman, A. O. (1970). *Exit Voice and Loyalty: Responses to Decline in Firms, Organizations, and States.* Harvard University Press.

Hirschman, A. O. (1980). "Exit, Voice, and Loyalty": Further Reflections and a Survey of Recent Contributions. *Milbank Memorial Fund Quarterly: Health and Society, 58*(3), 430–453.

Hayek, F. A. (2007). *The Road to Serfdom: Texts and Documents: The Definitive Edition*, Bruce Caldwell, (Ed.). University of Chicago Press.

Kukathas, C. (2003). *The Liberal Archipelago: A Theory of Diversity and Freedom.* Oxford University Press.

Lemke, J. S. (2016). Interjurisdictional Competition and the Married Women's Property Acts. *Public Choice, 166*(3), 291–313.

Lemke, J. (2020). Withdrawing Consent: Polycentric Defenses against Domination. *Independent Review, 25*(2), 265–278.

Lofthouse, J. K., & Herzberg, R. Q. (2023). The Continuing Case for a Polycentric Approach for Coping with Climate Change. *Sustainability, 15*(4), 3770.

Maletz, D. J. (2003). Making Non-Citizens: Consequences of Administrative Centralization in Tocqueville's "Old Regime." *Publius, 33*(2), 17–35.

Martin, A. (2019). Social Recontracting. In R. Q. Herzberg, P. J. Boettke, & P. D. Aligica (Eds.), *Ostrom's Tensions: Reexamining the Political Economy and Public Policy of Elinor C. Ostrom* (pp. 127–146). Mercatus Center at George Mason University.

McGinnis, M. (1999). *Polycentricity and Local Public Economies: Readings from The Workshop in Political Theory and Policy Analysis*. University of Michigan Press.

Mill, J. S. (1977). *The Collected Works of John Stuart Mill, Volume 18: Essays on Politics and Society*. London: Routledge and Kegan Paul.

Novak, M. (2021). *Freedom in Contention: Liberal Political Economy and Social Movements*. Lexington Books.

Nozick, R. (2013). *Anarchy, State and Utopia* (2nd edition), Basic Books.

Orgad, L. (2010). Illiberal Liberalism Cultural Restrictions on Migration and Access to Citizenship in Europe. *American Journal of Comparative Law, 58*(1), 53–105.

Ostrom, E. (1990). *Governing the commons: The evolution of institutions for collective action*. Cambridge University Press.

Ostrom, E. (1993). Covenanting, Co-Producing, and the Good Society. *The Newsletter of PEGS, 3*(2), 7–9.

Ostrom, E. (2005). *Understanding Institutional Diversity*. Princeton University Press.

Ostrom, E. (2010). Beyond Markets and States: Polycentric Governance of Complex Economic Systems. *American Economic Review, 100*(3), 641–672.

Ostrom, E. (2012). Nested Externalities and Polycentric Institutions: Must We Wait for Global Solutions Before Taking Actions At Other Scales? *Economic Theory, 49*(2), 353–369.

Ostrom, E., & Parks, R. B. [1987] (1999). Neither Gargantua nor the Land of Lilliputs: Conjectures on Mixed Systems of Metropolitan Organization. In M. D. McGinnis (Ed.), *Polycentricity and Local Public Economies: Readings from the Workshop in Political Theory and Policy Analysis* (pp. 284–305). University of Michigan Press.

Ostrom, V. (1991). *The Meaning of American Federalism: Constituting a Self-governing Society*. ICS Press.

Ostrom, V. (1997). *The Meaning of Democracy and the Vulnerability of Democracies: A Response to Tocqueville's Challenge*. University of Michigan Press.
Ostrom, V. (1999a). Polycentricity (Part 1). In M. D. McGinnis (Ed.), *Polycentricity and Local Public Economies: Readings from the Workshop in Political Theory and Policy Analysis* (pp. 52–74). University of Michigan Press.
Ostrom, V. (1999b). Cryptoimperialism, Predatory States, and Self-governance. In M. D. McGinnis (Ed.), *Polycentric Governance and Development: Readings from the Workshop in Political Theory and Policy Analysis* (pp. 166–185). University of Michigan Press.
Ostrom, V., Tiebout, C. M., & Warren, R. (1961). The Organization of Government in Metropolitan Areas: A Theoretical Inquiry. *American Political Science Review*, *55*(4), 831–842.
Rawls, J. (1999). *A Theory of Justice*. Revised Edition. The Belknap Press of Harvard University Press.

CHAPTER 7

How the Other Half Lives: The Emancipatory Contributions of the Chicago School of Sociology

Erwin Dekker

Social science is both a reflection of society and a reflection on society. Or to put it differently, it both seeks to document social change and to contribute to it. Research programs position themselves differently with respect to this dynamic. Some have taken up Marx' dictum that the goal of intellectual endeavors is not to interpret the world but to change it. Others have sought to restrict themselves purely to interpretation or even mere description in search of a neutral perspective. But work in intellectual history has time and time illustrated that social scientists can never fully escape their context (Danell et al., 2015; Leonard, 2010), and it has highlighted that even work that is intended to be merely descriptive can become appropriated by actors in society (Mackenzie, 2008). Given this fact, it is a relevant and important question how research programs have contributed to social change. It should be obvious that the most activist

E. Dekker (✉)
Mercatus Center at George Mason University, Fairfax, VA, USA
e-mail: edekker@mercatus.gmu.edu

M. Novak (ed.), *Liberal Emancipation*, Mercatus Studies in Political and Social Economy, https://doi.org/10.1007/978-3-031-94406-2_7

research programs are not always the ones which have contributed most and vice versa.

One prominent way in which social theory influences social developments is through reframing of issues, problems, identities, values, etc. Therefore, it makes sense to ask the historical question, which social science approaches or traditions have contributed to such reframing in a way which has furthered emancipation. We might even ask how they have contributed to emancipation by developing it conceptually, for instance, by broadening or specifying what emancipation entails. Successfully answering such questions depends on having some understanding of what we mean by emancipation. Emancipation has important economic dimensions, for instance, the improved economic opportunities for workers, women, and other marginalized groups. Yet, emancipation is hardly ever discussed within economics.[1] Even McCloskey's project on the dignity and respect for the bourgeois and later the proletariat does not theorize the idea of emancipation (Dekker & Kuchař, 2020; McCloskey, 2010). And emancipation is certainly not restricted to increased economic opportunities. Sociology has a longer tradition of conceptualizing emancipation; a recent study suggests that emancipation is: "the project of a reduction in the privileges of the dominant classes" (Boltanski, 2013: 154). This idea of emancipation is two-sided in the work of Boltanski, it can justify the worth of groups which were previously regarded as "less worthy," and it can also critique the "special worth" of privileged groups. As such the project of emancipation is liberal at heart and is concerned with an equality of status or dignity. It thus has both economic, social and symbolic dimensions. David Levy and Sandra Peart's have rightfully drawn attention to Frank Knight and James Buchanan's ideal of a society of dignified equals, which captures the dual nature of equality, both material and symbolic (Levy & Peart, 2020). This chapter argues that an analytically egalitarian social science is a combination of methodological commitments, *and* a familiarity with the diversity of perspectives present in complex (urban) societies.

A substantive notion of emancipation has the benefit of allowing us to see more clearly which developments have contributed to it, and which have sought to block or reverse this kind of emancipation. It has the downside of downplaying the extent to which the meaning of emancipation is discovered in the process of realizing it. But since we are at best making a start here at analyzing how social science contributes to emancipation, this limitation must be accepted. This substantive notion immediately makes clear that the history of social science is not a simple march of progress. A current wave of scholarship has shed light on the degree and extent to which thinkers during the Enlightenment period reinforced racial differences and helped justify social hierarchies (Eze, 1997; Sebastiani, 2013; Vermeulen, 2015). This pernicious influence was not restricted to the Enlightenment period, but continued well into the twentieth century and was arguably reinforced by the progressivist movement (Leonard, 2016). Critics of post-World War II development economists have drawn attention to the neo-colonial nature of the project, and its crypto-imperialism (Ostrom, [1986] 2012). Feminist scholars have made clear that the contributions of women to society and scholarship have long been downplayed or neglected (Watts, 2013). So, there are ample reasons to look for the social scientific approaches which have contributed positively to emancipation.

This chapter will look at a particular school of thought, the Chicago School of Sociology, both of the first and second generation, to see how they tried to shape social thought by flattening hierarchies and emancipate minority groups through their research (Bulmer, 1984; Fine, 1995). The Chicago School of Sociology is widely known for its qualitative approach to urban sociology and case-studies such as *The Polish Peasant*, *The Hobo*, *The Jack-Roller*, etc. They analyzed and presented the perspectives of social groups with low socio-economic and symbolic status, and their approach was intended to give voice to these communities through their methodological approach based on life-stories and other first-person perspectives. The second generation of the Chicago School, who worked during the 1950s is associated with symbolic interactionism. But their research, too, focused on marginalized groups, or what they called outsiders, such as drug users or those designated as mentally ill.

The reason for studying this school of thought is they had a significant emancipatory effect, particularly in the United States. But there are underlying reasons why they did so. The most important reason is their approach which sought to represent the world from the perspective of these marginalized groups. Subjective approaches in the social sciences are important because they do not impose an external frame on others but seek to respect the interpretation of the subjects they study. The Chicago School of Sociology is far from unique in adopting such an approach; think for instance of Austrian economics or various phenomenological approaches in sociology and anthropology, but the Chicago sociologists did it early and studied many urban groups which had not previously been studied. Second, the approach of the Chicago sociologists was deeply anti-paternalistic which reinforced the benefits of their perspectival approach. This resulted in an approach to social science which was inside-out (from the perspective of actors in society), rather than outside-in, the typical social scientific perspective of the disinterested and *external* observer (Boettke, 2022).

The first section of this chapter presents various positions research programs have taken vis-à-vis change in society, to argue why the Chicago School of Sociology is a relevant object of study for those interested in the emancipatory potential of social science. The second section presents their research program. The third section analyzes the ways in which it responded to the dominant progressive (and conservative) modes of thinking of the age. The fourth section discusses in more detail the perspectivism of the Chicago School and how it compares to the idea of analytical egalitarianism. The fifth section suggests that between the two generations of the School two competing predictions about the effects of emancipation of marginal groups: integration into mainstream society and social pluralism.

Social Science and Emancipation

In earlier work, I have distinguished between various roles of social scientists have adopted, based on their positioning as scientist or humanist and their activist (constructivist) or accepting (corrective) attitude. This allowed me to distinguish between positivists, social engineers, students of society, and emancipators. The positivists position themselves as scientists and seek to primarily describe and analyze society, accepting existing attitudes and institutions. The social engineers share the idea that social scientists are scientific in the same way that natural scientists are but regard it as their primary duty to improve society. So, while they are interested in description and analysis, they are mostly interested in evaluating the effectiveness of several types of reforms or interventions. They tend to align themselves with policymakers.

Students of society, like positivists, tend to accept the existing attitudes and institutions of their society, but their goal is interpretive. Their goal is to make sense of the world for themselves, as well as for others. Although they do point to what they regard as worrisome or hopeful tendencies, they tend to place themselves at some distance from processes of social change. Finally, emancipators share the sense-making goal of the students, but they are not content to merely study the development of society. Instead, they seek to be part of that change, typically by allying themselves with (social) entrepreneurs or social movements (Dekker, 2020; also Boettke & Horwitz, 2005).

The ability to change perspectives is not restricted to one or two of the four positions, but the type of alternative perspectives which are offered are different in kind. New perspectives which originate from the more scientific positions are likely to be rooted in empirical regularities or conceptualizations stemming from more speculative work. Marx notion of social classes, although he is not the first to use the concept, is a good example of a perspective which originates from his more speculative work, and which later became widely adopted by actors within society. But this perspective was according to Marx rooted in objective realities, in this case that of the relations of production, a good indication that we are dealing here with a perspective originating in a scientific perspective on the world.

The perspectives developed by those with a humanistic attitude tend to derive from subjective understandings of individuals or groups within society. Given the fact that sense-making is central, these perspectives are interpretive in nature and are typically situated, either historically or in relation to a particular position in society. This is not to say that these perspectives are free from speculation, to the contrary, one only has to think of idealist tendencies in the humanities. The work of the Chicago School of Sociology is not very speculative, but instead grounded in the perspectives of various individuals and groups within the city. They sought to offer new perspectives by giving voice to marginalized groups which were neglected, or underrepresented. The originality of the Chicago School was thus not in the perspectives that they developed, but rather in amplifying pre-existing perspectives which were not widely heard.

The outlook of the social engineers, positivists, emancipators, and students are ideal–typical characterizations based on what social scientists have done in the past one-hundred fifty years or so. The label "emancipator" might suggest that they are the only type of intellectual who helps to bring about a process of emancipation in society. But I think that would be a mistake for two reasons. First, as noted in the introduction, social thinkers have both facilitated and obstructed the process of emancipation. The extent to which "emancipators" contribute to substantive emancipation, understood as the reduction of privileges of the dominant classes, is dependent on the type of actors they align themselves with. This is no different for social engineers, who have in the past have repeatedly helped totalitarian regimes pursue their repressive goals.

Second, intended effects should never be equated with actual effects. It is trivially true that most social thinkers are not effective in contributing to social change. But more importantly the work of all four types of social scientists has the potential to contribute to emancipation, or its opposite, through unintended consequences. There are many concepts which were coined in descriptive and purely interpretive work, which have been appropriated by actors in society to mobilize a movement and bring about social change. Similarly, it is perfectly possible that concepts developed in more interpretive discourses are appropriated in engineering discourses to justify or reorient interventions.

In this chapter, I will argue that most of the work of the Chicago school of Sociology, especially among the first generation, was presented as interpretive work, which accepted the existing attitudes and institutions in society. They presented themselves as students of society and urban life, and yet they had both the ambition to raise the worth of marginalized groups in society and succeeded in doing so. The second generation of the Chicago School was more explicit about its emancipatory goals, and critical of various existing institutions in society, sometimes explicitly aligning themselves with outsiders. This did not necessarily make their efforts more successful since it allowed other social scientists to dismiss their work as overtly normative.

The Chicago School of Sociology

The heyday of the Chicago School of Sociology was in the 1920s when the department of sociology was the intellectual leader in the United States and arguably in the world. During this decade, the department led by Robert E. Park and Ernest Burgess produced a vast number of case-studies of distinct groups in the city of Chicago. These studies were based on the life-stories of individuals at the margins of society, through studies which relied heavily on what would later be called participant observation. This approach was pioneered in the landmark study by Thomas and Znaniecki (1918) *The Polish Peasant in Europe and America.*

This study came about in the context of extensive migration of Polish people to the United States and Chicago in particular, which was part of a much larger wave of European migration as well as migration from the

American South. Inspired by the work of Ferdinand Tönnies on community (*Gemeinschaft*) and society (*Gesellschaft*) Thomas and Znaniecki studied the organization, disorganization, and reorganization within the Polish community in the city. They relied on a wide variety of primary documents such as letters, diaries, and life-stories to sketch the inner-life, concerns, and aspirations of the Polish individuals both in Europe and the in the United States. Thomas believed that such documents provided direct access to the subjective experience of people, in the same way that the best novels could do. He preferred such documents from life over interviews, which he believed to be a less direct representation.

This study became a model for a considerable number of subsequent studies. The first major follow-up study was *The Negro in Chicago* by Charles S. Johnson and Park (published under the as a report of the Chicago Committee on Race Relations, 1922), a sociological reflection on the race riots of 1919 in the city. From 1923 onwards, the sociological studies from the department appeared in the Sociological Series of the University of Chicago Press. They included Nels Anderson's (1923) *The Hobo*, Ernest R. Mowrer's (1927) *Family Disorganization*, Frederic Thrasher's (1927) *The Gang*, Ruth Shonle Cavan's (1928) *Suicide*, Louis Wirth's (1928) *The Ghetto*, Harvey Zorbaugh's (1929) *The Gold Coast and the Slum*, E. Franklin Frazier's (1932) *The Negro Family in Chicago*, Cressley's (1932) *The Taxi-Dance Hall* and Walter Reckless' (1933) *Vice in Chicago*. A similar set of studies was produced for the Institute for Juvenile Research in Chicago, among them John Landesco's (1929) *Organized Crime in Chicago*, Clifford's Shaw's *The Jack-Roller* (1930) and his *The Natural History of a Delinquent Career* (Shaw and Moore, 1931).

The Chicago School of Sociology is frequently associated with a particular methodology, qualitative and subjectivist in its orientation. In the second generation this was developed into symbolic interactionism, which maintained the emphasis on subjective understandings as well as the agency of individuals within social structures or culture but expanded the analysis of the meaning attributed to social relationships. Some have argued that this characterization puts too much emphasis on a particular methodology which was frequently part of a multimethod approach in which comparative statistics were also used. A good example is the impressive volume by Drake and Cayton (1945) *The Black Metropolis* which is concerned with mapping the black community in Chicago, and does so through extensive statistical work, but it is preceded by an interpretative account which highlights the personal experiences of Black people in Chicago around World War II.

A related understanding of the efforts of the Chicago School of Sociology is to understand it as a form of urban anthropology. This interpretation is in fact suggested in the epigraph to that same volume on Chicago as Black Metropolis: "Anthropology, the science of man, has been mainly concerned up to the present with the study of primitive peoples. But civilized man is quite as interesting as an object of investigation, and at the same time his life is more open to observation and study. Urban life and culture are more varied, subtle, and complicated, but the fundamental motives are in both instances the same" (Park, cited in Drake & Cayton, 1945: v). And nearly all of the studies cited above were attempts to map the city anthropologically; in fact one of the few more theoretical elements of the research project of Park and Burgess was to develop a sociological theory of cities and urban life (Park et al., 1925). Burgess was open about the fact that he and Thomas were inspired to do this by the journalists and novelists who first explored "how the other half lived."[2]

A consequence of their methodology was to give voice to communities and individuals who were typically talked about, rather than heard. This was not a wholly unintended consequence; Thomas had already urged his students to "leave out the moralizing" (Thomas, cited in Cappetti, 1993: 23). This meant that they should present the perspectives of their subjects as valid and relevant, rather than as a consequence of immorality or bias. As such the studies normalized the behavior of the diverse groups living and working in the city. This is not to suggest that their approach was completely non-judgmental. A good example is the analysis provided by Clifford Shaw in *The Jack Roller*. After Stanley, a young delinquent, has told his own life in the pages of the book Shaw analyzes this life-history and the criminal behavior of Stanley. On the one hand, Shaw suggests that the Stanley's criminal activities, like jack-rolling, is only to be expected from young guys growing up in neighborhoods like the one Stanley came of age, because these activities have "become a more or less traditional aspect of the social life" (Shaw, 1930: 165). Yet only a paragraph later Shaw argues that Stanley in the account of his life exhibits a "definite tendency to excuse his misconduct by means of self-pity, fatalism, and by placing the blame on other persons" (ibid.). Yet these judgments are much less prominent than in other work from the same period.

To be able to more fully appreciate the uniqueness of the Chicago approach it helps to contrast it to some other prominent approaches in the social sciences of the period. A lot of secondary work on the school neglects this, because it is primarily interested in how the department in Chicago was able to establish a scientific form of sociology in the United States (Bulmer, 1984; Chapoulie, 2020; Cortese, 1995). This is indeed important, but in doing so it fails to sufficiently appreciate the distinctiveness of the Chicago approach during the Progressive era.

The Progressive Alternative

The most prominent strand of social theorizing in America during the early decades of the twentieth century was Progressivism, sometimes called the social gospel. It was influenced by older theological strands, the social temperance movement, and the ethical economics of the German Historical School (Bateman, 1998). As the Progressive label suggests it was optimistic about the prospects and potential of social reform, so its focus was often directly on what it perceived to be the major social problems of the day. It had little patience for the fact-value distinction and was primarily interested in the combination of moral improvement and actionable knowledge to improve the living, housing, and working conditions of the growing (lower) middle-classes. It frequently moralized about the lower social classes, those who were not Christian, or otherwise culturally (or racially) different. One of the major social facts of the 1920s was, of course, Prohibition, which was widely perceived to be a symbol of the Progressivist movement.

Even though its paternalism and overconfidence in the effects of social reform appear naïve in hindsight, it is important to acknowledge that the Progressive movement was a major impetus for empirical studies across the social sciences. Under the influence of the German Historical School, the Social Survey movement mapped the socio-economic conditions of large parts of the population. Although it was certainly activist in orientation, it confidently believed that if the extent of social ills were widely known, political action would automatically follow which meant they mainly focused on empirics. This movement was highly visible in Chicago through the famous Hull House settlement founded and managed by Jane Addams in the Near West Side of the city, close to the stockyards full of migrant workers (Addams, 1911; Deegan, 2017). At her initiative large-scale statistical studies were undertaken which, long before the

Chicago School of Sociology, mapped the city. In the "Hull-House Maps and Papers" from 1895, she and her collaborators presented statistical maps of the ethnic composition, wages, working conditions, and social and hygienic conditions in various neighborhoods.

The decision by the sociologists of the Chicago School to rely primarily on more qualitative methods closer to the lived experience of citizens was thus shaped in direct response to the Social Survey movement, which relied on quantitative measures which remained at considerable distance from the lived experiences of the Chicagoans. But this opposition should not be overdrawn, several of the studies mentioned above combined both methodologies, and saw the more qualitative methods mostly as a supplement, not an alternative to the quantitative methods.

Despite these complementarities in methodology the outlook of the two different strands of sociology could hardly have been more different. Jane Addams, known as "Saint Jane" in the Chicago press, stood for a new and better society, which would be more productive, peaceful, and just (Deegan, 2017: 6).[3] But this progressive attitude was combined with strong paternalistic tendencies, which manifested in hierarchical forms of thinking. A prominent form of this hierarchical thinking was the attempt to explain socio-economic differences and differences in morality as resulting from racial or genetic differences. Or worse, to advocate for the improvement of society by improving the genetic quality of the people, a research program known as eugenics (Leonard, 2016). Although Jane Addams was not directly involved, she welcomed this novel approach, "the new science of eugenics with its recently appointed university professors. Its organized societies publish an ever-increasing mass of information as to that which constitutes the inheritance of well-born children" (Addams, cited in Lombardo, 2002: 210).

The way Jane Addams welcomed eugenics is symbolic for the Progressive spirit. It embraced comparative statistics, but this framework was used at best indiscriminately across a wide variety of domains including morality, psychology, sociology, and economics. Some researchers emphasized primarily how differences in socio-economic conditions created outcomes, and therefore advocated for improvements in living and working conditions. But more often Progressive scientists attempted to locate innate genetic or psychological differences, such as those of "well-born children" between individuals to explain differences in social outcomes, and to argue for population policies to improve the quality of the "genetic stock." The Chicago sociologists, on the contrary, decided to provide voice to the badly-born children of the city.

Such views had direct relevance for how one looked at the city of Chicago, which grew faster than any city in the world during this period. In 1890 the city was home to about 1.1 million inhabitants; in 1920, it had nearly tripled to 2.7 million inhabitants. Nearly all this growth was due to migration. The major question, politically, was whether the migrants could adapt and integrate into American society. This so-called "Americanization debate" was a direct point of contention between the Progressives and the pioneering sociologist Thomas who attacked their ideas in his study *The Polish Peasant* (Wiley, 2011). In this book Thomas and Znaniecki argued that the Polish migrant came from vastly different social and economic circumstances, typical of peasants in Eastern Europe, but that they would adapt over time to American society. They strongly rejected essentialist explanations which suggested that something inherent to Polish, Lithuanian, Greek, Italian people, or their culture was incompatible with urban life in America.

This was part of a broader critical response to the tents of Progressivism, produced by the Chicago School of Sociology. They presented a sociological theory in which the diversity in human behavior, including many supposedly immoral or deviant behaviors, were the result of social interaction within communities, shaped through both the external constraints and the internal culture which emerged in social groups. But there was never a genetic or cultural hierarchy between individuals, nor an absence of individual agency in their perspective.

Just as important was the fact that they refused to use an external moral lens which allowed them to simply diagnose social ills, or even to determine from the outside which types of behavior were normal, and which were deviant. Theoretically the idea of social pathologies or ills which were in need of fixing derived from Emile Durkheim who "had suggested that a state of anomie, or normlessness, results from a breakdown in the regulation of goals; with such lack of regulation, individuals' aspirations become unlimited, and deviance may result" (Inderbitzin et al., 2018: 74). The Chicago School of Sociology replaced that explanation of anomie, with the varied perspectives of actors, whose norms and goals were dependent on social environments. What looked like unregulated or deviant behavior from one perspective, was well adapted behavior within another group. This was the major perspective shift that was accomplished in monographs like the Anderson's *The Hobo* and Shaw's *The Jack Roller*.

That which looked deviant to outsiders, was in fact the result of learned and broadly rational behavior among marginalized groups.

This perspective was not only used to explain the diversity of customs and norms in the ethnic groups in the city, but it was also applied to social groups like the homeless or youth criminals. Long predating the critical work of Foucault on the disciplinary power of the corrective system in society, the Chicago School developed a critique of the "age of correction" (Blackman, 2018). They refused to see phenomena like youth delinquency only as a form of moral depravity, and instead attempted to explain criminal behavior as both a response to circumstances and a form of socialized behavior.

This resulted in skepticism of progressive social reform on two grounds. First, it misdiagnosed the origins of the supposed social ills, and second, it relied on a moral perspective alien to the actors. As Ernest Burgess argued:

> ... We are readily disposed, because of our interest in the welfare of others, to impose upon them either our own standards of behavior, or standards of behavior higher than our own. Many persons quite sincerely voted 'dry' for the sake of their weaker brother but continued to drink 'wet.' The Southern planter might have a virtuous feeling in aiding prohibition legislation to protect his Negro tenant with the serene consciousness that his own stock of liquors would not be curtailed. Social workers are often expected to enforce standards of housekeeping and conduct upon clients of relief, which under similar conditions, they would find difficult to observe in their own households (Burgess [1935] 1974: 22).

His frequent collaborator and fellow leader of this early generation of sociologists framed it even more strongly to his students in a thinly veiled critique of Jane Addams: "the greatest damage done to the city of Chicago was not the product of corrupt politicians or criminals but of women reformers" (Burgess, cited in Bulmer, 1984: 74). This makes clear that the primary problem to Burgess and Park was not whether the reform was initiated by the state, the city government or by progressive movements, but rather that the moral and social reforms were forced upon groups. This shaped the morally inspired, anti-paternalistic stance of the sociologists of the Chicago School.

The Heterogeneity of Perspectives of Life in the City

Subjectivism in economics is primarily a methodological principle. It is an important element of the theory of value and of individual preferences more broadly, but hardly ever invoked to suggest that subjective perspectives of actors must be studied to understand the economy (Dekker & Kuchař, 2024). The Chicago School of Sociology did not explicitly adopt a methodological principle of subjectivism, but rather provided the perspective of those talked about, but not talked with. The methodology to provide such perspectives was not restricted to one type of data collection. Park encouraged his students to: "Go and sit in the lounges of the luxury hotels and on the doorsteps of the flophouses; sit on the Gold Coast settees and on the slum shakedowns; sit in the Orchestra Hall and in the Star and Garden Burlesk. In short gentlemen, go get the seat of your pants dirty in real research" (Bulmer, 1984: 97). Notice how Park contrasts the high and the low, emphasizing that a good understanding of social relations could only be attained if a variety of perspectives were analyzed. This crucially included perceptions that groups had of each other. This approach was the counterpoint to the social survey approach which had sought to provide comparable data across groups and different cities.

Even though this approach was more an eclectic practice in which perspectives were reconstructed based on letters, participant observation, and various other kinds of engagement with the group, it was understood that it had important implications for what counted as "social fact." Early on in the development of the school it coalesced into the famous Thomas quote that: "if a situation is defined as real, it is real in its consequences."[4] In other words, the perspectives of individuals and social groups were what shaped their behavior, not objective socio-economic or cultural circumstances. In the analysis of the race riots of 1919 the Chicago sociologists, for instance, paid ample attention to the way different ethnic groups were portrayed in the newspapers, and how this shaped (racial) prejudice.

Another key aspect of this attention to the importance of personal and group perspectives was that the action of individuals was never reduced to mere behavior but included their aspirations and dreams. Although not in use anymore, Thomas attempts to identify four universal drives in human behavior are a good example of this. He argued that all humans wish for security, recognition, response, and novelty. These universal, psychologically shared desires were broad enough to be useful to examine a wide variety of different perspectives. They were not psychological categories which could directly explain or predict human behavior, but they gained content within the social setting in which they were expressed. Colyer has argued that as such:

> … Thomas also embraced the wishes as a common denominator to humanity. That is, he rejected the arguments, anchored in Eugenics, that different groups of people are driven by wholesale differences in genetic, constitutional, or psychic makeup. Instead, he insisted that all people were at base, fundamentally the same (…) Humans are humans. Where we differ is in our desires, which are strongly socially conditioned, and our capacity to define or interpret our situations (Colyer, 2015: 259).

This is a difficult balance to strike, because on the one hand one wants to explain differences, and on the other hand one wants to start with commonality.

But surprisingly most of the secondary literature on the Chicago School neglects the moral orientation which clearly inspired the work. One of the few exceptions is the following characterization from Wiley: "This research elaborated, explained, and confirmed the egalitarian theory of the self. The subjective or intra-psychic point of view pervaded the research, even though there were also many demographic and statistical studies. These studies were not aimed at controlling the population. Instead they were done in a spirit of curiosity and wonder, revealing the fascinating varieties that grew in the corners of a community" (Wiley, 2011: 57).[5] His emphasis on the egalitarian nature of the project which it sought to achieve by studying those typically not heard and only talked about are really the core of the approach, which drove both the methodology, the choice of subjects as well as the conclusions which tended to be skeptical of outside interference.

This balance between a kind of methodological egalitarianism and the study of difference, has been analyzed in other contexts. Peart and Levy (2009) have called a similar attitude analytical egalitarianism, which assumes that human beings are equal for the purpose of analysis. Differences or changes in behavior and aspirations must therefore be explained from differences in circumstances, rather than in terms of innate biological or psychological differences. This methodological commitment was an important counterapproach to various strands of Progressivism, and it is crucial for a social science rooted in egalitarianism. If emancipation is the elimination of privilege, then we should expect an emancipatory social science to start from a more equal starting point than the one dominant in a particular society. This is exactly what the Chicago School of Sociology achieved.

There is, however, an interesting difference between the analytical egalitarianism that Levy and Peart identify, and the gradual inclusion of more diverse perspectives promoted by the Chicago sociologists. Levy and Peart identify a particular commitment, which is rationalist in origin and which they associate with various thinkers across the centuries. The Chicago School on the other hand gradually includes more groups into consideration. I think both approaches can reinforce each other, but it deserves some emphasis that supposedly (analytical) egalitarian perspectives of the past, have often looked one-sided, Euro-centric, gendered, or elitist to later generations. It is in other words easy to be led astray by adopting supposedly neutral or egalitarian perspectives, given the plurality of perspectives characteristic of complex modern societies. This suggests that a proper analytically egalitarian approach is unlikely to be achieved without the more empirical and gradual work which makes visible particular perspectives.

One potential disadvantage of such an approach is that it might end up neglecting crucial differences, not merely in terms of agency or innate abilities, but also in terms of the relations between groups. This tension was visible from the first major treatise produced by the Chicago School, *The Polish Peasant*. In the first decades of the twentieth century there was a lively political debate over the extent to which diverse groups could be Americanized. The Poles were considered to be only just above Black Americans in the genetic or psychological hierarchy presented by the Progressives. The social hierarchies "discovered" in quantitative social science, were invoked as evidence that groups like the Poles could simply not adjust to the American way of life. But Thomas and Znaniecki in their study of the Polish migrants in Chicago suggested clearly that they could and would gradually adapt to American culture. They argued that this would not lead to full assimilation but rather the emergence of what we would now call Polish Americans. This perspective was distinct and shaped by both cultural interactions in Poland as well as those in the second city of the United States. It provided a different outlook on American society and the other groups in Chicago, but also contained overlap with the perspectives of others.

This belief in integration was frequently coupled with the conviction that gradual integration would diminish differences between groups in society *and* lead to mutual acceptance. But this idea was certainly not universally shared, and how could it be in a city which was ethnically and racially segregated and in which social tensions between different nationalities were significant. Burgess recognized that cities were much more diverse and tolerant places than the rural towns were: "This diversity of urban areas and social types makes for a tolerance unknown in the rural neighborhood, which is expressed in the saying, 'It takes all kinds of people to make a world.'" But he refused to turn this into urban utopianism, recognizing that most diversity was made possible by the fact that social groups lived in different areas of the city. Burgess also distanced himself from the contact theory which suggests that interaction will lead to increased tolerance or even mutual respect: "But tolerance does not necessarily result in understanding and in social integration. One half of society does not know, and often does not seem to care, how the other half lives" (Burgess, 1974: 112).

The degree of toleration and overlap between perspectives is a crucial concern for sociologists of this generation. Although the Chicago School of Sociology dispensed with the naïve usage of normlessness as it had been employed by Durkheim and many of his followers, the question of what kept society together remained crucial. In Chicago that question was as pressing as ever in the 1920s, with a continuous large stream of migration as well as the race riots which had broken out in the city. One response to those developments might have been to despair about centrifugal forces which were tearing the city apart. The other was to seek to reimpose a certain set of norms from above and impose them through social policy and corrective institutions such as the reform schools, both widely employed. But the response of the Chicago School was instead to make visible the diversity of internal norms within the social groups of the city, to illustrate the varied but connected moral tapestry of the city.

This social analysis of the Chicago School thus presented a set of perspectives on the city and American life more generally which was novel, at least within the academic world.[6] These perspectives were given a voice and respectability they had not had before. But in their approach the Chicago sociologists also made a more implicit argument that a modern society could deal with a lot more pluralism than was commonly believed.

Skeptical of the idea that the groups had to be Americanized from above, they demonstrated that interactions within the city generated heterogenous perspectives, which nonetheless had some overlap and coherence. In this sense they presented Chicago as a multicultural city, which was gradually integrating, that image was transformed by the second generation of Chicago sociologists who worked after World War II.

Underdogs, Hegemonic Perspectives, and Emancipation

The history of emancipation shows that the elimination of some privileges exposes others. Therefore, emancipation is an ongoing process, and not just because there are frequent setbacks along the way. The pluralistic perspective of the 1920s was powerful in providing voice to various voiceless groups, and in broadening the set of perspectives considered in academic sociology. But from the vantage point of the postwar contributors to the Chicago School of Sociology there were two limitations to this approach. First it assumed convergence to the center; social groups wanted to integrate into mainstream society. Second it assumed a horizontal relationship between the different perspectives, or at least it did not seek to systematically challenge the dominant perspective in society. Instead, as we have seen, the early generation was more interested in showing the compatibility of these diverging perspectives with mainstream American culture.

In the 1950s there was a resurgence of the type of perspectival analysis of the 1920s. But this wave of scholarship, which also came out of the Chicago department of sociology, was more explicitly concerned with normalizing and destigmatizing the behavior of deviant groups within the city (Fine, 1995). Some of the leading scholars of this generation were Howard Becker and Erving Goffman, who explicitly studied subcultures, which were generated through processes of self-selection or through institutional pressures, such as the patients of a mental hospital (Barmaki, 2021; Goffman, 1961). Becker was interested in the way that social groups sought to differentiate themselves from mainstream society, and how mainstream society labeled certain groups as outsiders or less dignified (Becker, 1963). Emancipation came to mean something closer to self-expression, or even authenticity, rather than integration into mainstream society. This trend is also visible in earlier postwar studies by Harold Garfinkel (1949) and Harold Finestone (1957). As Gusfield summarized: "The second school shares with the first and identification with the less respected, less established elements in the society and a notable dose of skepticism and disrespect for the well-off, the authoritative and the official" (Gusfield, 1995: xiii).

An analysis of medical school by Howard Becker's was titled *Boys in White* (1961) which in its framing clearly challenged the elitist associations of medical school. In his presidential address for the Society of the Study of Social Problems Becker asked, "whose side are we on?" He came out strongly in favor of those who enjoyed less respect in society. He used the notion of the hierarchy of credibility to argue that some groups in society had less ability to define how things really are. Becker worked from a perspective of social constructivism, now supplemented that with the idea that those higher in the hierarchy of credibility had more power to shape this social construction of reality. To counter this power, he believed that sociologists had a duty to present the social world as it was experienced and interpreted by those lower in the hierarchy of credibility. Science he argued, frequently reinforced the hierarchy of credibility through its methodologies: "And thus we see why we accuse ourselves of bias only when we take the side of the subordinate. It is because, in a situation that is not openly political, with the major issues defined as arguable, we join responsible officials and the man in the street in an unthinking acceptance of the hierarchy of credibility" (Becker, 1966b: 243).

Although Becker took an extreme position on this matter, the sentiment was more widely shared among the second generation of the Chicago School. Erving Goffmann, for instance, suggested that his work was meant as a counterweight to those who: "are in a position to give official imprint to versions of reality" (Galliher in Fine, 1995: 172). Retrospectively one might suggest that this was also the purpose of the studies of the first generation which sought to challenge moralizing and racialized understanding of group differences by providing the outsider communities with a voice. In dignifying this voice, they at the very least challenged the hegemony of the dominant perspective, if not its (partial) validity.

There are, however, undeniable downsides to this position of the identification with the underdog or the deviant. Gouldner pointed out these dangers vividly when he accused Becker and some of his associates to be practicing a sociology of "the cool" among the hip, drug addicts, jazz musicians, cab drivers, prostitutes, night people, drifters, grifters and skidders (Gouldner, 1968: 104). He suggested that this introduced a tension if not an inconsistency in the work of Becker. For should the sociologist who recognizes the importance of perspectives, not simply take the perspective of whoever they happen to be studying, rather than to consistently take the position of the underdog? Becker responded partially to this critique through his emphasis on the hierarchy of credibility, and the fact that the underdogs frequently are not seen or listened to, while those higher up in this hierarchy find many outlets to express or impose their perspectives. But that response is only satisfactory to a degree, it legitimates attention to deviants, but not identification with them. And as Gouldner points out, most underdogs are not at the very bottom of the hierarchy of credibility, so their accounts might have to be checked in turn. To put a finer point on that criticism he suggests that the fascination with the "cool" deviants in particular implies a critique of "the uneducated middle classes" and their smug narrowness (Gouldner, 1968: 106).

A similar objection could be raised against the strong anti-paternalism of the first generation of Chicago sociologists. Although this position was understandable as a counter-reaction to the Progressivist movement, it risks collapsing into the simple acceptance of what is. Interestingly the first generation was quite aware of this danger, and therefore focused exactly on the aspirations of the groups they studied. As such they did not give up the notion of moral improvement, but instead suggested that it should come from within the community, rather than from outside.

One way to make this problem go away is to suggest that one researcher can only do so much. But as we have seen, the Chicago sociology program was a coordinated research effort in which there was at least a shared objective: to study those at the margins of society. One might still argue that their project existed within a wider ecology of sociological research the Chicago School merely provided a counterweight to other approaches. But I think Gouldner's worries, read through the lens of emancipation, requires a different response. What he worried about from this perspective is that siding with the perspective of outsiders serves primarily to delegitimize particular frames, while (inadvertently) reinforcing others. Studying the outsider can shed light on perspectives typically ignored or even suppressed, but siding with them can eventually only lead to new kinds of bias. Gouldner concludes that sociologist's ultimate allegiance should be to certain values. This is a contentious position, although it has a long tradition within social science (Dekker & Klamer, 2015; Hennis, 1994; Polanyi, 1958). It certainly is consistent with the starting point of this essay that social science can and should be emancipatory.

If emancipation is the value to which we aim, simply presenting a perspective, even a plurality of perspectives cannot be sufficient. Emancipation indeed requires a willingness to empathize with others, as well as a willingness to question our own perspectives. But there is a further step which is required, and that is the attempt to look for modes of convergence, mutual learning or at the very least a peaceful co-existence between different groups.[7] In other places Becker actually made arguments in this direction. He, for instance, sided with the idea that sociologists should contribute to "a conversation between the classes." His argument in that context is not about choosing sides, but rather about fostering mutual understanding with those 'down there', in which life-histories tell "us what it means to be a kind of person we have never met face to face (...) to [help us] comprehend what it means to live the life of a Negro junkie or Polish delinquent" (Becker, 1966a: xiv). This process of fostering mutual understanding is the emancipatory role that sociologists of the Chicago School take, and one that might provide inspiration for today.

It is important to see that this emancipatory function is epistemic. It concerns knowledge about different perspectives, which first checks our own biases and preconceptions. But when these epistemic skills of analyzing diverse perspectives and appreciating the variety of them is developed, it should enable us to see certain patterns of commonality or congruence as well as the tensions and contradictions between them. This type of knowledge is not instrumentally useful but does provide the building blocks of what is required to understand diverse groups, respect their differing perspectives, and to foster ways of peaceful co-existence.

An important question that arises from the subtle, but important, difference between the first and second generation is to what extent emancipation should be understood as integration into mainstream society, or rather as the ability of communities to develop their own norms, and where possible govern themselves. This question points toward a well-known tension within liberalism, between more uniform and rationalist forms of liberalism, and more pluralist forms (Levy, 2015). I don't think the Chicago sociologists resolve this tension in their work, but their work does illustrate the more sociological dimension of this tension. Their perspectivism furthermore suggests that at least to some extent the answer should depend on the aspirations of the group themselves, do they seek to integrate or differentiate, and to what extent are they able to realize these aspirations?

Conclusion

The direct effect of social science on public policy has been well documented and might be easier to pin down than the more indirect effect of social science on our understanding of others and more broadly the society in which we live. But to evaluate the emancipatory power of social science it is required to move beyond the study of its direct and indirect influence on public policy. This chapter has suggested one important way in which social science can have emancipatory effects, and that is by giving voice and dignity to voices which have been marginalized. Obviously, what this means is contextual, and I have argued that this was particularly significant in an age dominated by Progressivist social science which was prone to discredit alternative moral perspectives and tended to reinforce existing social hierarchies.

The Chicago School of Sociology managed to have this effect by adopting a stance somewhere between that of the student of society, predominant among the first generation, and the emancipator, predominant among the second generation. Its primary contribution was in presenting perspectives from diverse groups in society. They did this in a particular historical urban context, where they focused especially on ethnic minorities and criminals. But as Wiley has argued about their impact: "the human rights revolutions for Black people and other ethnic groups, women, gays-lesbians, the elderly, and the disabled in recent decades owe a lot to Chicago's theory of the self. For this was the notion that explained how these seemingly different groupings were fundamentally all the same. It explained their legal and moral equality, and, one might say, 'demanded' their civil liberties" (Wiley, 2011: 68).

But their contribution went beyond this. They recognized that social scientists are part of one among many groups in society, who function as something of an interpreter or intermediator between the different perspectives. Emancipation involves giving dignity to groups who are considered less worthy, but it also involves an effort at reconciliation or integration between different perspectives.

Wiley makes a strong claim when he suggests that the various civil and human rights are directly indebted to Chicago's egalitarian theory of the self, one which must be substantiated for different civil rights movements. But it is certainly true that the Chicago sociologists permanently altered the way that sociology was done, and one of their most visible effects was that they inspired a generation of novelists in Chicago to write about the same groups which had been studied by the sociologist (Cappetti, 1993). Another effect of (the second generation of) Chicago sociology has been to challenge supposedly objective or neutral perspectives. This approach is visible in later approaches which have sought to demonstrate the remaining biases, and inevitably normative nature of such perspectives. To what extent Chicago sociology has directly inspired such later developments is an important question for future scholarship.

Notes

1. One exception is the work of Wertheim (1974) in development economics, other uses of emancipation tend to be narrow and study the effects of the abolition of slavery. Although it should be acknowledged that we can find in anti-slavery writers broader notions of emancipation (i.e., Washington 2018).
2. This phrase was popularized Jacob Riis as the title of one of his pioneering photobooks documenting the urban lower classes.
3. Deegan observes that her pacifism during World War I harmed her reputation severely, to the point where the U.S. government labeled her "the most dangerous woman in America." This contributed to the subsequent neglect of her contributions and the continuities between her work and that of the Chicago School. This was further reinforced by the fact that W.I. Thomas who had extensively studied and published on women, was fired from the university after being arrested on the suspicion of soliciting a prostitute. Deegan draws a connection between his arrest and his involvement with his wife's pacifist efforts (Deegan 2017: 179–186). More broadly it has been suggested that the early sociologists of the Chicago School overemphasized the break with previous approaches, and actively ignored the work of some important predecessors such as W.E.B. DuBois (Morris 2017).
4. For details on the attribution of this quote to Thomas, see Wiley's (2011) footnote 1.
5. Another exception is the study by Smith (1988) who argues that the Chicago School were reformers within capitalism, in response to

an extensive literature that has faulted them for not having a critical agenda.

6. Some studies have rightly highlighted the interactions between the literary world and the sociologists in Chicago. Although they suggest most of the influence was from the sociologists upon the novelists (Cappetti 1993), it is clear that the early Chicago sociologists were inspired by the work of journalists and other writers (Køhlert 2011).
7. This type of convergence is also an important theme in the methodology of economics, in particular the convergence between everyday images of the economy and academic ones (Lavoie, 1995; Dekker & Kuchař, 2024).

References

Addams, J. (1911). *Twenty Years at Hull House: With Autobiographical Notes*. MacMillan.

Anderson, N. (1923). *The Hobo: The Sociology of the Homeless Man*. University of Chicago Press.

Barmaki, R. (2021). Erving Goffman's View of 'Deviance': 'Self' and 'Society' as the Sources of Deviancy and Conformity. *Deviant Behavior, 42*(2), 147–161. https://doi.org/10.1080/01639625.2019.1658845

Bateman, B. W. (1998). Clearing the Ground: The Demise of the Social Gospel and the Rise of Neoclassicism in American Economics. *History of Political Economy*, *30*(Supp.), 29–52.

Becker, H. S. (1961). *Boys in White: Student Culture in Medical School*. Transaction Books.

Becker, H. S. (1963). *Outsiders: Studies in the Sociology of Deviance*. Free Press of Glencoe.

Becker, H. S. (1966a). Introduction. In *The Jack-Roller: A Delinquent Boy's Own Story*. University of Chicago Press.

Becker, H. S. (1966b). Whose Side Are We On? *Social Problems, 14*(3), 239–247.

Blackman, S. (2018). Young Delinquency as a Social Product in an Age of Correction: The Chicago School's Struggle to Humanize Transgression. *Boyhood Studies, 11*(1), 88–91.

Boettke, P. J. (2022). David M. Levy and Sandra J. Peart, Towards an Economics of Natural Equals: A Documentary History of the Early Virginia School. *Public Choice, 192*(3), 401–405.

Boettke, P. J., & Horwitz, S. (2005). The Limits of Economic Expertise: Prophets, Engineers, and the State in the History of Development Economics. *History of Political Economy*, *37*(Supp.), 10–39.
Boltanski, L. (2013). *On Critique: A Sociology of Emancipation*. Polity Press.
Bulmer, M. (1984). *The Chicago School of Sociology: Institutionalization, Diversity, and the Rise of Sociological Research*. University of Chicago Press.
Burgess, E. W. (1974). *The Basic Writings of Ernest W. Burgess*. Community and Family Study Center.
Cappetti, C. (1993). *Writing Chicago: Modernism, Ethnography, and the Novel*. Columbia University Press.
Cavan, R. S. (1928). *Suicide*. University of Chicago Press.
Chapoulie, J. M. (2020). *Chicago Sociology*. Columbia University Press.
Chicago Committee on Race Relations. (1922). *The Negro in Chicago: A Study of Race Relations and a Race Riot*. University of Chicago Press.
Colyer, C. J. (2015). W. I. Thomas and the Forgotten Four Wishes: A Case Study in the Sociology of Ideas. *American Sociologist*, *46*(2), 248–268
Cortese, A. J. (1995). The Rise, Hegemony, and Decline of the Chicago School of Sociology, 1892–1945. *Social Science Journal*, *32*(3), 235–254.
Cressley, P. G. (1932). *The Taxi-Dance Hall: A Sociological Study in Commercialized Recreation and City Life*. University of Chicago Press.
Danell, R., Larson, A., & Wisselgren, P. (2015). *Social Science in Context: Historical, Sociological, and Global Perspectives*. Nordic Academic Press.
Deegan, M. J. (2017). *Jane Addams and the Men of the Chicago School, 1892–1918*. Routledge.
Dekker, E. (2020). On Emancipators, Engineers, and Students: The Appropriate Attitude of the Economist. *Review of Austrian Economics*, *33*(1), 55–68.
Dekker, E., & Klamer, A. (2015). About Doing the Right Thing as an Academic Economist. In G. F. DeMartino & D. N. McCloskey (Eds.), *Oxford Handbook of Professional Economic Ethics* (pp. 101–115). Oxford University Press.
Dekker, E., & Kuchař, P. (2020). Bourgeois Knowledge: The Incomplete Closure of the Epistemological Break in the Work of Deirdre McCloskey. *Journal of Contextual Economics–Schmollers Jahrbuch*, *140*(3–4), 301–317. https://doi.org/10.3790/schm.140.3-4.301.
Dekker, E., & Kuchař, P (2024). The knowledge gap in economics: What does the public know about the economy and what do economists know about the public? *OEconomia, History, Methodology, Philosophy*, (14–4), 703–737.
Drake, St. C., & Cayton, H. R. (1945). *Black Metropolis: A Study of Negro Life in a Northern City*. Harcourt, Brace and Company.
Eze, E. C. (1997). *Race and the Enlightenment: A Reader*. Blackwell.
Fine, G. A. (1995). *A Second Chicago School? The Development of a Postwar American Sociology*. University of Chicago Press.
Finestone, H. (1957). Cats, Kicks, and Color. *Social Problems*, *5*(1), 3–13.

Frazier, E. F. (1932). *The Negro Family in Chicago*. University of Chicago Press.
Garfinkel, H. (1949). Research Note on Inter-and Intra-Racial Homicides. *Social Forces, 27*(4), 369–381.
Goffman, E. (1961). *Asylums: Essays on the Social Situation of Mental Patients and Other Inmates*. Anchor Books.
Gouldner, A. W. (1968). The Sociologist as Partisan: Sociology and the Welfare State. *American Sociologist, 3*(2), 103–116.
Gunsfield, J. (1995). Preface. In G. A. Fine (Ed.), *A Second Chicago School? The Development of a Postwar American Sociology* (pp. vii–xvi). University of Chicago Press.
Hennis, W. (1994). The Meaning of 'Wertfreiheit' on the Background and Motives of Max Weber's "Postulate." *Sociological Theory, 12*(2), 113–125.
Inderbitzin, M., Bates, K. A., & Gainey, R. R. (2018). *Perspectives on Deviance and Social Control*. Sage.
Køhlert, F. B. (2011). *Chicago Literary Experience: Writing the City, 1893–1953*. Museum Tusculanum Press.
Landesco, J. (1929). *Organized Crime in Chicago*. Illinois Association for Criminal Justice.
Lavoie, D. (1995). The 'Objectivity' of Scholarship and the Ideal of the University. *Advances in Austrian Economics, 2*, 371–403.
Leonard, R. J. (2010). *Von Neumann, Morgenstern, and the Creation of Game Theory: From Chess to Social Science, 1900–1960*. Cambridge University Press.
Leonard, T. C. (2016). *Illiberal Reformers: Race, Eugenics and American Economics in the Progressive Era*. Princeton University Press.
Levy, D. M., & Peart, S. J. (2020). *Towards an Economics of Natural Equals: A Documentary History of the Early Virginia School*. Cambridge University Press.
Levy, J. T. (2015). *Rationalism, Pluralism and Freedom*. Oxford University Press.
Lombardo, P. A. (2002). Taking Eugenics Seriously: Three Generations of-are Enough? *Florida State University Law Review, 30*(2), 191–218.
MacKenzie, D. (2008). *An Engine, Not a Camera: How Financial Models Shape Markets*. MIT Press.
McCloskey, D. N. (2010). *Bourgeois Dignity: Why Economics Can't Explain the Modern World*. Chicago University Press.
Morris, A. (2017). *The Scholar Denied: W. E. B. Du Bois and the Birth of Modern Sociology*. University of California Press.
Mowrer, E. R. (1927). *Family Disorganization: An Introduction to Sociological Analysis*. University of Chicago Press.
Ostrom, V. [1986] (2012). Culture, Liberation Movements, and Human Development. In B. Allen & E. Ostrom (Eds.), *The Quest to Understand Human Affairs: Essays on Collective, Constitutional, and Epistemic Choice* (pp. 219–252). Lexington Books.

Park, R. E., Burgess, E. W., & McKenzie, R. D. (1925). *The City*. University of Chicago Press.

Peart, S. J., & Levy, D. M. (2009). *The Street Porter and the Philosopher: Conversations on Analytical Egalitarianism*. University of Michigan Press.

Polanyi, M. (1958). *Personal Knowledge: Towards a Post-Critical Philosophy*. Routledge & Kegan Paul.

Reckless, W. C. (1933). *Vice in Chicago*. University of Chicago Press.

Sebastiani, S. (2013). *The Scottish Enlightenment: Race, Gender, and the Limits of Progress*. Palgrave Macmillan.

Shaw, C. R. (1930). *The Jack-Roller: A Delinquent Boy's Own Story*. University of Chicago Press.

Shaw, C. R., & Moore, M. E. (1931). *The Natural History of a Delinquent Career*. A. Saifer.

Smith, D. (1988). *The Chicago School: A Liberal Critique of Capitalism*. St. Martin's Press.

Thomas, W. I., & Znaniecki, F. (1918). *The Polish Peasant in Europe and America*. Badger.

Thrasher, F. M. (1927). *The Gang: A Study of 1,313 Gangs in Chicago*. University of Chicago Press.

Vermeulen, H. F. (2015). *Before Boas: The Genesis of Ethnography and Ethnology in the German Enlightenment*. University of Nebraska Press.

Washington, B. T. (2018). *The Educational and Industrial Emancipation of the Negro*. Palala Press.

Watts, R. (2013). *Women in Science: A Social and Cultural History*. Routledge.

Wertheim, W. F. (1974). *Evolution and Revolution: The Rising Waves of Emancipation*. Penguin.

Wiley, N. (2011). The Chicago School : A political interpretation. In N. K. Denzin, L. H. Athens, & T. Faust (Eds.), *Blue Ribbon Papers: Interactionism: The Emerging Landscape* (pp. 39–74). Emerald Publishing.

Wirth, L. (1928). *The Ghetto*. University of Chicago Press.

Zorbaugh, H. W. (1929). *Gold Coast and Slum: A Sociological Study of Chicago's Near North Side*. University of Chicago Press.

CHAPTER 8

The Classical Liberal Response to Critical Race Theory: Material Gains, Expressivity, and Divisions of Power

Fabio Rojas

Critical race theory (CRT) is a response to an obvious fact about modernity. The societies we inhabit today are built on a history of conquest, colonialism, and imperialism. Today, an individual's chances at success and access to resources often appear to be highly correlated with race, gender, and other social distinctions that were crucial in the societies that became the United States and Western Europe. What makes CRT different than other intellectual traditions is that it is highly skeptical of "liberal" responses to enduring social inequality and many writers advocate anticapitalist alternatives.

On the first count, writers associated with CRT tend to see their work as unmasking the pernicious effects of liberal policies. Specifically, critical

F. Rojas (✉)
Virginia L. Roberts Professor of Sociology, Indiana University, Bloomington, IN, USA
e-mail: frojas@iu.edu

M. Novak (ed.), *Liberal Emancipation*, Mercatus Studies in Political and Social Economy, https://doi.org/10.1007/978-3-031-94406-2_8

race theorists tend to argue that liberal solutions to racial inequality exacerbate the problem (Ray, 2019), distract people from confronting racism (Bonilla-Silva, 2003), or perpetuate racialized inequalities in schooling and jobs (Delgado & Stefancic, 2017). A consistent theme in this literature is that liberal solutions to social problems make things worse for minorities and intentionaly, or unintentionally, reinforce the superiority of Whites. One well-known example is Bonilla-Silva's argument that people use the language of color-blind justice to deflect discussions away from racial inequality. In *Racism without Racists*, Bonilla-Silva (2003: 33) says that the new racism in the United States is, in part, by the use of civil rights rhetoric to reduce, or undermine, efforts to overturn racial inequality. Describing modern American political culture, he says that there is an "avoidance of racial terminology and the ever-growing claim by whites that they experience 'reverse racism'" and there is an "elaboration of a racial agenda over political matters that eschews direct racial references."

On the second count, many writers closely ally themselves with movements and policy solutions that have a strong anticapitalist or socialist flavor. Major writers in this tradition often say their own work operates in tandem with Marxist analyses. Patricia Hills Collins (2014: 9) sees her scholarship as being in parallel with radical political theory: "[f]eminism advocates women's emancipation and empowerment, Marxist social thought aims for a more equitable society, while queer theory opposes hetero-sexism." In his bestseller, *How to Be an Antiracist*, Kendi (2019) directly addresses this point. In discussion of how his own anticapitalism stems from the writers like W.E.B. DuBois, Angela Davis, and Robin Kelly, Kendi (ibid.: 177–178) notes that Du Bois asserts that "an antiracist anticapitalism could seal the horizontal class fissures and vertical race fissures and, importantly, their intersections with equalizing racial and economic policies for working people. Later, Kendi (ibid.: 179) dismisses conservative critics of his anticapitalist positions as "fearmongers" who inaccurately label him as a Marxist but also says critics and proponents of liberalized markets defend "the freedom to exploit freedom into economic ruin."

Critical race theory has generated many responses among academics, popular writers, and politicians that range from extremely friendly to complete rejection. Within the academy, critical race theory is now a very popular framework that has many adherents among legal scholars, humanists, and social scientists. CRT is valued for its appeal as an explanation for enduring racial differences. It's also a theory that is very attractive to academics who tend to have progressive or socialist sympathies. CRT, like Marxism or more radical feminisms, tend to describe modern society as an essentially exploitative system (e.g., Collins, 2014; Ray, 2019).

In contrast, conservative writers and politicians completely reject CRT. A number of states with conservative governors and legislators have passed laws that ban the teaching of CRT in schools (e.g., Hamilton, 2021). Other states have actively intervened in universities to demand that students not be required to learn CRT or related ideas. Academic writers have taken a different, but equally skeptical, approach. For example, McWhorter (2021) has claimed that CRT is an un-scientific ideology that is more like a religion for the Left than a social scientific theory.

The purpose of this chapter is to articulate a third response to CRT based on classical liberal principles. Since CRT views social life through a lens of zero-sum social conflict, the theory is fundamentally incompatible with classical liberalism's focus on pluralism and cooperation (e.g., Kukathas, 2003). Also, CRT is at odds with classical liberalism because many of CRT's well-known advocates openly advocate socialism or are deeply suspicious of ideas that lie at the core of the liberal vision such as free markets, race neutrality in law, and ethical individualism (Rojas, 2020). A basic point is that CRT writers often assume that a concern with enduring inequality and repression automatically leads to anticapitalist conclusions. On the contrary, many classical liberals have seen liberty as a helpful response to racial repression and the abuse of power by the wealthy (Hart et al., 2017).

Classical liberals should appreciate that CRT has a partially correct grievance against modernity. It *is* true that modern societies descended from imperialist nations, and it is true that an individual's racial identity is often a barrier to success and thorough inclusion in society. It is clearly true that many people use the rhetoric of race neutrality to avoid discussions of race-based privilege (Bonilla-Silva, 2003). At the same time, CRT often makes a profound error by assessing the value of liberal institutions primarily in those terms. Just because an institution might have an illiberal history doesn't mean that its modern version lacks merit, nor is it the case that a principle, such as race-based neutrality, is always used to evade much needed arguments that precludes the possibility that it has many desirable features.

This chapter formulates a classical liberal response to CRT that acknowledges the dynamics of racial inequality while pointing out that liberal institutions are still highly desirable. Three criteria for evaluating liberal institutions are offered. First, one can ask about the material benefits that a given institution grants racial and ethnic minorities. That is, do liberal institutions generate material improvement for people who are at the bottom of society's status hierarchy? I label this the "material improvement" criteria. Second, classical liberalism values tolerance and social pluralism. Thus, one can judge an institution based on whether racial and ethnic minorities are allowed to cultivate their own distinctive identities and social practices. This is labeled the "expressivist" criteria. Third, classical liberals are often concerned about how antagonistic state and non-state actors that target minorities might be limited through a division of authority. Inspired by James Madison's argument about the division of power in a democracy, I call this the "Madisonian" criterion.

How Critical Race Theorists Evaluate Institutions

Critical race theory and related ideas such as critical legal theory and intersectional feminist theory tend to be very skeptical of the institutions favored by classical liberals, such as capitalism, racial neutrality, and free speech. It is impossible to succinctly summarize such a large literature. For this essay, it's sufficient to identify a few major claims and contrast them with the criteria of material improvement, pluralism, and the division of power.

First, many critical race theorists believe that liberal institutions have the intended or unintended effect of reinforcing racial differences (Delgado & Stefancic, 2017; Ray, 2019). This can happen in many ways. For example, CRT writers will often use a sort of path dependence argument. Initially, an institution may allocate resources based on race. Then, the future outcomes generated by that institution may become identities with low status, which then prevents that minority group from improving their position.

Neighborhoods might be viewed in this way from the point of view of CRT. Neighborhoods would initially reflect racial divisions in a society. In the United States, African Americans were often segregated into areas separated from Whites. In a few extreme cases, such as Detroit, walls were erected. Then, the concentration of low income minority groups would result in substandard schools, sparse employment, and a stress inducing environment. These would result in worse educational outcomes, which would then be associated with racial characteristics. The picture portrayed by CRT advocates is one of a vicious cycle of racial distinctions that lead to stratified outcomes, which are then associated with those same distinctions (e.g., Brown & Homan, 2024).

Second, CRT writers often claim that race neutrality does not occur in practice. It is very common for writers, especially legal scholars, to argue that many policies that appear to be race neutral have a disproportionate impact on minorities. Perhaps the most famous example is 1990s era drug laws, which imposed penalties for forms of narcotics that were more commonly found in minority communities. The law itself does not target a specific minority group but by focusing on particular forms of drugs, it indirectly imposes higher penalties and more time in prison for minorities (Fornili, 2018).

Third, CRT advocates often criticize liberal institutions for serving as a mask, or distraction, from racial inequality. For example, critics of free speech norms will often argue that a focus on speech rights distracts from the fact that speech may directly damage people or that hateful speech can contribute to an environment where minorities are persecuted (Moore & Bell, 2019). Thus, it is a mistake to uncritically support or defend abstract rights. Rather, one has to understand that rights can be exercised in ways that perpetuate racial inequality and indirectly condone historical injustices.

A fourth theme in many CRT writings is that contemporary institutions have roots in highly violent and exploitative systems such as slavery, segregation, and apartheid. For example, a number of writers have claimed that forms of business organization, as well as various accounting practices, were created to assist with the management of plantations (e.g., Desmond, 2021). Other writers focus on the claim that police departments, and other law enforcement agencies, have their roots as slave patrols (e.g., Spruill, 2016). Another claim that emerged is that specific organizations were created using slave labor or used the profits from slavery. In 2016, critics levied charges against Georgetown University and pointed out that the school used funds from slave sales to finance the school (Swarns, 2016). A similar claim is made in the context of residential segregation. Modern housing policy is under suspicion because federal policy in the mid-twentieth century resulted in "redlining," where loans for housing were driven by the goal of having all white neighborhoods (Solorzano & Velez, 2016). These varied examples all suggest that the legitimacy of modern institutions, such as higher education in the

Georgetown case or housing allocation in the redlining case, is contaminated because these institutions at some point were entangled in slavery and segregation. This point should elicit sympathy from classical liberals. For example, Nozick (1974) did note that some property rights claims might be questioned because the initial establishment of title involved violence and theft.

Hypocrisy is a theme that sums up various CRT arguments. An institution may claim to be race neutral but it reproduces inequality. Or, an ideal, such as free speech, is used to truncate discussions of racial inequality and facilitate hate speech. Derrick Bell famously argues that pro-Black policies are only permitted if they help a White majority. Consistent with the theme of hypocrisy, the "interest convergence" thesis suggests that policies that appear to help minorities are self-serving (Bell, 1980). The institutional life of modern societies is one where our economic and political systems create harmful distinctions, maintain them, and then pretend as if everything is just fine.

A Classical Liberal Perspective

CRT is, at its core, a theory of social conflict that employs a Foucauldian perspective in the sense that the repressive nature of political and economic institutions can be uncovered through genealogical analysis and the goal is an "unmasking of power." Classical liberalism offers a different perspective on evaluating institutions. While some classical liberal authors completely reject CRT and related ideas such as intersectionality (Magness, 2020a), many scholars recognize the reality of racial inequality and they understand that the hypocritical and evasive practices documented by scholars in that school require explanation and criticism (Levy, 2017; Rojas, 2020). However, the crucial difference is that classical liberalism has a very different sense of what institutions do and how they should be evaluated.

A core idea is that markets are the way that people produce wealth and increase their standard of living. Much of classical liberalism takes Adam Smith's view of markets as a starting point. People have differing desires and needs, but prices and the pursuit of profit allow for productive cooperation. Modern classical liberal writers, such as McCloskey (2006), note that liberalized markets have resulted in historically unprecedented increases in the standards of living for billions around the world. Markets work.

The appreciation of economic freedom leads to an important argument. The material improvement produced by markets is not an abstract statistical fact. It represents important things like having enough calories to eat every day, the reduction of child mortality through improved sanitation and medical care, and comforts that make everyday life more enjoyable. Classical liberals might respond to critical race theorists by disputing the exploitative nature of labor markets but a more powerful, and persuasive, response is this: "The material benefits of markets are so large that we have to take them seriously, even if there are racial inequalities among the recipients of wealth."

This leads to the first of the three criteria that are the focus of this chapter: the criteria of material improvement. We should evaluate an institution on its ability to provide tangible benefits to people, especially ethnic minorities. Intuitively, this criterion should take precedence over a criteria of complete equality. For example, one might achieve equality by placing everyone in poverty, but that is a form of equality few would support. This insight suggests that the meeting of basic material needs and raising living standards should be a focal point of normative analysis.

I also note that there is an argument to be made about the relative importance of material improvement for minorities because they are most likely to find themselves subject to extreme poverty or material deprivation. In the United States, African Americans, Latinos, and Native Americans are much more likely to be classified as living in poverty and having worse living conditions (US Census Bureau, 2022). People in that circumstance would find disproportionate benefit from additional income, purchasing power, and improved technologies. In economic jargon, the marginal utility of money is likely to be greater for people with less income. A dollar for a rich man is barely a thought, but it's the world for someone in poverty.

An appreciation for pluralism and expression motivates the second criteria examined in this chapter. A core theme in classical liberal thought is that people with extremely different world views and religions need to meaningfully co-exist with each other (Kukathas, 2003). Numerous principles stems from this insight, such as freedom of speech, religious tolerance, and norms for civic engagement. In other words, we shouldn't view the social world as a theater for a Hobbesian struggle against others. Rather, we need to appreciate that other people have intrinsic value, even those with views that might be repulsive or alien to us, and there needs to be a way to peacefully and productively interact with them. This insight about the necessity of living with a wide range of people results in an appreciation for tolerance and pluralism. We need to co-exist and we need to be accepting of otherness.

Pluralism and tolerance are related to expressivity. Once a community establishes a culture of tolerance, minorities within that community may want to use that openness to assert their distinctiveness. This has many forms such as speaking a different language, attire, gesture, religion, and schooling. Thus, a community that states its desire to foster norms of co-existence will naturally invite its minorities to engage in behaviors that will contrast with the mainstream. Motivated by this insight, we can evaluate an institution based on its permissiveness and variety of cultural expression. Does a specific political or economic regime allow minorities to freely express their social identity without fear of harassment? In the evaluation of institutional regimes, I denote this the "expressiveness" criterion.

Third, classical liberals have often been concerned that an antagonistic majority would use the tools of the state to harass minorities through regulation. The well-known articulation of this idea is James Madison's *Federalist Paper 10*, which famously argued that political power should be divided because people are inherently partisan. By creating multiple sources of authority, antagonistic actors are less able to persecute others. In modern times, public choice economists, such as Gordon Tullock, recognized that racial antagonism represented a "special problem" for constitutional analysis (Magness, 2020b). Since public choice economists tended to focus on how rules can emerge from interactions among rational actors, the idea that a racial majority could bully a minority group through the state was a problem that needed a resolution.

Progressive scholars have also focused on this problem. If the point of a democratic community is to allow individuals and subgroups to protect their rights and pursue their interests, it is highly problematic when a majority uses their superior numbers to enact legislation that is directly targeted at ethnic minorities. The legal scholar Guinier (1992), and others, for this reason have argued that democratic systems should implement practices that amplify the weight of particular voting blocks. This might include creating Congressional districts that cluster Black voters or systems that assign some extra weight to minority votes. While critics have seen such proposals as anti-democratic, they are meant to address the problems of a purely majoritarian system where any group that can assemble 51 percent of all votes has the ability to endlessly harass a minority group.

Given this discussion, we can recognize that it is important to understand that pure majoritarian democracy might invite racial repression. Democratic political systems need additional rules to ensure that minorities acquire some systemic protections. In reference to Madison's defense of divided powers, we can evaluate an institution in "Madisonian" terms if it has such protections.

The criteria of improved material conditions for minorities, expressiveness, and Madisonianism are worth contrasting with the sort of criteria employed by critical race theorists and egalitarians. For example, CRT and egalitarian writers are often focused on ensuring that institutions provide the same outcomes for everyone. While that may be desirable, it is not the only goal worth pursuing and it may be secondary, or complimentary, to other goals. It would be highly desirable to have an institution where everyone receives large identical benefits. But that does not contradict another point: institutions that produce large tangible, but unequal, gains for large segments of the population may also be worth defending and promoting.

Material Well-Being

Here, and in the sub-sections that follow, we consider how liberal institutions appear when evaluated with these criteria. A single essay, or book chapter, does not permit for a complete exploration of these issues, but first steps can be taken. Perhaps the most simple and direct case is material wellbeing. Within classical liberal thinking, free markets bear the normative burden of proof. Nearly every utilitarian defense of classical liberalism focuses on the high productivity of liberalized markets. Writers often point out that societies with more economic freedoms as measured by the Freedom Index have lower poverty rates, higher GDP, and more time for leisure (Iceland & Silver, 2024).

The perspective of many CRT writers is that capitalist societies still exhibit a high degree of racial inequality, racial differences endure, and that increases in statistics such as GDP are beside the point. The response is simply to point out that we should care about both increases in baseline wellbeing and relative differences. Furthermore, those improvements in absolute terms are extremely important because many minority groups are likely to have high rates of poverty and lack basic amenities. According to the criteria of material improvement, we would only discount the productive capacity of markets if minorities did not benefit at all.

In the United States, African Americans had very high poverty rates with correspondingly low incomes. One of the most remarkable facts is that from the mid-1900s to 2024, African American poverty rates drastically declined from 40% in the 1950s in to 18% in 2020. In real terms, incomes increased in the middle of the African American income distribution increased from $4,000 in the mid-1900s to $46,000 in inflation adjusted terms (US Census 2022: Table H3). Understanding poverty among ethnic groups in other nations with liberalized economies is complicated. Sometimes, the comparison is straightforward, such as in Australia. In the 1990s, aboriginal poverty was estimated to be above 40 percent (Australian Institute of Family Studies, 1993) in the 1950s but has declined to 19 percent in the mid-2010s (Australian Council of Social Service, 2014). In other cases, such a comparison is difficult to make. Many nations with liberalized economies also have welfare states, which resulted in the reporting of very low overall poverty rates that include data from all racial and ethnic groups. In the United Kingdom, social scientists initially found extremely low poverty rates in the 1950s but then needed to revise their estimates (Gazeley et al., 2017). Still, there is evidence that ethnic minorities do experience important improvements. One finding is that the standard of living in Northern Ireland has increased, with relative poverty declining in the early 2000s to about 16 percent of the Northern Irish population (Department of Communities UK, 2023).

One might ask a similar question for immigrants in nations with more open economies. One striking finding is that immigrants in the United States have experienced steep declines in poverty rates in the 2010s (Batalova & Fix, 2023). This may be a composition effect. The stricter regulation of migration might select for individuals with more valuable labor market skills. While this might be true, it likely isn't the only explanation as the decrease in poverty among migrants mirrors that native born people. In other words, migrants have higher poverty rates, but that decreased at the same time as the decline in poverty rates for native born people.

We can also look at the European Union, where many nation-states have admitted large numbers of immigrants. As in the United States, migrants from outside the EU have higher poverty rates than people born in the EU and the probability of being in poverty depends on many factors, especially the generosity of the welfare state. The trends in poverty vary a great deal by country. Some nations, including larger states like the UK and Germany, have seen poverty rate reductions among migrants, while others like France, have seen increases (Kunychka et al., 2023; OECD and European Commission, 2023).

The empirical issue is complicated and a single essay like this can't survey all the evidence. Still, despite these measurement issues and the complexity of the data, an important point remains. Nations with relatively open economies, such as the United States and various Western nations, have often seen decreases in poverty rates among native born and foreign born minority populations. The trend is not completely uniform, but it is there and it is substantial. The effect of wealth might be direct. Racial minorities are less likely to be poor because they can participate in more efficient labor markets. Poverty reduction also occurs via welfare state mechanisms and represents an indirect impact of wealth. Nations with more open markets and larger GDPs are more able to fund welfare states through taxation.

With respect to CRT, the central point is that liberal markets do not operate as a mechanism that excludes racial minorities from wealth creation. Rather, minorities are often the beneficiaries of wealth creation associated with more open economies, directly through labor market participation or redistribution via the welfare state. The data presented here is meant to reframe the criticism levied by critical race theorists. Life is unfair and it is true that racial inequalities can reflect the legacies of repressive social institutions, but if we care about the day-to-day life of racial minorities, then our policy prescriptions must include a robust appreciation of liberalized markets and economic growth.

Expressiveness

I begin this section with an auto-ethnographic moment. A few years ago, I went to the mall in my town and entered the Target department store. The electronics department is located next to the entrance I used and the large television screens captured my attention. There was an advertisement for the book, *How to Be an Antiracist* by Kendi (2019), displayed on multiple screens. At first, I was a little surprised that a book on racism should be so prominently featured in a big-box store. Then, I appreciated the larger significance of this advertisement. Antiracist discourse was being shown to thousands of people who talked through this mall. In bookstores, malls, and popular culture across America, people talked about all the ways one could end racism. At that time, I viewed the popularity of antiracism talk as a passing cultural trend, but I was mistaken. The fact that people bought products that featured antiracism was remarkable. Even more remarkable was the fact that, apparently, business executives approved antiracist talk and believed they could make a profit selling merchandise with this theme.

This leads to an important observation. Contemporary societies, especially American society, is highly tolerant in the sense that it allows ethnic minorities to publicly dispute racism and it allows them to develop social practices that heighten their distinctiveness. In the US, markets routinely focus on Black interests. For example, Johnson Publications produced Black themed magazines *Ebony* and *Jet* for seventy one years (Seidel, 2019). Black Entertainment Television has produced content oriented toward Black audiences for decades (Pulley, 2004). During the Black power era, there was a celebration of an afrocentric aesthetic represented by new styles of clothing and popular entertainment (Van Deburg, 1992). Beyond that, it's important to note that the United States contains ethnic enclaves where people offer goods and services aimed at specific audiences. American cities often contain neighborhoods that represent diasporic communities, whether they be "Chinatowns" in places like San Francisco in the twentieth century or the older German and Polish neighborhoods of the nineteenth century.

The expressivity of ethnic groups is not limited to market contexts. We find ample evidence of expressiveness in schools and popular culture. Many education scholars have noted that multiculturalism is now a feature of school curricula in many nations (Cole, 2012). The idea is that schools should teach the history of many ethnic groups, not just the dominant one, especially in nations with a history of European colonialism such as Australia. In popular culture, there is compelling evidence that antiracist talk is now a more prominent feature in social interactions. Social media platforms and news media are more likely in the 2020s to use the vocabulary of antiracism than in the early 2000s (Dunivin et al., 2022). These trends not only reflect the activities of antiracist activist groups, such as Black Lives Matter, but a growing interest in these ideas among academics, journalists, and educators.

Many of the trends discussed in this chapter are well known, but they grow in importance when contrasted with the CRT depiction of liberal institutions. For example, Bell's (1980) interest convergence thesis argues that concessions made to minorities only occur when they benefit

White majorities. At best, this is an incomplete story. The Black press, for example, as represented by Johnson publications or Black Entertainment Television were not White concessions, but rather entrepreneurial efforts carried out by African American businesspeople. They are rooted in property rights and the norm of a free press, more than a negotiation with a White majority. Critics of antiracism and "wokeness" have claimed that antiracism's popularity among progressive White audiences reflect a sort of guilt or form of virtue signaling (McWhorter, 2021). Even if true, that doesn't counter the fact that the popularity of antiracist ideas is itself an important form of cultural expression that is facilitated by liberal norms such as freedom of speech and civil discourse.

Madison and the Division of Power

The division of power is crucial for ethnic minorities who fear violence and harassment from the majority. Different nations, or political systems, can be assessed in terms of how well they protect minority groups from hostile actors who can muster 51 percent of the vote. In some cases, the division of power may reflect a basic feature of constitutional design. American history contains a great example—the Civil Rights movement. The movement was certainly enabled and helped by the complex, multi-layered system of governance that is the United States. We can look at selected moments in the movement's history to understand how and when the division of powers helped the movement for Black rights. The key issue is that public opinion data showed that the Civil Rights movement did not receive a majority of support from American citizens (Lee, 2002). Yet, the movement managed to gain stunning victories and those victories received some help from America's fragmented political system.

For example, a key observation about the Civil Rights movement of the 1960s was that there was an important divergence between the Southern states and the rest of the nation in the mid-twentieth centuries, which was a result of activism aimed at sympathetic Northern White audiences (Lee, 2002). The split of power between the states and Federal allowed sympathetic Whites to support Civil Rights activists in the South. One example was the intervention of the Federal government in school desegregation, such as in Little Rock, Arkansas. Another was to have the Federal government investigate violence against activists in Southern states. Of course, the ultimate example of split power was when the Supreme Court overturned segregation in *Brown v. Board of Education* in 1954. The split between Northern and Southern whites was extreme (Saad, 2016).

At other times, the division of power is indirect and implicit. To illustrate this point, I'll use the recent political dispute of school curricula in the United States. In the years 2022–24, several conservative American politicians campaigned against the inclusion of critical race theory, and other related schools of thought, in high school and college courses (Ray & Gibbons, 2021). There are some states where these proposals were carried out and these ideas became state policy.

Due to the institutional complexity of the United States, there is little danger that these ideas will be completely suppressed. As noted above, privately owned corporations are happy to make profits selling millions of books that discuss antiracism. Within the educational sector, private universities are free to set their own curriculum. The public universities of conservative states may ban the teaching of some ideas, while states with progressive legislators have public universities who are happy to teach critical race theory. The important point is that a society with a vibrant public sector and multiple independent public institutions can create the space for racial and ethnic minorities to assert the political rights and cultural expression.

Classical Liberalism Versus Mills' Black Radical Liberalism

This chapter has argued that critical race theorists might not properly recognize that liberal institutions provide tangible benefits to racial and ethnic minorities. One response to this position might be similar to that offered by Mills' in *The Racial Contract* (1997) and *Black Rights/White Wrongs* (2017). The first book critiques liberalism from the perspective of what contemporary writers might call anti-Blackness. For Mills, liberalism, as defined by a range of writers like John Locke and Immanuel Kant, assumes that non-Whites don't merit rights. He argues that the lack of attention to the rights of non-Whites renders the liberal project highly suspect. He correctly notes that there is an absence of concern for Black rights and, in some cases, liberal writers consistently affirmed the inferiority of non-White colonial subjects. Most fundamentally, Mills argues that the conceptual of project of liberalism is a reflection of the world of

European intellectuals rather than a more far encompassing theory that was applied to all people.

Black Rights/White Wrongs approaches things from a different, but related, perspective. Through a collection of essays and interviews, Mills attempts to construct a form of "black radical liberalism" by critiquing the political theory of Kant, Rawls, and others. A common theme is genealogical. He focuses on their lack of attention in Western canon to White domination over non-Whites and the fact that many saw Black and Native peoples as naturally subservient. In terms of positive social theory, Mills relies on a combination of Marxian and Du Boisian ideas. From Marx, he relies on exploitation theory. From Du Bois, he focuses on "White payoff," which today might be called "White privilege" theory. That is, Whites occupy a superior social position from which they benefit a great deal of benefits.

The classical liberal perspective offered in this chapter agrees with Mills on some points, but drastically diverges from others. In terms of agreement, most scholars who identify with classical liberalism (e.g., Kukathas, 2003; Levy, 2017) would concur that Western political thought outrightly denigrated non-Whites and relegated them to non-human status. They might also agree with Mills' intellectual anthropology. Most Western intellectuals took the superiority of Europe as a given fact and actively affirmed it.

The sort of pragmatist classical liberalism presented in this chapter points to a divergence with Mill's black radical liberalism. The criterion of material improvement is one point of departure. We can ask about the institutions that improve the lives of non-Whites and that answer is not related to what Kant or Rawls might have said about non-White people. We have an independent base of evidence to draw on. Earlier in this chapter, I drew on basic statistics from the US Census to document large increases in the financial status of Black Americans. We also have historical knowledge. The type of socialism favored by Du Bois and Mills has not yielded societies that have produced gains for most people, much less ethnic minorities within societies.

Another issue with the Black radical liberalism promoted by Mills is that it nowhere directly addresses the problem of antagonistic majorities. On level, this is simply a disciplinary difference. Mills was a philosopher who was interested in addressing political theory as it exists in that profession. He offers very little in terms of institutional design. The deep lesson of public choice theory is that the type of governance we get depends on the rules we set. Thus, if we set up a political system with a very strong centralized state (e.g., socialism) or that favors a numerical majority (e.g., direct democracy), then people who capture the levers of the state will be able to bully ethnic minorities. As noted earlier in this chapter, and in other writings, socialist states have a terrible track record with minorities. Democracies are not immune to this problem either, as we've seen in the United States during the Jim Crow era.

My views is that Mills' position is most persuasive as a corrective to the mainstream of thinking within political philosophy. A "deracialized" Kant is probably an improvement over the Kant that lived in eighteenth century Germany and a properly contextualized Rawls that ignored race is better than the one who inhabits the world of ideal theory. But that's not enough to obtain an argument about which institutions would be desirable. It's also not enough to argue, as Mills and DuBois do, that racial privilege is real. Rather, one needs to develop an understanding of which social practices can be deployed to mitigate a tyrannical majority. To do that, political theory then needs to offer a criteria by which to judge social practices and that is why I have argued that traits like material improvement, expressivity, and division of power are important to consider.

Conclusion

The purpose of this essay is to identify a type of tunnel vision found in CRT and related schools of thought. Writers in these areas often focus on durable racial inequality, liberal hypocrisy, and a history of repression to the exclusion of other virtues. These claims are often rooted in very sensible observations. Western nations did exploit non-White people and subjugated them for centuries. The effects of segregation and colonial have endured. People do use civil rights rhetoric to avoid talking about racism and defend their own status. Yet, by themselves, these points do not lead to conclusions that CRT writers often express. To properly argue that liberal institutions should be abandoned in favor of alternatives, one needs to show that these alternatives produce what people need and that liberal alternatives are so grossly lacking in merit that they should be dismantled. An institution that produces unequal outcomes, or whose legitimacy is tainted through association with repression and exploitation, maybe have enough merit that is deserves promotion and reform, especially if the alternative itself has an incredibly poor, or even worse, performance.

This is the reason that this essay offered three criteria for evaluating social institutions. The main reason that people defend liberalism, whether it be economic freedom, or freedom of speech, or civil rights, is not that they always help all people equally or that their history of free of sin. Rather, people defend liberalism because of its large-scale benefits to people and they conform to the idea that we should allow people to pursue what is important to them. Thus, this essay suggests that institutions should be evaluated in terms of increases in tangible material benefits that minorities have, the ability to express themselves, and a social system's division of power, which allows minorities to assert their interests and offers some protection from tyrannical majorities. This perspective results in a more positive evaluation of liberal institutions like free markets, free speech norms, and polycentric governance than is suggested by CRT with its focus on relative differences.

These arguments were illustrated with selected examples from Western nations that have these liberal institutions. A more extended assessment can be carried out that systematically collects data on these liberal institutions and measures the correlation with the well-being of minorities. Indeed, while economists have documented the positive effects of liberalized markets, systematic surveys of other liberal social institutions are less commonly found, but there is literature correlating economic freedom with political rights. More can be done in spirit to provide a more balanced assessment of liberalism, freedom, and openness as a form of governance and a way of life.

Acknowledgements I thank the anonymous peer review process and the editor, Mikayla Novak, for providing helpful criticism and guidance for this chapter.

References

Australian Council of Social Service. (2014). *Poverty in Australia 2014*. https://www.acoss.org.au/images/uploads/ACOSS_Poverty_in_Australia_2014.pdf

Australian Institute of Family Studies. (1993). Aboriginal Australians and Poverty. *Family Matters 35*. https://aifs.gov.au/research/family-matters/no-35/aboriginal-australians-and-poverty

Batalova, J., & Fix, M. (2023). Understanding Poverty Among Migrants and Their Children. Migration Policy Institute. https://www.migrationpolicy.org/sites/default/files/publications/mpi-poverty-declines-immigrants-2023_final.pdf

Bell, D. A. (1980). Brown v. Board of Education and the Interest-Convergence Dilemma. *Harvard Law Review, 93*(3), 518–533.

Bonilla-Silva, E. (2003). *Racism without Racists: Color-Blind Racism and the Persistence of Racial Inequality in the United States*. Rowman & Littlefield.

Brown, T. H., & Homan, P. (2024). Structural Racism and Health Stratification: Connecting Theory to Measurement. *Journal of Health and Social Behavior, 65*(1), 141–160.

Collins, P. H. (2014). *Black Feminist Thought: Knowledge, Consciousness, and the Politics of Empowerment* (2nd ed.). Routledge.

Cole, W. M. (2012). Ethnocentric Curricula and the Politics of Minority Incorporation at Tribal and Historically Black Colleges. *Diaspora, Indigenous, and Minority Education, 6*(2), 63–84.

Delgado, R., & Stefancic, J. (2017). *Critical Race Theory: An Introduction* (3rd ed.). New York Press.

Department of Communities UK. (2023). The Northern Ireland Poverty and Income Inequality Report 2021–22 is released. Media release, March 30. https://www.communities-ni.gov.uk/news/northern-ireland-poverty-and-income-inequality-report-2021-22-released

Desmond, M. (2021). Capitalism. In N. Hannah-Jones, C. Roper, I. Silverman, & K. Silverstein (Eds.), *The 1619 Project: A New Origin Story* (pp. 165–187). One World.

Dunivin, Z. O., Yan, H. Y., Ince, J., & Rojas, F. (2022). Black Lives Matter Protests Shift Public Discourse. *Proceedings of the National Academy of Sciences, 119*(10), Article e2117320119.

Fornili, K. S. (2018). Racialized Mass Incarceration and the War on Drugs: A Critical Race Theory Appraisal. *Journal of Addiction Nursing, 29*(1), 65–72.

Gazeley, I., Rufrancos, H. G., Newell, A., Reynolds, K., & Searle, R. (2017). The Poor and the Poorest, 50 Years On: Evidence from British Household Expenditure Surveys of the 1950s and 1960s. *Journal of the Royal Statistical Society Series a: Statistics in Society, 180*(2), 455–474.

Guinier, L. (1992). The Representation of Minority Interests: The Question of Single-Member Districts. *Cardozo Law Review, 14*(5), 1135–1174.

Hamilton, V. E. (2021). Reform, Retrench, Repeat: The Campaign Against Critical Race Theory, Through the Lens of Critical Race Theory. *William and Mary Journal of Race, Gender, and Society, 28*(1), 61–102.

Hart, D. M., Chartier, G., Kenyon, R. M., & Long, R. T. (2017). *Social Class and State Power: Exploring an Alternative Radical Tradition*. Springer.

Iceland, J., & Silver, E. (2024). Does Economic Liberalism Reduce Poverty? In F. Rojas & C. Stern (Eds.), *Sociology and Classical Liberalism: Freedom is Something We Do Together* (pp. 21–43). Rowman & Littlefield.

Kendi, I. X. (2019). *How To Be An Antiracist*. One World.

Kukathas, C. (2003). *The Liberal Archipelago: A Theory of Diversity and Freedom*. Oxford University Press.

Kunychka, M., Grešš, M., Raneta, L., Dziura, B., & Sinković, D. (2023). Possible changes over time: poverty among migrants in the European Union. *Economic Research – Ekonomska Istraživanja, 36*(3), 2264377.

Lee, T. (2002). *Mobilizing Public Opinion: Black Insurgency and Racial Attitudes in the Civil Rights Era*. University of Chicago Press.

Levy, J. T. (2017). Black Liberty Matters. Niskanen Center, September 20. https://www.niskanencenter.org/black-liberty-matters

Magness, P. W. (2020a). *The 1619 Project: A Critique*. American Institute for Economic Research.

Magness, P. W. (2020b). The Anti-discriminatory Tradition in Virginia School Public Choice Theory. *Public Choice, 183*(3), 417–441.

McCloskey, D. N. (2006). *The Bourgeois Virtues: Ethics for an Age of Commerce*. University of Chicago Press.

McWhorter, J. H. (2021). *Woke Racism: How a New Religion has Betrayed Black America*. Portfolio.

Moore, W. L., & Bell, J. M. (2019). The Limits of Community: Deconstructing the White Framing of Racist Speech in Universities. *American Behavioral Scientist, 63*(13), 1760–1775.

Mills, C. W. (1997). *The Racial Contract*. Cornell University Press.

Mills, C. W. (2017). *Black Rights/White Wrongs: The Critique of Racial Liberalism*. Oxford University Press.

Nozick, R. (1974). *Anarchy, State, and Utopia*. Basic Books.

Organisation of Economic Co-operation and Development (OECD) and European Commission. , 2023Organisation of Economic Co-operation and Development (OECD) and European Commission. (2023). *Indicators of Immigrant Integration 2023: Settling In*. OECD Publishing.

Pulley, B. (2004). *The Billion Dollar BET: Robert Johnson and the Inside Story of Black Entertainment Television*. Wiley.

Ray, R., & Gibbons, A. (2021). *Why are States Banning Critical Race Theory?* Brookings Institution. https://www.brookings.edu/articles/why-are-states-banning-critical-race-theory

Ray, V. (2019). *On Critical Race Theory: Why It Matters and Why You Should Care*. Penguin.

Rojas, F. (2020). Intersectionality: Friend or Foe of Classical Liberalism? Cato Unbound. https://www.cato-unbound.org/2020/05/28/fabio-rojas/intersectionality-friend-or-foe-classical-liberalism

Saad, L. (2016). Gallup Vault: 60 Years Ago, the End of "Separate but Equal." Gallup, November 11. https://news.gallup.com/vault/197372/gallup-vault-years-ago-end-separate-equal.aspx

Seidel, J. (2019). Johnson Publishing Co., the Ex-publisher of Ebony and Jet, Files for Bankruptcy. Chicago Sun-Times. April 10. https://chicago.suntimes.com/2019/4/10/18407771/johnson-publishing-co-the-ex-publisher-of-ebony-and-jet-files-for-bankruptcy

Solorzano, D., & Velez, V. (2016). Using Critical Race Spatial Analysis to Examine the Du Boisian Color-Line Along the Alameda Corridor in Southern California. *Whittier Law Review, 37*, 423–437.

Spruill, L. H. (2016). Slave Patrols, "Packs of Negro Dogs" and Policing Black Communities. *Phylon, 53*(1), 42–66.

Swarns, R. (2016). 277 Slaves Were Sold to Georgetown. What Does It Owe Their Descendants? New York Times. April 16. https://www.nytimes.com/2016/04/17/us/georgetown-university-search-for-slave-descendants.html

US Census Bureau. (2022). Historical Income Tables: Households. https://www.census.gov/data/tables/time-series/demo/income-poverty/historical-income-households.html

Van Deburg, W. L. (1992). *New Day in Babylon, The Black Power Movement in American Culture, 1965–1975*. University of Chicago Press.

CHAPTER 9

Emancipation and "The Woman Question"

Jayme Lemke

Subjectivist social and political theorists like F. A. Hayek, J. M. Buchanan, Elinor Ostrom, and Vincent Ostrom considered participation in choice processes to be essential both to personal flourishing and to cultivating one's ability to contribute to the social world. This is most apparent in Buchanan's 1979 article, "Natural and Artifactual Man," in which he connects his work on the relationship between cost and choice to the intentional crafting of one's own person. In essence, choice is a process through which an individual becomes the possible version of themselves that they would most like to be. Likewise, early liberal contributors to the study of women's rights—including Mary Astell, Mary Wollstonecraft, John Stuart Mill, and many others—argued that women's personal development was everywhere impeded and distorted by their exclusion from opportunities to act and learn in politics, in markets, in intellectual circles, and in everyday life. Women were blocked from making particular choices—and sometimes from making choices at all—in ways that limited their ability to become and *even to be able to imagine* the version of themselves they would want to become.

J. Lemke (✉)
Mercatus Center at George Mason University, Fairfax, VA, USA
e-mail: jlemke@mercatus.gmu.edu

M. Novak (ed.), *Liberal Emancipation*, Mercatus Studies in Political and Social Economy, https://doi.org/10.1007/978-3-031-94406-2_9

This is nowhere more obvious than in discussion of women's intellectual aptitude and practical competency, perhaps the most vigorously fought for women's rights issue in Europe and the United States prior to the nineteenth century. Before feminists fought for equality, women's suffrage, and the right to own property, they fought for education, access to intellectual spaces, and the right to decline to participate in social and political institutions that taught women to direct their personal growth towards becoming more appealing as a marriage partner. The first step in this process was settling "the woman question"—essentially—convincing societies led by male aristocrats that women were not inferior to men, that they had the intelligence, aptitude, and character to learn, and that the exercise would not be destructive to them or to society.[1]

Early writings, some of which may now be considered proto-feminist, sought to prove women's intellectual capacity by reference to widely known great women. Christine de Pizan's books, pamphlets, and novels, written in the late fourteenth and early fifthteenth centuries in late Medieval France, used examples such as the famed Archaic Greek poet Sappho and the great Queens of medieval Europe to argue in favor of women's capabilities. She also demonstrated with her own choices and work the fact that women could learn and did have a thirst for knowledge (Becchio, 2024: 36–37; Forhan, 2017). De Pizan was far from the only woman to direct her pen towards this cause. In the words of historian Gerda Lerner, "women have for millennia been forced to prove to themselves and to others their capacity for full humanity and their capacity for abstract thought. This has skewed the intellectual development of women as a group, since their major intellectual endeavor had to be to counteract the pervasive patriarchal assumptions of their inferiority and incompleteness as human beings" (Lerner, 1993: 10). As such, after de Pizan came French writers Marie de Gournay [1641] (2002) and Olympe de Gouges, Dutch writer Anna Maria van Schurman [1641] (2013), and English writers Bathsua Makin, Hannah Woolley, Lady Mary Chudleigh, and Mary Astell (Becchio, 2024; Broad, 2015; Lerner, 1993), all vocal advocates for women and women's education in the seventeenth century.

In the eighteenth century, Mary Wollstonecraft's *A Vindication of the Rights of Woman*—one of the great treatises of liberal feminism—considered poor education and social norms prioritizing marriage to be the greatest impediments to women's advancement. In Wollstonecraft's view, women were taught by parents, peers, and educators that marriage was the only real accomplishment for a woman. The pursuit of other projects and bodies of knowledge was—if not outright forbidden at law—discouraged as overly taxing, unfeminine, or just a waste of time. Any kind of *action* other than domestic was particularly discouraged. It might have been fine to read about a craftsman, politician, businessman, or religious leader from the safety of home where nobody else could see—but women should not actually *do* any of these things.

Importantly, when Wollstonecraft talked about education she was not just talking about learning from books and teachers: "[m]en and women must be educated, in a great degree, by the opinions and manners of the society they live in… till society be differently constituted, much cannot be expected from education" (Wollstonecraft [1792] 1993: 86). In this opinion, she anticipates F. A. Hayek and the other theorists who would follow his lead in considering social customs and norms to be a way that knowledge is conveyed through societies and across generations (Hayek, [1960] 2011). Wollstonecraft, like Hayek, Buchanan, and other subjectivist social theorists, saw learning as directly connected to action and to the exercise of ones' own mental capacities:

> … whatever effect circumstances have on the abilities, every being may become virtuous by the exercise of its own reason … Consequently, the most perfect education, in my opinion, is such an exercise of the understanding as is best calculated to strengthen the body and form the heart. Or, in other words, to enable the individual to attain such habits of virtue as will render it independent. In fact, it is a farce to call any being virtuous whose virtues do not result from the exercise of its own reason (Wollstonecraft, [1792] 1993: 86).

In this chapter, I argue that emancipation enables people to more fully engage in the choice and learning required to become the version of themselves they want to become. A critically important implication of subjectivist arguments about the inseparability of beliefs, choices, and actions is that if human beings cannot choose for themselves, they are also severely constrained in their ability to cultivate their values and morals—a reality of which the seventeenth and eighteenth century advocates for women's education were all too aware. As Mary Wollstonecraft succinctly put it, "[w]ithout knowledge, there is no morality." The political economist might add, without choice, there is neither. An emancipated life is one that can change who we are at our very core.

Emancipation makes it possible for people to become the version of themselves they would most like to be—not out of unlimited possibilities, but out of the set of possibilities that are both imaginable and achievable—and as such has important implications for both social progress and personal flourishing.

First, I begin by discussing the relationship between action and the humanity of the actor in the more subjectivist strains of political economy. In particular, I consider the hypothesis that action cannot be independent from who we are and how we think. Cost is only realized in the moment of choice,[2] and likewise our values and who we are at our core are also only realized when we are able to choose to put ourselves into action. Then in section three, I survey a set of underutilized arguments from classical liberal feminists about the ways in which limitations on choice deprive women of opportunities to learn and grow. In section four, I explore the implications of combining subjectivist and early feminist theory for women's personal growth, ability to engage in cooperative ventures, and capacity to make broader social contributions. In conclusion, exclusion from choice processes is a barrier to growth, and this fact was well understood by the classical liberal feminists who argued in defense of women's intellectual and practical capabilities.

Personal Impact of Choice Qua Choice in Subjectivist Political Economy

One of the unique contributions of Austrian and Virginia political economy has been in challenging the way choice is traditionally thought about in economics. Specifically, rather than viewing choice as a mechanistic response to stimuli, as if human beings are rats in a maze, choice is conceived of as being constitutive of ourselves and our reality.

The human experience is a subjective rather than objective phenomena. A core implication is that it is the meaning that individuals attach to alternative choices that makes one choice seem more desirable than another rather than any externally identifiable criteria. As such, it is the perception of meaning and the beliefs and experiences that shape that perception that make up the true facts of the social sciences—the facts that are the relevant object of study for the social scientist seeking to better understand social phenomena and the human experience (Lachmann, [1986] 2020: 43–48; Thomas & Thomas, 1928).[3] In an early treatment of this idea, F. A. Hayek framed the issue as human beings defining the value of an object according to that object's relationship to their plans: "Money is money, a word is a word, a cosmetic is a cosmetic, if and because somebody thinks they are" (Hayek, [1943] 2014: 80). In this sense, the value of an exchange is in a very real sense internally determined by our own perceptions of the world. This is not to say that human activity is disconnected from physical reality, which of course it is not, as evidenced by the fact that we rarely walk through walls instead of doors or eat refrigerator parts instead of the food inside. However, the way that physical reality influences our choices is always through the lens of cognition, which is inevitably biased by our own perceptions—the angles at which we as individuals are able to view the world around us. As Mises wrote, "[t]he popular saying according to which economics deals with the material conditions of human life is entirely mistaken. Human action is a manifestation of the mind" (Mises, [1949] 2007: 142).

Consequently, and of particular relevance to the seventeenth and eighteenth century arguments for women's education and skill development, the interpretation of information—whether consciously or unconsciously—is part of action (Lachmann, [1986] 2020: 50). The information and techniques for processing information that an individual already possesses will shape their ability to interpret, synthesize, and act upon new information. For instance, if women are denied the opportunity to study chemistry or to work with chemicals as part of a trade, we should not be surprised if as a result they are less likely to be able to identify potential uses for a newly available chemical compound. In such cases, "the information received cannot be transformed into useful knowledge" (ibid.). The fact that people will process information in different ways and thereby gain access to very different pieces of potentially useful knowledge is one of the reasons why progress depends on the contributions of a great many, and why, as Adam Smith observed, the ability of a society to capture the gains of the division of labor will depend upon the extent of the market (Smith, [1776] 1982).

Further, the interpretation and processing of knowledge always takes place within the context of an institutional environment of established laws, regulations, norms, and customs. Ludwig Lachmann played a particularly important role in teasing out the connections between subjectivity of interpretation and the institutional environment (Lemke & Lingenfelter, 2017). For example, understanding participation in a market is fundamentally about trying to understand what participation means to the participant and how those beliefs will shape their interactions with and responses to others. We have to elucidate "the nature of those problems economic agents endeavor to solve when they acquire, use, store or replace knowledge. What part do these activities play in making, carrying out and revising those plans which guide action?" (Lachmann, [1986] 2020: 49). If how and why we "acquire, use, store or replace knowledge" matters for how we create and carry out plans, then institutions that establish different epistemic systems according to gender will shape action in a gendered way.

Institutions can serve as signposts around which people orient their plans: "[i]n a complex society such as our own, in which the success of our plans indirectly depends on the actions of millions of other people, how can our orientation scheme provide us with firm guidance? The answer has to be sought in the existence, nature, and functions of institutions" (Lachmann, [1971] 2007: 49). Even the most basic of human plans can often only be fulfilled with the cooperation of others. My ability to eat a sandwich depends upon the owner opening up the café, the cook showing up for work, and all of the other patrons refraining from grabbing the sandwich out of my hands and taking it for themselves. In the absence of an institutional basis of respect for the property rights of all involved, none of this can happen. This is why for Lachmann, "the existence of such institutions is fundamental to civilized society" because they enable us to make plans despite our near total ignorance of the plans and purposes of the other people upon whom our plans depend (ibid.: 50; Vaughn, 1992).

The fact that a stable set of institutions can facilitate coordination by virtue of its stability alone does not make that institutional set immune to criticism. Institutions can be stable in their encouragement of sub-optimal and even anti-social behavior. If such institutions emerged through individual action, we may call them perverse spontaneous orders (Martin & Storr, 2008). If such institutions are imposed by the few onto the many by virtue of either government or other threats of violence, then order results from the strength and consistency of oppression within the relevant hierarchy.

Whether institutions are emergent, designed, or some combination thereof, they can hold multiple meanings according to one's position in society (Lachmann, [1971] 2007: 62). One implication of this is the rules of the institutional order will not always be general in character, but instead may depend on your religion, race, gender, sexuality, or social class (Lemke, 2015). When social norms, customs, or political/legal regimes create and enforce restrictions on freedom of choice that only apply to women, the institutional signposts and the resulting order become patriarchal in character. To adapt a phrase from James M. Buchanan's "Natural and Artifactual Man" (Buchanan, [1979] 1999: 259), patriarchal institutions make it uniquely difficult for women to become the women they want to become by enforcing limits on what women are allowed to learn and what they are allowed to experience.

When Buchanan wrote that man "wants liberty to become the man he wants to become" (ibid.), he argued that we are "imagining being[s]" (ibid.: 250) who are capable of perceiving many possible and at times wildly fantastic visions for ourselves. Even after we face the realities of the various physical, social, cultural, and political limits that might make these imaginings difficult or impossible to realize, there are still many paths forward left to choose from. These "prospects of becoming are sufficient to channel action" and "[w]e move through time, constructing ourselves as artifactual persons" (ibid.: 251). There are very real constraints on the material we have available to us as we proceed with the construction of ourselves, but that creative process of changing how we work with what we have is always available to us, and we cannot avoid altering and shaping those materials whether we do so intentionally or not.

Although he expresses a desire not to spend too much time on the issue, Buchanan recognizes the role education plays in learning how to value opportunities: "the ranking of prospects requires valuation. 'Push-pin is not as good as poetry.' The role of education is to provide persons with both an array of imagined prospects and some means of valuation" (ibid.: 254–255). Further, "choice also implies a moral responsibility for action … Man must bear the responsibilities for his own choices because of his artifactual nature, because he has available to him alternative 'choosables,' to use Shackle's term, because man makes his own history" (ibid.: 257).[4] This is also a theme that will emerge from the work of the eighteenth century writers on women's education discussed in the next section, who were deeply concerned about the fact that women were deprived of both choice and responsibility for the consequences of their actions. They saw this insulation from choice and responsibility as having deleterious impacts on women's ability to develop their moral character.

The ultimate conclusion of Buchanan's essay is that without the freedom to make one's own choices, an individual cannot transform their imaginative capabilities into actions that will enable them to learn and develop through the exploration of different prospects over time.

Buchanan views this as the reason why individuals value their personal freedom, and a core reason why people have an interest in living within a free society. Further, Buchanan see a connection between this potential for self-creation and the growing Enlightenment emphasis on person freedom, rights, and responsibilities: "[a]rtifactual man, along with his institutions of social order, was embodied in the wisdom of the eighteenth century" (ibid.: 252). Perhaps it therefore should not come as a surprise to see the same artifactual understanding of humanity and human development represented in the works of the seventeenth and eighteenth century advocates for women's education.

Choice in Early Liberal Feminist Theory

Some may be surprised to learn that the twentieth century subjectivist theorists discussed in the previous section were advancing an argument remarkably similar to that advanced by many seventeenth and eighteenth century feminists. Early contributors to liberal feminist thought, including Mary Astell, Mary Wollstonecraft, and John Stuart Mill, were concerned with how prohibitions on women's participation in public spaces altered the personalities and even the humanity of men and women alike. These observers were keenly aware of how women had been affected by being so consistently excluded from choice processes. Women were not completely controlled, but there were also many ways in which their choices were not their own. Property ownership, market activity, and political participation were all areas of life that many women were either legally barred from or only participated in with the permission of their husbands and fathers. As such, women were far less likely than men to stand in that moment of choice where it becomes clear what your true valuations are.

The choice environments that women did participate in were often very different from the large public networks in which men participated. For instance, as will be discussed in detail shortly, many of the early feminists talk about the choices women make in order to make themselves as desirable as possible to potential husbands. While those boys and young men with the means to receive an education were focused on the classics, girls and young women instead received only the rudiments of math and language skills while devoting most of their attention to skills relevant to household management (Gordon, 2015: 18; Skedd, 1997). This emphasis on learning for marriage was exacerbated by the way limits on property ownership, education, and professional work cut off alternative ways for women to support themselves. In isolating women within the household, they were also cutting them off from the learning that would have come with interaction and choice within broader social systems.

These early feminists were not concerned just with the lack of quality education, but with the presence of what they considered to be poor quality and even maladaptive learning. In 1622, Marie de Gournay argued that women's education was so poor that it should be considered "a marvel" that women have accomplished as much as they have: "[i]f, therefore, women attain less often than men to the heights of excellence, it is a marvel that the lack of good education—indeed, the abundance of outright and blatantly bad education—does not do worse and prevent them from doing so entirely" (de Gournay, [1622–1641] 2002: 81). Over 150 years later, Mary Wollstonecraft directed her ire towards the superficiality and dependence women were encouraged to cultivate when the outside world determined for them that the highest attainment possible in life was success in marriage: "strength of body and mind are sacrificed to libertine notions of beauty, to the desire of establishing themselves—the only way women can rise in the world—by marriage. And this desire making mere animals of them, when they marry they act as such children may be expected to act" (Wollstonecraft, [1792] 1993: 74). Lerner (1993: 10) later described this as the "condition of trained ignorance."

Mary Astell, a seventeenth century English moral philosopher roughly thirty years junior to John Locke, constructed two ideal types in her demonstration of how women were shaped by their learning environments. The first type of woman is mentally weak, lacks good judgment, depends on others for her happiness, and is constantly worried that she may fall out of the favor of men. Astell saw English society as actively cultivating this type of woman at every turn. The second type of women is mentally resilient, judicious, relies on reason, and is able to recognize that happiness is a function of her own choices and state of mind. A major impetus of her written work was to figure out how to move society from pushing women into the first type and instead support the development of the second type of woman (Broad, 2015: 1–6).

These arguments in defense of women's capabilities continued into the first generation of philosophers recognized as feminist by modern standards. Mary Wollstonecraft, the progenitor of liberal feminism, centered her arguments about women's social, political, and economic wellbeing around the matter of education. She viewed the narrow form of education women received as having deleterious effects on their characters, marriages, children, and societies. First, women's attention was being directed to pursuits that encouraged them to be narrow-mindedly focused on the acquisition of a husband. Second, this narrow-minded focus meant that a good number of the available minds were being directed away from projects with the potential to make significant contributions to human progress. Third, the fact that young men and women were developing their minds in such different ways made it difficult for them to see eye to eye, thereby limiting the potential for a relationship founded in mutual sympathy and cooperation as equals. She believed "all the writers who have written on the subject of female education and manners from Rousseau to Dr. Gregory, have contributed to render women more artificial, weak characters, than they would otherwise have been; and consequently, more useless members of society" (Wollstonecraft, [1792] 1993: 87).[5] In her view, the "disorderly kind of education" (ibid.: 88) women received was a primary cause of both women's incapacities and the societal acceptance of their subjugation. Women were trained to act in ways considered ignorant, and then had that ignorance used to justify their further infantilization: the education "which women have hitherto received has only tended, with the constitution of civil society, to render them insignificant objects of desire—mere propagators of fools!" (ibid.: 74).

Lest it be assumed that Wollstonecraft speaks only for the privileged young ladies forced to learn the piano-forte in order to impress gentlemen, it's worth acknowledging that Mary Wollstonecraft was not of nobility or inherited wealth. She worked for a living and had direct experience of a variety of socio-economic strata. She was born in Spitalfields, one of the most violent of London's villages. Her father was an alcoholic and gambler who took the family on a turbulent ride from working class to aspiring gentlemen farmer to barely eking out a living (Gordon, 2015: 11–22). Edward Wollstonecraft was cruel to his children—he even hung the family's dog in front of them for no apparent reason—and sexually abusive to their mother. It takes no great imagination to see how her abusive father's control of and cruelty towards her mother would have heightened Mary's awareness of the dangers of relying too much on marriage as a source of safety and financial security. Likewise, when their family's brief years as middle-class farmers enabled her to go to school, she experienced firsthand the disappointment of being limited to "needlework and simple addition" while her brother was learning "history, mathematics, and Latin" (ibid.: 18). Her own life experience and observations made her keenly aware that girls of all social backgrounds were being taught to marry and manage households, and she was no stranger to hard work.

One hundred years later still—demonstrating how incredibly long it took women and feminists to convince their societies of women's intellectual aptitude—John Stuart Mill finds himself still needing to defend the idea that women have the potential to make contributions elsewhere than in domestic spaces. He addressed *The Subjection of Women* (Mill, [1869] 1970) to those who believe "that the greater nervous susceptibility of women is a disqualification for practice, in anything but domestic life" (Mill, [1869] 1970, 60). Like Wollstonecraft, he sees this impression and other apparent idiosyncrasies of the female sex as the result of cultivation—"nervous energy run to waste" in the absence of "definite ends" to direct it towards—rather than inherently connected to gender. This situation is further exacerbated by the "conscious or unconscious cultivation" (Mill [1869] 1970, p. 60) that discourages women, particular those of the upper class, from undertaking too great of an effort at any pursuit. In short, women are not even encouraged to learn how to *try*.

Mill adds to this the observation that women who do attempt to defy the mold may risk getting themselves ignored completely if they are too contrary. Unlike a million subjects who all want to overthrow one king—not that this exercise is without it's difficulties—every wife has in their household a husband with his own vested interests in the family hierarchy: "[w]hatever gratification of pride there is in the possession of power, and whatever personal interest in its exercise, is in this case not confined to a limited class, but common to the whole male sex" (Mill, [1869] 1970: 12). Changing norms around women's educational opportunities therefore confronted the dual problem of men benefitting from the authority over those closest to them, while women are kept "in a chronic state of bribery and intimidation combined" by the fact that most improvements—and threats—to their circumstances are in the hands of their male family and neighbors (ibid.: 12). Consequently, women may keep parts of themselves secret for fear of upsetting the men who have such control over their daily lives. Even among those women who succeeded in writing for publication, "yet very few of them dare tell anything, which men, on whom their literary success depends, are unwilling to hear" (ibid.: 26). This point is validated by the experiences of those who were willing to speak out. Once Wollstonecraft was revealed as the author of *A Vindication of the Rights of Man* ([1792] 1993), reviews of the book—which had originally been overwhelmingly positive—turned to critiques of Wollstonecraft's impertinence at speaking to issues outside the proper domain of women (Gordon, 2015: 152–153; Janes, 1978).[6]

How Deprivation of Choice Impedes Personal Growth, Cooperation, and Societal Progress

At least three hypotheses about the personal and societal implications of limiting women's scope of choice can be drawn from the works of the advocates for women's education introduced above. First, deprivation of learning opportunity limits personal growth—the opportunity to encounter new knowledge and interpret it in a way that shapes ones' future development. To borrow the terminology of Buchanan ([1979] 1999]), there is less scope for the imagination and development of moral valuation that would enable women to intentionally craft themselves into the women they'd like to become. Second, educating and training men and women in such different ways introduces barriers to cooperation between those socialized as men and those socialized as women.[7] This has a detrimental impact on marriage relationships and families that has the potential to extend to all social interactions. Third, although freedom for personal development is the main point of this essay, the writers in question were keenly aware that these impediments to personal growth and cooperative endeavor wind up becoming social losses. The contribution never made, whether because it could not be discovered or could not be communicated to others, is a lost opportunity for all members of the current society as well as future generations.

Personal Growth

On one level, it is intuitive that those with access to more information will be able to interpret the world around them in a way that is more accurate and conducive of the successful accomplishment of plans. The notable feminist theorists of the seventeenth and eighteenth centuries often used the language of morality and character in their contributions to this debate. In short, the general view that emerges—with much nuance across individual contributors, of course—is that the cultivation of a stronger, wiser, more prudential set of character traits requires one to be able to act for themselves and learn their own hard lessons about the practical and moral consequences of their actions.

Evidence from Wollstonecraft's text suggests that she, like the political economists described previously, viewed the self as a kind of intentional creation: "I wish to shew that elegance is inferior to virtue, that the first object of laudable ambition is to obtain a character as a human being, regardless of the distinction of sex" (Wollstonecraft [1792] 1993: 73). Further, freedom to act is a necessary prerequisite for cultivation of the self to take place: "[l]iberty is the mother of virtue, and if women be, by their very constitution, slaves, and not allowed to breathe the sharp invigorating air of freedom, they must ever languish like exotics [tropical flowers], and be reckoned beautiful flaws in nature" (ibid.: 103).

For Wollstonecraft, the women of her time were narrow-minded and inadequately prepared for many of life's pursuits relative to their male peers. However, this had nothing to do with women's innate nature, and everything to do with the fact that they chose and acted in an environment that was dramatically constrained in its potential for learning:

> … Taught from their infancy that beauty is woman's sceptre, the mind shapes itself to the body, and, roaming around in gilt cages, only seeks to adorn its prison. Men have various employment and pursuits which engage their attention, and give a character to the opening mind; but women, confined to one, and having their thoughts constantly directed to the most insignificant part of themselves, seldom extend their views beyond the triumph of the hour (Wollstonecraft, [1792] 1993: 112).

Confined to their not-entirely-metaphorical cages, women "are provided with food and raiment, for which they neither toil nor spin; but health, liberty, and virtue, are given in exchange" (ibid.: 125). The costs of dependence are quite high when compared to the ability to cultivate oneself under conditions of freedom.

For Wollstonecraft, the cultivation of character requires action. Only then can genuine learning of what is wise and what is right take place, "for how can a rational being be ennobled by any thing that is not obtained by its own exertions?" (ibid.: 120). Further, this kind of personal development is cumulative. Having the opportunity to grow is beneficial because of the growth that took place, and the desire for further growth that emerges as the capacity for discomfort and change are expanded: "who sacrifices pleasure when it is within the grasp, whose mind has not been opened and strengthened by adversity, or the pursuit of knowledge goaded on by necessity?" (ibid.: 124). Likewise, Mary Astell writes, "[w]e must judge finally for ourselves … because if we determine amiss *we* must answer for it" (Astell, quoted in Broad, 2019: 173, emphasis in original).[8] These can be interpreted as statements about learning how to learn. Philosopher Jacqueline Broad argues that Astell's emphasis on choosing, acting, and ultimately bearing responsibility for oneself adds up to "a feminist theory of autonomy: a theory that for women to acquire true self-determination in their moral choices and actions, they must be permitted the conditions that enable careful self-examination and self-government" (Broad, 2019: 724).

Crucially, learning how to learn requires action, but Wollstonecraft and others saw girls and women as being regularly induced to inaction and the cultivation of dependency. In her observation, girl children in particular are never left to their own devices, and as such "rendered dependent—dependence is called natural" (Wollstonecraft, [1792] 1993: 109). The girl "condemned to sit for hours together listening to the idle chat of weak nurses, or to attend at her mother's toilet" will inevitably imitate the only behavior she sees, and as such will "amuse herself by adorning her lifeless doll, as they do in dressing her, poor innocent babe!" (ibid.: 109). We can see in this evidence of a theory in which learning is contingent on our experiences as well as the direct lessons we receive.

This is consistent with Mill's explanation for why great Queens are to be found even during eras in which women were particularly oppressed:

> … princesses, being more raised above the generality of men by their rank than placed below them by their sex, have never been taught that it was improper for them to concern themselves with politics; but have been allowed to feel the liberal interest natural to any cultivated human being, in the great transactions which took place around them, and in which they might be called on to take a part (Mill, [1869] 1970: 57).

For Mill, this was clear evidence that women had the potential to be great in all facets of life. If women during Mill's time seemed more inclined to succeed in the practical matters of day-to-day domesticity than in leadership and entrepreneurial roles, it was because their intellectual development and daily activity supported the former over the latter. Men lacking such education—whether obtained through school, self-education, or practical experience—would be similarly unable to produce great intellectual or practical achievements out of the ether: "[n]obody ever perceived a scientific law of nature by intuition, nor arrived at a general rule of duty or prudence by it. These are results of slow and careful collection and comparison of experience; and neither the men nor the women of intuition usually shine in this department, unless, indeed, the experience necessary is such as they can acquire by themselves" (ibid.: 57–58). Again, experience is essential to the processing of knowledge; human beings cannot integrate new knowledge with experiences they have not had.

The very concept of reaching one's "full" potential doesn't quite make sense from a subjectivist perspective. The limited perspective available to a person in the process of living makes it impossible for them to see and compare alternative paths from some sort of God's eye view. Even if they could, they cannot know that the metric they are using to compare is "right" other than through the lens of their own subjective perception, which can change over time as choices are made. This is not a purely academic point—the unknowability of the direction in which potential lies is itself an important argument for the creation and preservation of space in which individuals can experiment and learn from the results of those experiments.

Community and Cooperation

The benefits of developing a skill are not limited to the immediate context within which the skill is first practiced. This is why Ostrom (1997) emphasized the extended benefits of learning the science and art of association. The development of the capacity to cooperate will spill over into other areas of life, just as the ability to process and integrate new knowledge will cross environments. Consequently, in a world where political and economic resources are primarily in one gender's control, the ability of men and women to communicate clearly is essential for women to be able to make contributions that require cooperation across genders.

Again, the heart of this idea can be found in Wollstonecraft, who believed that the strange nature of women's education impeded both their own personal growth and their ability to interact and cooperate with others: "how can woman be expected to cooperate unless she know why she ought to be virtuous? Unless freedom strengthen her reason till she comprehend her duty, and see in what manner it is connected with her real good?" (Wollstonecraft, [1792] 1993: 66) She regularly addresses this argument towards men, who in their defenses of separate spheres often expressed frustration at their own attempts to understand and communicate with women. For Wollstonecraft, they should not have been so surprised. They had supported an institutional system and set of social customs that discouraged women from acquiring independence and maturity of character: "[m]en, indeed, appear to me to act in a very unphilosophical manner when they try to secure the good conduct of women by attempting to keep them always in a state of childhood" (ibid.: 85).

Both Wollstonecraft and the great economist and moral philosopher Adam Smith seem to have viewed the education that boys and girls received as so vastly different that it was something akin to being taught two different languages. In Wollstonecraft's argument, she draws on Adam Smith's ideas about the importance of sympathy and mutual understanding in the building of community (Leddy, 2016: 274). How could a husband and wife work together in mutual respect if the intellectual gap between them was so great that they could not truly understand each other? Such a dividing wedge would indeed make it difficult for women to make meaningful contributions, intellectual or otherwise, in a world where positions of authority were held near-exclusively by men. Adam Smith likewise decried the way men were denied opportunities to develop the human sympathies that he viewed as critically important to moral life. In *Theory of Moral Sentiments*, Smith argued that young men were being failed by the fact that they were not taught to understand the human condition better by reading the sentimentalist novels recommended to women (Leddy, 2016; Smith, [1759] 1994: 143).

It was not only the relationship of the husband and wife that was affected by this lack of mutual sympathy. Children were affected as well. In order to make this point, Wollstonecraft expresses an argument that will come to be embraced by proponents of separate spheres and rejected by her more feminist future readers: educating children is primarily women's responsibility, and since uneducated women cannot successfully raise educated children, society and polity will suffer if women are not permitted robust opportunities for learning.

In this discussion, Wollstonecraft gives the example of a woman who has not learned to think for herself but only ever followed her husband's direction. Even if that direction is kind and helpful, "alas! She has never thought, much less acted for herself" (Wollstonecraft, [1792] 1993: 116). If anything should happen to him, she will be left in the dark, with no ability to guide her children and not even good principles upon which to select another husband. Although this particular argument stands in tension with women's liberation because of the assumption that women are solely or primarily responsible for child rearing, Wollstonecraft was merely stating a point of fact for her time. Whether she liked it or not—and whether they liked it or not—she lived in a society where women would be primary caretakers. The remainder of her arguments make it abundantly clear that she had no interest in upholding separate spheres (Becchio, 2024: 49–55), even describing those who supported the subjugation of women as "tyrants" who are "eager to crush reason" when they "*force* all women, by denying them civil and political rights, to remain immured in their families groping in the dark" (Wollstonecraft, [1792] 1993: 67; emphasis in original).

Another channel through which the suppression of women's learning harms cooperation and community is that it teaches women and men alike to navigate tyranny rather than freedom. Neither role—that of oppressor or oppressed—is likely to lead to behavior that is conducive of cooperation. Strict hierarchies support the giving and following of orders—one reason why Wollstonecraft compares women's educational status to that of military recruits who are taught to do what they're told rather than to be able to think for themselves (ibid.: 81, 88–89). Wollstonecraft argues that women, having learned the law of power and submission, will now "make their children and servants endure their tyrannical oppression. As they submit without reason, they will, having no fixed rules to square their conduct by, be kind, or cruel, just as the whim of the moment directs; and we ought not to wonder if sometimes, galled by their heavy yoke, they take a malignant pleasure in resting it on weaker shoulders" (ibid.: 115–16). This is why Vincent Ostrom (1997), in *The Meaning of Democracy and Vulnerabilities of Democracies*, emphasizes the need to learn democratic ways of relating to each other. Social dilemmas will be more effectively resolved if the participants are actively involved in coming up with and implementing the solution. This is at core a claim about the epistemic and motivational limits of human beings that is very consistent with other subjectivist theory and with proto-feminist arguments about why it is so harmful to prevent women from education and learning by doing. We don't know what we want separately from our participation in choice processes.

The issue of women's rights was only one context within which Wollstonecraft applied her critique of tyranny. Her political writings were sharply critical of Rousseau and other thinkers she saw as employing the rhetoric of freedom but in practice merely replacing one hierarchy with another: "[b]ut one power should not be thrown down to exalt another—for all power inebriates weak man; and its abuse proves that the more equality there is established among men, the more virtue and happiness will reign in society" (Wollstonecraft, [1792] 1993: 80). For Wollstonecraft, the subjugation of women was but a variant of the political oppression that was so often the target of Enlightenment critiques.

A common response to concerns about male tyranny at the time was to argue that women had great influence over men—possibly even too great, which is why male leadership in the household needed to be firmly enforced. In response, Mill observes that one of the many flaws of this argument is that it is the women who are most likely to need protection who are least likely to be able to obtain it by their own cajoling, begging, or blackmailing: "But this instrument of self-protection—which may be called the power of the scold, or the shrewish sanction—has the fatal defect, that it avails most against the least tyrannical superiors, and in favor of the least deserving dependents" (Mill, [1869] 1970: 37). In addition to being a flawed logic, the theory that wily feminine influence serves as an effective counterbalance to masculine rights and power misses the point about people relating to each other on an egalitarian rather than hierarchical basis. Even if the relative plusses and minuses of each spouses bargaining position equaled out perfectly, they would still be negotiating within an institutional structure of gender hierarchy, thereby developing the skills of command and control rather than the skills of cooperation and mutual exchange.

Social Progress

Finally, in addition to the direct harms to women and their families, the denial of educational opportunities will be an impediment to social progress overall. As usual, we can begin with a motivating insight from Mary Wollstonecraft: "[i]t is difficult for us purblind mortals to say to what height human discoveries and improvements may arrive when the gloom of despotism subsides, which makes us stumble at every step" (Wollstonecraft, [1792] 1993: 101).

John Stuart Mill clearly agrees, and in fact his primary focus in *The Subjection of Women* is how flawed the logic of subjugation is and the harm it causes all people. In John Stuart Mill's writings on women's rights, he focuses on the way that women's experiences—limited both by law and social convention—did not afford them the same opportunities to learn and grow as their male peers. This lack of opportunity and the resulting lost contributions are, for Mill, one of the great missed opportunities of the age: "the principle which regulates the existing social relations between the two sexes—the legal subordination of one sex to the other—is wrong in itself, and now one of the chief hindrances to human improvement; and that it ought to be replaced by a principle of perfect equality, admitting no power or privilege on the one side, nor disability on the other" (Mill, [1869] 1970: 3).

Mill's interpretation of the "woman question" is that it is social practices and institutions that have created the apparent divide between men and women, and that history cannot show women's true potential because they have been kept always in bondage: "the opinion in favor of the present system, which entirely subordinates the weaker sex to the stronger, rests upon theory only; for there never has been trial made of any other" (ibid.: 6). As a result, "[w]hat is now called the nature of women is an eminently artificial thing—the result of forced repression in some directions, unnatural stimulation in others" (ibid.: 22). This framing is similar to Wollstonecraft's claim nearly 100 years before that "it cannot be demonstrated that woman is essentially inferior to man because she has always been subjugated" (Wollstonecraft, [1792] 1993: 104).

In other words, Mill—like many great classical liberals before and after—adopts what might now be considered a new institutionalist position on social construction rather than a gender essentialist position.[9] This institutional perspective leads Mill to make an economic argument that is simple on the surface, but often overlooked in practice when it comes to questions of granting all people equal rights to participate in markets and other public spaces. In short, he argues that if women lack the capacity to work as professionals, succeed in education, serve as political leaders—whatever the task at hand may be—then they will not be able to keep those jobs. Given a reasonably competitive institutional environment, if women are destined to fail, they will simply fail on their own. They don't need a law or custom to bar them from participation to ensure it happens:

> ... Nobody thinks it necessary to make a law that only a strong-armed man shall be a blacksmith. Freedom and competition suffice to make blacksmiths strong-armed men, because the weak-armed can earn more by engaging in occupations for which they are more fit ... if the principle

> is true, we ought to act as if we believed it, and not to ordain that to be born a girl instead of a boy, any more than to be born black instead of white, or a commoner instead of a nobleman, shall decide the person's position through all life (Mill, [1869] 1970: 19).

Likewise, if it is contrary to the nature and aptitudes of women to succeed at any but domestic pursuits, there is no need to fear that they will flock to and flourish in these unnatural corners. Further, Mill recognizes in his discussion that the impact is not solely a social matter but also a personal one, in which denial of admission to competitive systems can decrease market productivity but also impact the entirety of a life.

To be denied admittance to a competitive environment is unnecessary if a person will truly never be able to compete, and injurious to the progress of the market if they do have the ability to make contributions that outcompete the other available offerings. Hayek emphasized that one of the most important features of markets is the creativity and experimentation they enable. He argued that standing in the present, we have very little idea what the future will bring and what ideas, products, and ventures will be most conducive to success in that future period (Hayek, [1960] 2011). In the face of this great uncertainty, to impede the creativity and experimentation of roughly fifty percent of the population seems like a serious mistake if one's focus is on social progress and the mass of benefits it has the potential to bring.

Conclusion

In short, both the subjectivist strand of political economy and the early classical liberal feminists were developing arguments about the inseparability of values and choice. Human perceptions and values are not developed in a vacuum, but instead are experienced simultaneously with the actions we do or do not take over the course of our lives. A person who is systematically denied the ability to make choices for themselves is put in a position where their beliefs and values develop in a separate mind from that which is making the choice. If my husband decides for me what I read, or whether I can go to school, I never experience that moment of becoming aware that there are ideas I might like to explore. I never have the opportunity to even consider becoming an economist.

One way of thinking about the contributions of early classical liberal feminists is as early forays into the question of how it changes both social outcomes and people themselves when individuals are denied the right to directly participate in processes of choice. Direct participation in choice processes plays a critical role in value formation and, ultimately, in people becoming who they are best suited to be. These processes involve a great degree of trial and error, and women have been excluded from both social life and opportunities to *become* themselves because of their presumed inferiority or fragility.

The legal and social constraints that used gender status to limit a person's range of choice also limited who they could become and what they would be able to contribute to a rapidly changing world. Buchanan (2005) suggests that people have somehow learned not to be fully adult in their relationship with the state. Nineteenth century women living under coverture were taught much the same thing—that it is better not to be fully adult, but to let their fathers and husbands handle the business. Further, husbands and wives spent centuries learning from their relationships with each other how to navigate systems of tyranny. The emancipatory project of liberalism requires gender relations that are instead consistent with self-construction and cooperative egalitarian relations.

Obstacles to embodying one's full humanity in the absence of choice are, of course, not the exclusive domain of women living under patriarchy. The core argument—that preventing people from making their own choices will also prevent them from learning, growing, and becoming themselves—applies to all people who are denied the opportunity to see and experience life fully for themselves. The case I have made here leaves many questions open for further inquiry, including how different forms and experiences of emancipation vary. Future research, I hope, will extend the conversation outlined here in order to make our understanding of the experience of emancipation ever more robust.

Notes

1. A comprehensive survey of debates on "the woman question" is beyond the scope of this paper, but Kathleen Canning (2006) provides an overview of debates across Europe, Helsinger et al. (1983) provide a selection of core written arguments from Britain and North America, and Offen (2017) offers detail on the French debate.

2. James Buchanan persuasively made the argument that since all cost is ultimately opportunity cost, cost and choice are inseparable (Buchanan, [1969] 1999). There is no such thing as being able to understand the cost or the value of an object without the context of the person making the choice and their perceptions in that moment of what will (or will not) pay off for them.
3. In sociology, the theory that we act according to perception rather than objective reality is known as the Thomas Theorem. Interestingly given the context of this chapter, the credit for the theorem was given exclusively to W.I. Thomas for nearly 50 years despite the original text being co-authored with Dorothy Swaine Thomas (Smith, 1995).
4. Buchanan refers here to G.L.S. Shackle's (1972) book *Epistemics and Economics*.
5. Wollstonecraft here refers to the Scottish physician Dr. John Gregory, who wrote a popular book on women's education – specifically, suggesting they not let on that they've had too much of it.
6. When Wollstonecraft's husband William Godwin published his memoirs and a selection of previously unpublished writings of Mary's after her death, the negative reaction became stronger. What Godwin saw as romantic and humanizing, critics saw as hysterical and sex-crazed: "If one looks up "Prostitution" in the index of *The Anti-Jacobin Review*, the entry reads, "see Mary Wollstonecraft." Experts warned parents against letting their daughters read Wollstonecraft's books, claiming her words could promote suicide, foster licentiousness, and destroy the very fabric of decent society (Gordon 2015: 513).
7. Royal women and others of sufficiently elite status are sometimes treated practically as a kind of "honorary" man. And of course, women who disguise themselves as men in order to take advantage of particular opportunities can be found throughout history. See for example Norena Shopland's (2021) *A History of Women in Men's Clothes*. Conversely, men in occupations or social positions that are looked down upon may be treated as less-than and deprived of status and opportunity to learn.
8. There is a religious connotation to this statement. Many women in philosophy in the West were Christian, if for no other reason than that religious pursuits were more permissible than other intellectual

outlets for many centuries (Hutton 2021). For this reason, Mary Astell's work has been controversial within feminist philosophy for the perceived tension between a quest for autonomy and the Christian requirement of submission to God. Jacqueline Broad (2019) argues that the issue is more complex, and that we can learn about individual agency from Astell's work.

9. Gender essentialism is the belief that differences in men and women's behavior can be explained primarily by their different biological characteristics. An institutional perspective, in contrast, believes that social scientific analyses of gender should focus on social construction and acculturation.

References

Becchio, G. (2024). *The Doctrine of the Separate Spheres in Political Economy and Economics: Gender Equality and Classical Liberalism*. Palgrave Macmillan.

Broad, J. (2015). *The Philosophy of Mary Astell: An Early Modern Theory of Virtue*. Oxford University Press.

Broad, J. (2019). Selfhood and Self-Government in Women's Religious Writings of the Early Modern Period. *International Journal of Philosophical Studies, 27*(5), 713–730.

Buchanan, J. M. [1969] (1999). *Cost and Choice: An Inquiry in Economic Theory*. In G. Brennan, H. Kliemt & R. D. Tollison (Eds.), *The Collected Works of James M. Buchanan*(Vol. 6). Liberty Fund.

Buchanan, J. M. [1979] (1999). Natural and Artifactual Man. In G. Brennan, H. Kliemt & R. D. Tollison (Eds.), *The Logical Foundations of Constitutional Liberty: The Collected Works of James M. Buchanan*(Vol. 1, pp. 246–259). Liberty Fund.

Buchanan, J. M. (2005). Afraid to Be Free: Dependency as Desideratum. *Public Choice, 124*(1–2), 19–31.

Canning, K. (2006). The 'Woman Question.' In S. Berger (Ed.), *A Companion to Nineteenth-Century Europe, 1789–1914* (pp. 193–208). Blackwell Publishing.

de Gournay, M. l. J. [1641] (2002). The Equality of Men and Women. In R. Hillman & C. Quesnel (Eds.), *Apology for the Woman Writing and Other Works* (pp. 69–95). University of Chicago Press.

Forhan, K. L. (2017). *The Political Theory of Christine de Pizan*. Routledge.

Gordon, C. (2015). *Romantic Outlaws: The Extraordinary Lives of Mary Wollstonecraft and Mary Shelley*. Random House.

Hayek, F. A. [1960] (2011). *The Constitution of Liberty: The Definitive Edition*. In R. Hamowy (Ed.), *The Collected Works of F. A. Hayek (*Vol. 17). University of Chicago Press.
Hayek, F. A. [1943] (2014). The Facts of the Social Sciences. In B. Caldwell (Ed.), *The Market and Other Orders: The Collected Works of F. A. Hayek*(Vol. 15, pp. 78–92). University of Chicago Press.
Helsinger, E. K., Sheets, R. L., & Veeder, W. (1983). *The Woman Question: Society and Literature in Britain and America, 1837–1883*. Manchester University Press.
Hutton, S. (2021). Radicalism, Religion and Mary Wollstonecraft. *Intellectual History Review, 31*(1), 181–198.
Janes, R. M. (1978). On the Reception of Mary Wollstonecraft's: A Vindication of the Rights of Woman. *Journal of the History of Ideas, 39*(2), 293–302.
Lachmann, L. M. [1971] (2007). *The Legacy of Max Weber: Three Essays by L. M. Lachmann*. Ludwig von Mises Institute.
Lachmann, L. M. [1986] (2020). *The Market as an Economic Process*. Mercatus Center at George Mason University.
Leddy, N. (2016). Mary Wollstonecraft and Adam Smith on Gender, History, and the Civic Republican Tradition. In G. Kellow & N. Leddy (Eds.), *On Civic Republicanism: Ancient Lessons for Global Politics* (pp. 269–281). University of Toronto Press.
Lemke, J. S. (2015). An Austrian Approach to Class Structure. *Advances in Austrian Economics, 19*, 167–192.
Lemke, J. S., & Lingenfelter, J. (2017). A Practical Approach to Understanding: The Possibilities and Limitiations of Applied Work in Political Economy. *Advances in Austrian Economics, 22*, 81–102.
Lerner, G. (1993). *The Creation of Feminist Consciousness: From the Middle Ages to Eighteen-Seventy*. Oxford University Press.
Martin, N. P., & Storr, V. H. (2008). On Perverse Emergent Orders. *Studies in Emergent Order, 1*(1), 73–91.
Mill, J. S. [1869] (1970). *The Subjection of Women*. MIT Press.
Mises, L. v. [1949] (2007). *Human Action: A Treatise on Economics*. Liberty Fund.
Offen, K. (2017). *The Woman Question in France, 1400–1870*. Cambridge University Press.
Ostrom, V. (1997). *The Meaning of Democracy and the Vulnerability of Democracies: A Response to Tocqueville's Challenge*. University of Michigan Press.
Shackle, G. L. S. (1972). *Epistemics and Economics: A Critique of Economic Doctrines*. Cambridge University Press.
Shopland, N. (2021). *A History of Women in Men's Clothes: From Cross-Dressing to Empowerment*. Pen and Sword History.

Skedd, S. (1997). Women Teachers and the Expansion of Girls' Schooling in England, c. 1760–1820. In H. Barker & E. Chalus (Eds.), *Gender in Eighteenth-Century England: Roles, Representations and Responsibilities* (pp. 101–125). Routledge.

Smith, A. [1759] (1994). *The Theory of Moral Sentiments*. Liberty Fund.

Smith, A. [1776] (1982). *An Inquiry into the Nature and Causes of the Wealth of Nations*. Liberty Fund.

Smith, R. S. (1995). Giving Credit Where Credit Is Due: Dorothy Swaine Thomas and the 'Thomas Theorem.' *American Sociologist, 26*(4), 9–28.

Thomas, W. I., & Thomas, D. S. (1928). *The Child in America: Behavior Problems and Programs*. A. A. Knopf.

van Schurman, A. M. [1641] (2013). A Dissertation on the Natural Capacity of Women for Study and Learning. In D. M. Clarke (Ed.), *The Equality of the Sexes: Three Feminist Texts of the Seventeenth Century* (pp. 79–118). Oxford University Press.

Vaughn, K. I. (1992). The Problem of Order in Austrian Economics: Kirzner vs. Lachmann. *Review of Political Economy*, *4*(3), 251–274.

Wollstonecraft, M. [1792] (1993). *A Vindication of the Rights of Woman and A Vindication of the Rights of Man*. Oxford University Press.

CHAPTER 10

A Radical Liberal Approach to LGBTQ Emancipation

Nathan P. Goodman

In *Obergefell v. Hodges* (2015), the United States Supreme Court ruled that state governments could not prohibit same-sex marriages, as such prohibitions violated the equal protection clause of the Fourteenth Amendment to the U.S. Constitution. Other rulings had similarly applied liberal legal principles to protect the civil liberties of lesbian, gay, bisexual, transgender, queer, and questioning (LGBTQ) people. For instance, *Lawrence v. Texas* (2003) ruled that sodomy laws violated the right to privacy. Such laws had largely been used to criminalize consensual sex among gay and bisexual men. These types of rulings suggest the emancipatory potential of a liberal legal system, in which federal courts constrain the power of state and local governments, preventing them from violating the civil liberties of minority groups.

Yet not all LGBTQ scholars and activists are so sanguine about liberal legal orders. For instance, Spade (2015) argues that excessive focus on formal legal equality can leave behind the most vulnerable and

N. P. Goodman (✉)
Mercatus Center at George Mason University, Fairfax, VA, USA
e-mail: ngoodman@mercatus.gmu.edu

M. Novak (ed.), *Liberal Emancipation*, Mercatus Studies in Political and Social Economy, https://doi.org/10.1007/978-3-031-94406-2_10

marginalized members of the LGBTQ community. Even if the laws on paper appear to respect LGBTQ rights, the most vulnerable members of LGBTQ communities may still be vulnerable to police violence, incarceration, deportation, and other legally sanctioned oppression. Even if this violence arises from laws that do not appear to violate formal constitutional guarantees of equal protection or privacy, this state violence is still clearly oppressive. A strategy that focuses merely on what the law says about LGBTQ people, rather than on a more thorough examination of power, the distribution of wealth and opportunities, and state violence, is likely to leave the most vulnerable members of the LGBTQ community behind.

Spade's work is part of a broader literature that contests mainstream liberal approaches to LGBTQ politics, instead advocating a more revolutionary approach to queer and trans liberation (Daring et al., 2012; Conrad, 2014; Stanley & Smith, 2015). These scholars argue that liberal reforms promote inclusion within systems that remain fundamentally violent, oppressive, and unequal. Rather than seeking inclusion within these systems, they advocate challenging these systems. For example, they argue that rather than focusing on ensuring that LGBTQ soldiers can openly serve in the military, efforts should instead be aimed at ending imperialist wars. Rather than seeking to establish and enforce hate crime statutes that impose mandatory minimum sentences for those who target victims based on sexual orientation or gender identity, they argue that such statutes further strengthen oppressive systems of policing and mass incarceration. They want these systems abolished, not strengthened.

Throughout this literature, the word "liberal" largely takes on a pejorative tone. Liberalism is seen as something to resist, an embodiment of the system we live under as well as reform movements that merely seek inclusion within that system. However, I will argue that liberalism and radical queer and trans politics can be complementary. While radical queer and trans scholars and activists see themselves as challenging liberalism, I contend that many of their arguments can fruitfully inform a *radical liberal* politics that seeks to abolish prisons, borders, police, militarism, and the state itself. This radical liberal variety of anarchism is part of the left-wing market anarchist tradition, which traces its roots to nineteenth century thinkers who called their ideas by various names, including liberalism, individualist anarchism, and mutualism (Chartier & Johnson, 2011).

To make the case for a radical liberal approach to LGBTQ emancipation, I draw on a political economy tradition known as "mainline economics" (Boettke, 2012; Boettke et al., 2016; Mitchell & Boettke, 2017). Mainline economics applies rational choice theory, which focuses on the purposeful actions of individuals. However, mainline economists emphasize that individuals always act within an institutional context. This includes not just formal legal institutions, but also informal institutions such as social norms. Using institutional analysis, mainline economists analyze how individual purposive action under alternative institutional arrangements can give rise to different patterns of social cooperation, including social cooperation and coordination that arises from the bottom-up without central command. This social scientific approach allows us to examine how existing liberal institutions have enabled some expansion of LGBTQ freedom, while also enabling us to analyze the institutional incentives and feedback mechanisms that underly the oppressive systems queer radicals seek to resist. Moreover, it gives us a framework for analyzing the likely implications of alternative institutional arrangements that have not yet been observed. We can use this to offer a plausible account of how a radical liberal variety of left-wing market anarchism could enable social cooperation, human flourishing, and LGBTQ emancipation.

The chapter proceeds as follows. First, I discuss several ways that liberal institutions have helped expand LGBTQ freedom. Then I elaborate on the radical critique of liberal LGBTQ politics, exploring some of the dysfunctions that radical queer and trans politics identifies in existing liberal states. I then show how insights from mainline economics can complement these radical critiques by giving us a social scientific framework for analyzing prevailing systems of power. However, simply demonstrating dysfunctions in existing liberal societies is not sufficient to justify an alternative institutional arrangement. Using both empirical and theoretical insights, I argue that some proposed radical alternatives would be far worse for LGBTQ emancipation than existing liberal states, however flawed they may be. However, I argue that radical liberalism can offer a way forward that abolishes existing dysfunctional institutions while enabling emancipatory politics, human flourishing, and queer and trans liberation.

The Role of Liberalism in Expanding LGBTQ Freedom

Perhaps the most obvious way that liberalism has expanded and protected the freedom of LGBTQ people is via formal constitutional law. In the United States, the Fourteenth Amendment's legal guarantee of equal protection under the law has been especially relevant, as have precedents that establish a constitutional right to privacy. These constitutional principles have been used to overturn sodomy laws, bans on same-sex marriage, and various other restrictions on the autonomy of LGBTQ people.[1] By stopping these overtly anti-LGBTQ laws, liberal constitutional constraints protect individuals from formal, legally legitimized discrimination or restriction based on their sexual orientation or gender identity.

Yet in addition to directly protecting LGBTQ rights, liberal institutions also had greater space for LGBTQ civil society and social movements, largely due to constitutional rights to freedom of speech, press, and association. Of course, these freedoms have not always been consistently respected within nominally liberal societies. For instance, *ONE* Magazine, a gay magazine associated with the homophile movement, faced investigations, harassment, and censorship from both the U.S. Post Office and the FBI. However, legal challenges to this censorship eventually culminated in a Supreme Court ruling upholding the magazine's First Amendment right to publish. A similar case, *Manual Enterprises, Inc. v. Day*, addressed whether physique magazines that showcased male bodybuilders were obscene. In both cases, "homosexuals used the First Amendment to establish the right of public magazines to exist in the public sphere, demonstrating the importance of traditional First Amendment theories and doctrines as instrumental in allowing LGBTQ citizens to identify with and create a subculture and social movement" (Shepard, 2020: 670).

While expression, including via magazines and other written outlets, was important for emerging LGBTQ subcultures and movements, so too was association within civil society more generally. This civil society grew throughout the 1970s, as "[o]ver 1,000 community-based organizations serving LGBT people emerged in the 1970s, following the opening of the first LGBT community center in Los Angeles in 1969" (Martos et al., 2017: 4). Many of these organizations were involved in delivering healthcare that fit the unique needs of the LGBTQ community.

Yet organization through community groups, non-profit organizations, and other elements of civil society was only part of LGBTQ community formation. Many of the social spaces that have shaped and defined LGBTQ communities are operated as profit-seeking businesses. As Virgil Storr emphasizes, markets are social spaces (Storr, 2008). Workplaces, coffee shops, bookstores, bars, and various other commercial spaces are often important spaces where people build community and form social relationships with one another. One illustrative way to see this in the LGBTQ context is to consider the Stonewall Inn, a gay bar in Greenwich Village that was raided by the NYPD vice squad, which then resulted in the pivotal Stonewall Riots. The Stonewall Inn had been purchased by Tony Lauria, a mobster, and operated as a profit-making business for the mafia. Lauria and the mob were not socially minded LGBTQ allies, but alert entrepreneurs who seized a profit opportunity associated with serving an underserved and criminalized community (Goodman, 2023). Gay bars have continued to serve as an important social space for gay communities (Ghaziani, 2024). Markets have been important also in offering identity-related goods that help members of the LGBTQ community network with one another. For instance, particular types of fashion goods have been used by members of LGBTQ communities to signal their identity and express themselves (Malamet & Novak, 2023).

These types of market-driven spaces, services, and goods that serve LGBTQ communities are more likely to arise under conditions of relative economic freedom. In addition to providing these types of specialized goods and services, market societies generate opportunities for mutually beneficial exchange between people who are different from one another. This creates incentives for voluntary and positive association and contact across different identity groups. It therefore should not be surprising if economic freedom is associated with tolerance towards and emancipation of LGBTQ people. Empirical research seems to support this hypothesis. Using a cross-sectional regression analysis, Berggren and Nilsson (2013: 181) find that "the Economic Freedom Index is robustly positively correlated with tolerance towards homosexuals." Moreover, "first-difference regressions confirm that increases in economic freedom makes people more open-minded to and accepting of homosexuals, especially when these increases come about through more stable monetary arrangements" (ibid). More recent research has reinforced this finding. For instance, comparing economic freedom across U.S. states and rates of tolerance for a variety of groups (including homosexuals), Berggren and Nilsson

(2016) find that increases in economic freedom in U.S. states contribute to increased tolerance later. Berggren and Nilsson (2020) summarize a wider body of evidence on this subject.

Liberal rules offer wide scope for social and economic experimentation and association. This includes a lot of space for people to hold illiberal or bigoted values and promulgate those values. But it also leaves space for marginalized and stigmatized people to find one another, express themselves, form or patronize businesses, and organize through both civil society and politics. It also encourages interaction across differences, which can contribute to changing social attitudes and increasing toleration. The pluralism of a liberal society, combined with legal rules based on individual rights, have allowed substantial moves in the direction of LGBTQ emancipation.

The Radical Critique of LGBTQ Liberal Politics

To radical critics of liberal reformist approaches to LGBTQ liberation, the use of liberal institutions to promote equal protection, formal legal rights, and inclusion in the existing order is insufficient. The existing order is characterized by oppression, inequity, systemic violence, and exploitation. It must be resisted, not simply reformed or made more consistent with its stated constitutional principles.

There are several types of arguments offered for this view. One pertains to the extent to which formal legal protections translate into real, material improvements in the well-being of marginalized people. Supreme Court rulings, pieces of civil rights legislation, hate crimes legislation, and other aspects of law are ultimately words on paper. Dean Spade argues that typical law reform strategies rely "on the belief that if we change what the law says about a particular group to make it say 'good things' (e.g., creating laws that say you are not allowed to fire someone just because they are trans) and not 'bad things' (e.g., eliminating laws that explicitly criminalize people for cross-dressing or having certain kinds of sex) then those people's lives will improve" (Spade, 2015: 9). He contends that this emphasis on the letter of the law can conceal the broader operation of social systems, and how these social systems impact the well-being of LGBTQ people:

> … This analysis misunderstands how power functions and can lead to approaches to law reform that actually expand the reach of violent and

> harmful systems. In order to properly understand power and transphobic harm, we need to shift our focus from the individual rights framing of discrimination and 'hate violence' and think more broadly about how gender categories are enforced on all people in ways that have particularly dangerous outcomes for trans people. Such a shift requires us to examine how administrative norms or regularities create structured insecurity and (mal) distribute life chances across populations. This attention to the distribution of life chances acknowledges that even when laws are changed to say different things about a targeted group, that group may still experience disproportionate poverty as well as lack of access to health care, housing, and education. Those law reforms do nothing to prevent violences like criminalization and immigration enforcement. Legal systems that have official rules of nondiscrimination still operate in ways that disadvantage whole populations—and this is not due solely, or even primarily, to individual bias (ibid.).

Rather than trying to establish rules that explicitly prohibit treating LGBTQ people badly, Spade suggests looking more broadly at the institutional context within which people live and how that shapes the opportunities available to them. This institutional context includes not just the formal words on paper, but also informal rules and norms.

It's also clear that Spade recognizes state violence as just as objectionable as ordinary criminal violence. Some LGBTQ civil rights activists see establishing hate crimes laws, hiring LGBTQ police officers, and otherwise using the state's criminal justice system as the key to protecting queer and trans people from violence. Yet Spade emphasizes that policing, imprisonment, and immigration enforcement are fundamentally violent activities. Moreover, they are violent activities that LGBTQ people, especially transgender people, have been especially vulnerable to. Some of this was historically a result of overt criminalization via sodomy laws, laws restricting cross dressing, and so on. However, even after court rulings that overturned these laws, members of the LGBTQ community remained vulnerable to state violence. Some of this resulted from employment discrimination, housing discrimination, families kicking LGBTQ youth out, and other situations that resulted in poverty and economic precarity (James et al., 2016).

In such precarious situations, various criminalized activities may be the most effective available way to survive and make a living. For instance, a 2015 nationwide survey of transgender respondents found that: "[o]ne in five (20%) have participated in the underground economy for income at some point in their lives—including 12% who have done sex work in exchange for income—and 9% did so in the past year, with higher rates among women of color" (ibid.: 14). When police detain, arrest, and incarcerate individuals for participating in the underground economy, these police officers use violence or the threat of violence. However, in addition to this socially legitimized and regularized violence, transgender people working in the underground economy are vulnerable to additional, extralegal police misconduct. "[r]espondents who interacted with the police either while doing sex work or while the police mistakenly thought they were doing sex work reported high rates of police harassment, abuse, or mistreatment, with nearly nine out of ten (86%) reporting being harassed, attacked, sexually assaulted, or mistreated in some other way by police" (ibid.).

Once incarcerated, members of the LGBTQ community face additional violence in jails, prisons, and immigration detention centers. LGBTQ inmates, especially transgender inmates, are especially vulnerable to sexual violence by fellow inmates as well as by guards (Brown & Jenness, 2020). LGBTQ immigrants may find that an arrest leads to immigration detention and deportation, which may result in them being sent to a country where they face much higher risk of violence or repression. Observing this state violence leads radical queer and trans scholars to support an abolitionist analysis of policing and the prison-industrial complex. They tie this to the history of LGBTQ rights movements, noting that the movement is often seen as beginning with the Stonewall Riots, when LGBTQ bar patrons fought back against a police raid (Bassichus et al., 2011).

As a result of their abolitionist perspective, radical LGBTQ scholars are critical of hate crimes legislation, which involves establishing harsher criminal sentences for those convicted of hate crimes and giving more resources to police. The Sylvia Rivera Law Project, a group which advocates self-determination for transgender and gender nonconforming people, opposed the Matthew Shepard and James Byrd, Jr. Hate Crimes Prevention Act. In addition to opposing the legislation because it strengthened an oppressive criminal justice system, they also opposed the fact that it was bundled with the military budget, including funding for wars in Afghanistan and Iraq (Sylvia Rivera Law Project, n.d.).

This opposition to state violence also motivates opposition to efforts to include LGBTQ citizens in organizations that carry out state violence. While many LGBTQ rights groups worked for reforms that would allow LGBTQ soldiers to serve openly in the armed forces, radical critics argue that this is an ill-conceived goal. The military engages in unjust violence around the globe. Rather than asking for permission to participate in a violent organization that perpetuates injustice, radical queer and trans activists favor participation in anti-war, anti-militarist, and anti-imperialist movements. As Spade puts it, "the notion that a lesbian and gay political stance should focus on military inclusion rather than demilitarization is a grave, divisive mistake" (Spade, 2015: 70).

Radical queer and trans scholars have also diverged from mainstream LGBTQ rights movements on questions related to same-sex marriage. Rather than seeking inclusion in existing marriage law, they argue that marriage reinforces patriarchal power relations, is unfairly privileged by the state over other relationship forms, and functionally does more to protect those who are already well-off than the most vulnerable in our society. For instance, one reason to support same-sex marriage is so that gay couples who have children can maintain custody of their children. However, Spade argues that this does not go far enough, as the child welfare system breaks apart vulnerable families even when the parents are married. Likewise, marriage enables someone to share health insurance benefits or immigration status with their partner. But this will be insufficient in some contexts, such as those where neither partner has health insurance or a legally recognized right to reside in the country. As Spade writes:

> … Framing issues related to child custody through a lens of marital recognition…means ignoring the racist, sexist, and classist operation of the child welfare system and passing up opportunities to form coalitions across populations targeted for family dissolution by that system. Black people, indigenous people, people with disabilities, queer and trans people, prisoners, and poor people are targeted in child welfare systems. Seeking 'family recognition' rights through marriage, therefore, means seeking such rights only for queer and trans people who can actually expect to be protected by family law and child welfare systems. Since the availability of marriage does not protect straight people of color, poor people, indigenous people, prisoners, or people with disabilities from having their families torn apart by child welfare systems, it is unlikely to do so for queer poor people, queer people of color, queer indigenous people, queer prisoners, and queer people with disabilities. The quest for marriage seems to have far fewer benefits, then, for queers whose families are targets of state violence and who have no spousal access to health care or immigration status, and seems

> to primarily benefit those whose race, class, immigration, and ability privilege would allow them to increase their well-being by incorporation into the government's privileged relationship status. The framing of marriage as the most essential legal need of queer people, and as the method through which queer people can obtain key benefits in many realms, ignores how race, class, ability, indigeneity, and immigration status determine access to those benefits and reduces the gay rights agenda to a project of restoring race, class, ability and immigration status privilege to the most privileged gays and lesbians (ibid.: 31).

The core argument here is not an argument that legalizing same-sex marriage is worse than the status quo, but that activists' scarce resources and political energies should be devoted towards efforts to help the least advantaged by dismantling systems of social control. One fear was that a politics single-mindedly focused on reforms such as legalizing same-sex marriage would stop agitating to address the underlying issues marriage equality was meant to fix once same-sex marriage is legalized. This would leave the most vulnerable members of the LGBTQ community vulnerable and abandoned by mainstream LGBTQ rights nonprofits. A focus on what the law formally says about LGBTQ people leaves out consideration for LGBTQ people whose marginalization is largely a result of patterns of human activity other than formally unequal laws.

While this is true as far as it goes, it is important not to lose sight of the role that access to marriage, adoption rights for same-sex parents, and more have played for improving the lives of LGBTQ people and their families. Many LGBTQ people can more easily make stable plans, share health insurance, extend immigration benefits to their spouses, adopt children or keep custody of their children, and more (Craig & Goodman, 2023). While LGBTQ radicals are right to point out that some are excluded from these benefits even when the formal law improves, we also should not lose sight of those whose lives and dignity have materially improved due to legal reform.

That said, LGBTQ radicals embrace a set of critiques that extend to a range of established institutions, and as a result they push for the abolition of a variety of existing institutions. Proponents of this radical perspective are informed by a variety of analytical frameworks and advocate a range of institutional and social changes to address the systemic problems they're concerned with. For instance, Dean Spade's work is informed by Foucault and by critical race theory (Spade, 2015). Some radical LGBTQ activists embrace Marxist analysis and advocate Marxist-Leninist revolution (e.g., Feinberg, 1999, 2009). However, many others advocate various forms of anarchism (Daring et al., 2012; Spade in Chua et al., 2024). What is not common among these radical theorists, however, is an embrace of "liberalism." In the next section, however, I argue that a research agenda largely promulgated by liberal scholars, namely mainline economics, can be quite fruitfully applied to address the issues radicals care about.

How Mainline Economics Complements the Radical Critique

Mainline economics refers "a set of positive propositions about social order that were held in common from Adam Smith onward" (Boettke, 2012: xvii). One of these propositions is that human beings engage in purposeful action. This basic premise, which is the foundation of "rational choice" theory, implies that individuals respond to incentives, or costs and benefits. By analyzing how individuals pursue their plans given the incentives and constraints they face, we can engage in social scientific research that is grounded in methodological individualism. Methodological individualism should not be confused with atomistic individualism, however. Individuals are shaped by their social environment. In particular, the incentives, constraints, and knowledge that individuals have are all shaped by the institutional context they operate within. Institutions refer to the formal and informal rules that structure human interactions. Mainline economists use institutional analysis to study how individuals act and interact within different social contexts. Their interactions can give rise to emergent or spontaneous orders, patterns of social cooperation that arise without central control, command, or design (Boettke et al., 2016).

Scholarly work within the mainline tradition is quite useful for understanding the systems of power that radical queer and trans scholars and activists critique. Much of this analysis stems from a research program known as public choice theory. Public choice theorists analyze the incentives that shape decisions within the political process. They study how the rules of the political process, such as voting rules and constitutional rules, shape the incentives of voters, legislators, presidents, bureaucrats, police, lobbyists, and others involved in politics. Mainstream economists in the middle of the twentieth century had already developed a detailed theory of market failures, or situations in which the incentives individuals faced within markets would lead to suboptimal outcomes. Often these mainstream economists presumed that the presence of a market failure was sufficient evidence that state action could improve the situation. Yet the state in this context was treated as an exogenous, unitary actor. The incentives faced by individual participants in the political process were assumed away. Government was treated as if it were a "benevolent despot." Public choice theorists pointed out the politicians, bureaucrats, and voters are people with their own individual ends, and therefore they respond to incentives. A pattern of political incentives can therefore give rise to "government failure" just as a pattern of incentives can give rise to "market failure."

Public choice economists highlight how private interests, such as businesses, expend resources to exert political influence and secure special privileges from the state. This process is known as rent-seeking. This process results in complex and often close-knit relationships between nominally private and nominally public organizations, giving rise to what Richard Wagner (2016) calls an "entangled political economy." In this context, it may be unhelpful to draw a sharp distinction between "government failure" and "market failure." Instead, societal dysfunctions can be understood as instances of "institutional mismatch," defined as situations where "the rules governing an economic problem are inferior to a feasible alternative set of rules" (Furton & Martin, 2019: 198). By an "economic problem," Furton and Martin (ibid.) simply mean a problem that arises when "individuals' ends may be in conflict, or in which individuals may cooperate to advance one another's goals."

This framework can help us understand how oppressive systems operate, as well as why they predictably serve the interests of some while marginalizing and oppressing others. Randall Holcombe's work on "political capitalism" is illustrative here (Holcombe, 2018). Holcombe's analysis draws on Nobel laureate Ronald Coase's work on "transaction costs" (Coase, 1960). Transaction costs refer to the costs associated with identifying potential trading partners, negotiating an agreement, and enforcing that agreement. Holcombe points out that within our political system, some people face relatively low transaction costs when it comes to making political agreements with one another. For instance, legislators in the U.S. House of Representatives know one another, work together, and make deals with one another regarding the provisions of legislation. Lobbyists with experience in Congress face similarly low transaction costs when it comes to making deals. By contrast, most people would face very high transaction costs when it comes to making political deals, which means that their interests and values are unlikely to be reflected in public policies. A small ruling class gets to make deals among themselves that have adverse effects for the rest of the population.

This helps explain the organization of state violence in our society. Executives and lobbyists for defense contractors such as Lockheed Martin, Raytheon, and Boeing face low transaction costs when it comes to making deals with public officials. Often they are former public officials themselves, as a revolving door operates between the Pentagon, congress, and politically connected businesses and lobbying firms. This further lowers the transaction costs associated with making political exchanges. Those who benefit from militarized policies reap concentrated benefits from these policies, which gives them strong incentives to invest time and resources advocating for militarism. By contrast, many of the costs of militarism are widely dispersed throughout society, which reduces the incentive for ordinary people to invest time and energy in anti-militarist activities. As for those most directly impacted by militarism, they face incredibly steep costs when it comes to influencing U.S. policies. Many of them reside abroad, and even those who live in the U.S. are often poor, marginalized, and living a precarious life wherein they have relatively few resources to spend on efforts to influence national politics. These dynamics give rise to an entrenched military-industrial complex that rarely faces strong, well-organized political opposition (Coyne & Goodman, 2022a; Goodman, 2024a).

America's militaristic foreign policy then contributes to the militarization of domestic policing. The weapons and hardware used abroad eventually come home, where they are given to state and local police officers as part of the Department of Defense's 1033 Program. These weapons are then used by SWAT teams, a type of militarized police strike force that was invented by military veterans who were simply reusing coercive techniques they learned in foreign wars. This "boomerang effect," in which coercive techniques deployed abroad boomerang back home to undermine domestic liberty, is a predictable result of military veterans and officials learning from their experiences and using the tools at their disposal in a manner consistent with their incentives (Coyne & Hall, 2018).

Members of marginalized minority groups are especially vulnerable to the violence enabled by police militarization. One reason for this is that their voice in the political arena is more limited. They have fewer resources to use to try to influence politics, and they are less likely to have connections to the politically powerful, which means that they face higher transaction costs associated with political exchange. In addition to being limited in their ability to exercise voice in politics, they are also more constrained in their ability to exit jurisdictions with violent police departments and move somewhere less oppressive. If you do not have savings or good employment opportunities, the costs of moving to a new jurisdiction can simply be prohibitively high. Their limited access to both voice and exit renders marginalized people especially vulnerable to state violence by militarized police (Coyne & Hall-Blanco, 2016).

A similar process occurs in the U.S. borderlands, as weaponry, skills, and tactics developed for U.S. wars abroad come home and are used by the Border Patrol (Coyne & Goodman, 2022b). The militarization of the U.S. Border Patrol has included the development of a powerful SWAT team known as the Border Patrol Tactical Unit (BORTAC), the development of a large fleet of drones that surveils the borderlands, and extensive contracts between the Border Patrol and major defense contracting firms. This militarization undermines privacy and civil liberties in the borderlands, pushes migrants into dangerous desert routes that lead them to premature deaths, and results in tight-knit crony relationships between defense contractors, the Department of Homeland Security, and Congress (Coyne & Goodman, 2020). It also fuels the militarization of policing and expansion of surveillance in the domestic interior, as BORTAC agents and CBP drones assist police throughout the United States (Goodman, 2024b).

These are just a few of the ways that mainline economics can illuminate the systems of state violence and unequal power that characterize our world. Mainline economics can also fruitfully help us understand why transgender and gender nonconforming people are so vulnerable to these systems of power and violence. One way to understand this is to recognize that gender roles are themselves a type of institution. Individuals use gender roles and gendered expectations to align their expectations of one another, which enables them to coordinate their plans with one another (Craig & Goodman, 2023). In a world where gender is used for this purpose, those who are gender nonconforming will tend to face higher costs when it comes to making agreements. Moreover, those who use gender as a means of simplifying and coordinating their plans are likely to seek to enforce gender roles upon those who deviate from them. This enforcement of institutionalized gender roles does not always rely on formal rules that explicitly reference gender. Instead, it often relies upon individuals with discretionary power, such as police officers and prison guards, acting in a manner that is consistent with the informal institutions that structure their lives. This is why changing the rules on paper is not enough. To truly achieve queer and trans liberation, formal and informal rules must change in a manner that enables queer and trans people to live autonomous and flourishing lives.

Economics as a Constraint on Utopias

If radical institutional changes are needed to challenge militarism, policing, and repressive gender roles, what form should these changes take? What strategy and aims should we pursue in our efforts to build a better world? Mainline economics is vital to answering this question because economic reasoning helps us analyze what institutional arrangements are feasible and what their likely consequences are.

Many radical queer and trans scholars and activists see *capitalism* as an underlying cause of grave oppression. As a result, they seek to replace capitalism with an alternative system of political economy. For some, such as the late Leslie Feinberg (1999, 2009) this alternative takes the form of Marxism-Leninism, in which a revolutionary vanguard seizes power and leads a dictatorship of the proletariat that plans the economy and fundamentally restructures society. For others, such as Dean Spade and the various contributors to the *Queering Anarchism* anthology, the preferred alternative is a form of social anarchism, in which society is organized based upon bottom-up non-market social relations, such as mutual aid and gift economies.

To discern whether these alternatives are conducive to LGBTQ emancipation, it is not enough to demonstrate that existing liberal capitalist representative democracies feature systemic oppression. One must also engage in comparative institutional analysis and examine whether the alternative system would be better or worse. Too often, radicals offer trenchant critiques of the existing order, but then offer idealized accounts of their proposed alternative institutions. Moreover, sometimes they neglect to discuss specifics of alternative institutions. Marx's claim that he would not write "recipes for cookshops of the future" is one example of such an approach.

However, social science offers us tools for analyzing the likely consequences of institutions. These include empirical tools and theoretical tools. For assessing Marxist-Leninist institutions, we can start with empirical examination. How have LGBTQ rights, and civil liberties generally, fared within Marxist-Leninist states? In two words: *not well*. But two words are hardly enough to convince a committed revolutionary.

So, let's look at the facts. Repression of LGBTQ people is common across history, and many states engaged in severe homophobic and transphobic repression prior to their Marxist-Leninist revolutions. Nevertheless, the revolutions often made this repression even more severe, rather than ameliorating it. Consider the case of Cuba. Prior to the revolution, "there were well known LGBT-friendly bars in Cuban cities, such as the St. Michel, the Dirty Dick, and El Gato; however, Cuba had strict laws that criminalized homosexuality and targeted gay men for harassment" (Majied, 2015: 29). In addition to a commercial market for LGBTQ-friendly bars, many gay men in pre-revolution Cuba worked as sex workers who serviced tourists. Repression and harassments were serious problems, but markets created incentives for some spaces to welcome and cater to LGBTQ people. The revolution changed that:

> ... In 1959 the Cuban revolution erased the profit incentive for the superficial tolerance of homosexuality. Any tolerance of LGBTQ people by the more vehemently homophobic majority of Cubans dissolved. There was significant migration of LGBTQ persons who could afford to leave for Miami or to other parts of the United States and the world. It was at this point that existing homophobia and heterosexism became more systemic and institutionalized. Issues of sexuality became explicit in political discourse, and laws began to emerge targeting transgender men or those who were believed to be homosexual. Female homosexuality received less attention, presumably because of machismo and the heightened focus on the behavior of men. Between 1959 and 1980, gay men endured experiences ranging from limited job opportunities to detention in street sweeps to incarceration in labor camps. Having long hair or flamboyant hairstyles, wearing tight pants or colorful shirts, and exhibiting mannerisms perceived to be effeminate were sufficient to place one under suspicion of being gay. These supposed hallmarks of homosexuality helped identify those who would be targeted by antihomosexual sentiment and legislation. Furthermore, visibility and gender transgressions themselves constituted a central part of the problem identified by the revolution (ibid.: 30).

Suspected homosexuals were reported by informants, including "family members, work associates, or friends organized into neighborhood watch groups or 'Committees for the Defense of the Revolution'" (Ocasio, 2002: 80). In 1965, repression was escalated by "the inauguration of the Unidad Militar para el Aumento de la Producción (Military Unit for the Increase of Production-UMAP), a system of work and rehabilitation camps for social misfits, including homosexuals" (ibid.).

While Cuba's repression is particularly well known, similar repression has occurred (and continues) in other Marxist-Leninist states. Consider the case of China. Along some margins, China's policies have been better than Cuba's. For instance, "[h]omosexuality is not illegal in China and has never been explicitly illegal since the founding of the People's Republic of China (PRC) in 1949" (Chia, 2019: 29). Moreover, "consensual sex between same-gender adults had been deemed non-criminal since 1957" (ibid). However, "homosexual men were still arrested by local police for 'hooliganism' under art160 of the 1979 PRC Criminal Law," which remained in place until 1997 (ibid). In addition, rights and recognition for same-sex couples remain quite limited. "The PRC Marriage Law (2001) currently limits marriage to that between a man and a woman. Same-sex couples in China do not have any form of partnership recognition under the PRC Marriage Law and there are no legal protections for cohabiting same-sex couples" (ibid). In addition, there have been high profile stories of censorship directed against LGBTQ content in Chinese media (Chia, 2019).

Marxist-Leninists might argue that the repression seen in these contexts is a result of local culture, rather than distinctive pathologies in Marxist-Leninist politics. Yet the concentrated power and machinery of state repression that a "dictatorship of the proletariat" requires naturally creates dangers of repression. Indeed, the very arguments that LGBTQ radicals apply to police and prisons in the American context seem likely to be an even more severe problem in contexts where police and prisons are even less restrained by the formal constitutional limits associated with liberal democracies. Marxism-Leninism concentrates coercive power in the hands of an elite vanguard and treats repressive state violence and coercion as core to its theory of change. Such an arrangement will clearly pose a danger to any marginalized, stigmatized, or persecuted minority group.

Of course, many radicals can reasonably say that they do not want anything like Marxism-Leninism. If the root cause of these dysfunctions in Marxist-Leninist states is the level of centralized power and unconstrained authoritarian control, then socialists of a more democratic, libertarian, or anarchist bent can plausibly say that their proposed alternative would look quite different. Is there some fundamental insight from social science that places limits on the feasibility and desirability of their proposals as well? I argue that there is: the economic calculation problem.[2]

Resources, including resources used for production, are scarce. They have competing uses. Therefore, using them for one productive project entails foregoing the benefits of another productive project. Given the multiplicity of possible projects we could pursue, and the variety of production techniques people could choose to use for those projects, they need some way to decide how to allocate scarce resources among competing ends. Moreover, these productive goods are heterogeneous. Therefore, while a piece of productive property can be used for multiple different kinds of projects, it cannot be easily shifted to producing just any other good. Mining equipment used to extract metal from the ground cannot be easily repurposed into farm equipment. This means that if scarce resources are used for productive projects that turn out to be unwanted, there are real costs to shifting production plans. Decisions about which production plans to pursue therefore have real costs, costs that would be concealed by treating capital as homogeneous, as some neoclassical economists do. Given the opportunity cost of pursuing one production project over another, how are people to choose among the diverse range of possible projects? How are they to assess which have benefits that exceed the costs? This is the problem of economic calculation.

In a market economy with institutions of private property rights, individuals and firms purchase, rent, own, and sell productive property. The exchanges they make give rise to exchange ratios, or prices, of these productive goods. These prices act as knowledge surrogates, communicating easily digestible information about how much value others in the market attach to alternative uses of the goods. Profit and loss feedback helps the owners of firms discern whether consumers value their products more or less than alternative uses of the inputs that they have used. That feedback also creates an incentive to adjust one's productive plans if they are not creating value. Of course, markets are imperfect, characterized by externalities, information asymmetries, and distortions wrought by the political capitalist system we live in. However, even disequilibrium prices act as important knowledge surrogates, and as a lure for alert entrepreneurs to promote adjustments away from disequilibrium. Moreover, the presence of political capitalism does not give us reasons to jettison price feedback altogether, but instead reasons to resist the state-secured system of privilege that distorts markets in the interests of politically connected capitalist rent seekers.

Unfortunately, the socialist program of central planning does jettison price feedback, at least for the goods used within production processes. Even so-called "market socialists" propose abolishing property rights in the means of production, instead replacing them with a mix of central planning and trial and error. Markets, in this system, are reserved for consumption and labor decisions. By eliminating the institutional foundation that exchange of productive property rests upon, socialist planning prevents exchange ratios (or prices) from emerging for these productive goods. This means giving up the guides that help individuals coordinate their plans with one another and pursue projects that create value for others.

When the process of market coordination via price feedback is abandoned, socialists need some alternative mechanism to coordinate productive plans. They often opt for central planning, which centralizes power in the hands of an elite group who then face all the problems of discretionary coercive power that radicals rightly recognize in the American police, prison wardens, and military commanders. The results include shortages, gluts, and other resource misallocations that impoverish the population. Moreover, the economy becomes militarized and regimented (Lavoie, 1985b). In some cases, the economy, while nominally subject to central planning, decentralizes de facto decision-making into the hands of politically connected individuals who control plants and resources. In this way, socialism devolves into a system of mercantilism or political capitalism (Anderson & Boettke, 1997).

The inability to engage in economic calculation means that a system that attempts to abolish private property or institute central economic planning is unable to raise productive forces, coordinate plans, and thereby guide society towards a world of plenty in which people can flourish free from exploitation, class antagonism, and alienation. That world is not within the realm of possibility. Therefore, while central planning is possible, it is not possible for it to achieve the lofty and admirable goals of socialists.

This applies to all forms of socialism that attempt to replace coordination via the market process with coordination via central planning, not just those that explicitly embrace a dictatorship of the proletariat. As Lavoie (1985b) explains, the knowledge problem impacts not just comprehensive planning, which attempts to plan the entire economy, but also various forms of noncomprehensive planning, such as industrial policy. Indeed, Lavoie devotes an entire chapter to discussing various proposals for planning via "economic democracy."

Whether social anarchist proposals are subject to this critique is a more complicated question. After all, social anarchists are not proposing a central planning board to coordinate production and distribution. Their preferred arrangements are still polycentric, and therefore leave room for individuals and groups to act on their local, context-specific knowledge. However, to whatever extent social anarchism entails jettisoning exchangeable rights to productive property, it is likely to prevent the emergence of prices for productive property. The knowledge discovered and communicated through prices is therefore unlikely to be discovered and communicated. In such a context, local decisions can still proceed based on local knowledge, but coordination and cooperation across wider groups of people that cannot directly communicate with one another is likely to be hampered. When the extent of social cooperation, productive specialization, exchange, and coordination is limited in this way, people will likely be substantially poorer. Under such conditions of poverty, fewer people, including queer and trans people, will be able to flourish and thrive. The productive specialization that has given rise to LGBTQ-empowering forms of commerce and civil society would be hampered. Moreover, to achieve coordination in the absence of markets and central planning, communities would likely turn to tradition as an alternative coordination mechanism (Lavoie, 1985b). Traditions are often a useful coordinating mechanism, but they can be stultifying and oppressive for those whose values, goals, and identities do not fit well with them. We might therefore expect coordination based on tradition to further the marginalization of at least some queer and trans people. Thus, any proposal that aims to entirely jettison exchangeable property rights to productive property is likely to exacerbate oppression, not emancipate queer and trans people.

Yet while mainline economics hereby imposes a set of constraints upon the ways we can escape the current morass of imperialism, coercively imposed gender conformity, political capitalist exploitation, and mass imprisonment, this does not mean that a radical break from the existing order is impossible. Instead, it means that this radical break, to achieve liberatory ends, must maintain opportunities for bottom-up, decentralized coordination of individuals' diverse plans. In the next section, I discuss one possible way forward for this kind of bottom-up radicalism.

Towards Radical Liberalism and Emancipation for All

The notion of "radical liberalism" may strike many as laughable or incoherent. After all, the term "liberal" often evokes notions of milquetoast support for the existing system, of asking elites to implement reforms rather than pursuing fundamental institutional change (Lavoie 1977; Byas, 2017). Yet it was not always this way. After all, liberalism began as a radical movement for social change, creating a massive break from the old order, the ancien regime, the aristocracy, the power of throne and altar (Rothbard, 1965; Lavoie, 1985b). Moreover, as shown previously, the analytical tradition of mainline economics offers a scientific basis for analyzing fundamental institutional dysfunctions associated with militarism, borders, police, prisons, political capitalism, and other institutional arrangements that reformists often simply take for granted. In this sense, it can provide the basis for what Lavoie (1985b) calls a "scientific radicalism." Social science in this liberal tradition shows us why fundamental changes to the underlying institutional incentives and feedback mechanisms, not mere tinkering around the edges, are required to end the pathologies we see around us. This scientific radicalism can take the form of a "radical liberalism" that takes the liberal emphases on positive sum social cooperation, market-driven experimentation and trade tested betterment, individual rights, voluntary cooperation in civil society, relations of political equality, open democratic discussion, and political decentralization with checks and balances to their logical conclusions (Lavoie, 1993; Byas, 2017).

The version of radical liberalism that I support is a kind of individualist anarchism, in the tradition of nineteenth century individualist anarchists such as Benjamin Tucker, Voltairine de Cleyre, and Lysander Spooner (Long, 2020). These anarchists advocated a society built on voluntary association, in which the state-granted monopoly privileges associated with political capitalism were leveled and any valuable services currently provided by the state were instead provided by voluntary associations. Many of these individualist anarchists said explicitly that their views were a more radical and consistent variation upon classical liberal ideas of their time. For instance, Benjamin Tucker described his views as "consistent Manchesterism," in reference to Manchester's classical liberal free-traders (Tucker, 1888), and elsewhere called himself an "unterrified Jeffersonian democrat" (Tucker, 1893). Voltairine de Cleyre connected anarchism with American liberal notions of individual liberty (de Cleyre, 1932). Tucker beautifully expounded on the bottom-up, positive sum social cooperation that is at the heart of a liberal vision of spontaneous order and cooperation without command:

> … The history of humanity has been largely one long and gradual discovery of the fact that the individual is the gainer by society exactly in proportion as society is free, and of the law that the condition of a permanent and harmonious society is the greatest amount of individual liberty compatible with equality of liberty. The average man of each new generation has said to himself more clearly and consciously than his predecessor: My neighbor is not my enemy, but my friend, and I am his, if we would but mutually recognize the fact. We help each other to a better, fuller, happier living; and this service might be greatly increased if we would cease to restrict, hamper, and oppress each other. Why can we not agree to let each live his own life, neither of us transgressing the limit that separates our individualities? It is by this reasoning that mankind is approaching the real social contract, which is not, as Rousseau thought, the origin of society, but rather the outcome of a long social experience, the fruit of its follies and disasters. It is obvious that this contract, this social law, developed to its perfection, excludes all aggression, all violation of equality of liberty, all invasion of every kind. Considering this contract in connection with the Anarchistic definition of the State as the embodiment of the principle of invasion, we see that the State is antagonistic to society; and, society being essential to individual life and development, the conclusion leaps to the eyes that the relation of the State to the individual and of the individual to the State must be one of hostility, enduring till the State shall perish (Tucker, 1890).

This vision of bottom-up, positive sum social cooperation that grows out of respect for individual liberty was mirrored by later liberal scholars in the mainline economics tradition. For instance, F.A. Hayek famously wrote of the market order as a "catallaxy," which he defined as a process of turning enemies into friends (Hayek 2021, 309–310). Ludwig von Mises likewise emphasized the "Ricardian law of association" and the social cooperation furnished by an institutional context of respect for individual liberty and private property rights (Mises, 1949).

The individualist anarchist tradition seems promising given our earlier discussions of liberal moves towards queer emancipation and radical critiques of liberal states. The individualist anarchist would abolish the centralized, repressive, discretionary, and violent power of police, prisons, borders, and empire, which LGBTQ radicals condemn as oppressive forces that brutalize the marginalized. Yet at the same time, the individualist anarchist would radicalize existing liberal commitments to economic freedom, markets and entrepreneurship, and space for experimentation and voluntary association.

However, some liberals may balk at the proposal. They may question its feasibility. After all, Mises, Hayek, and other similar liberal thinkers did not embrace Tucker's anarchist conclusions. This is largely because they believed that a state equipped to enforce general rules, especially rules pertaining to the protection of property and contract, was necessary for sustaining the market order and the social cooperation it begets. Were they correct? Tucker and de Cleyre did not think so. More importantly, an emerging research program in mainline economics provides social scientific reasons to believe that social order, social cooperation, and the protection of rights are possible without a centralized state. This research program, which Peter Boettke ([2005] 2018) has dubbed "analytical anarchism," uses historical case studies, institutional analysis, and economic theory to analyze situations of endogenous rule formation. These situations occur when individuals or groups cannot rely upon a state's formal legal system to protect their rights or solve their governance dilemmas, and therefore they instead endogenously devise governance arrangements that work for them. Boettke and Candela (2020) summarize a large portion of this literature, showing that both inclusive mechanisms that bring people together and exclusive mechanisms based around selective groups can be used to provide governance that sustains social cooperation from the bottom-up.

The radical queer and trans movement's emphasis on prison and police abolition, as well as their efforts to organize individuals who face violence and criminalization by the state, means that they have direct experience engaging in this type of endogenous and bottom-up governance. To the extent that the most marginalized members of the queer and trans community see the police and the criminal justice system as a threat rather than a service provider, they will seek out alternative mechanisms to keep their communities safe. For instance, the Audre Lorde Project, an organization run by LGBTQ people of color, has operated a safe neighborhood campaign that works to deescalate and prevent hate violence without calling the police (Goh, 2018). Similar projects in which marginalized people build alternatives to state administered governance have been documented by Mariame Kaba and other prison abolitionists through a project called "One Million Experiments."[3] This name resonates with the emphasis mainline economists place on bottom-up processes of experimentation and discovery, rather than top-down one-size-fits-all solutions.

But even if a radical liberal anarchism of the sort that the nineteenth century individualists embraced seems possible, some radical queer and trans activists may worry that it winds up supporting existing unjust distributions of wealth and life chances. Yet consistent with Holcombe's analysis of political capitalism, the nineteenth century individualist anarchists recognized that existing inequality and economic injustice rests upon state-granted monopoly privileges, especially "four of principal importance: the money monopoly, the land monopoly, the tariff monopoly, and the patent monopoly" (Tucker, 1893). Tucker argued that ending such state granted monopoly privileges would empower ordinary people and erode precisely the exploitative and unequal relations that socialists wished to resist. Members of queer radical movements have likewise sought to end unjust state-secured monopolies. For instance, activists affiliated with AIDS Coalition to Unleash Power (ACT-UP) have opposed pharmaceutical patents and FDA restrictions that limit HIV patients' access to medicine (Szijarto, 2023). Radical transgender activists have often supported routing around the monopoly privileges that medical professionals have when it comes to prescribing gender affirming hormones and related treatments (Rotondi et al., 2013). These activists engage in mutual aid, routing around state-erected barriers to entry and ensuring that their fellows have access to the healthcare they need. This strategy directly challenges state secured monopoly privileges and moves us in the direction of a genuinely free market, rather than the captured political capitalist system we live under.

Many radical queer and trans movements emphasize direct action and mutual aid projects that leverage local knowledge to directly help the most vulnerable, rather than imposing top-down plans via efforts to seize control of a state that is hostile to queer and trans survival. These strategies are far less vulnerable to the pitfalls we identified in the previous section. Rather than imposing centralized economic planning, they empower individuals to use their local knowledge, cooperate from the bottom-up, and help their community. In this respect, the vibrant and positive sum practical anarchism of radical queer and trans liberation movements is already consistent with the radical liberal vision I outline here. They might never choose to speak of it in those terms, as they may associate "liberalism" with a stodgy status quo rather than an emancipatory project. But they already live their lives in a manner that is consistent with bottom-up discovery, endogenous rule formation, the pursuit of the positive sum, and efforts to live our lives as dignified equals. Ultimately, that is more important than labels. While social anarchists and other LGBTQ radicals may at times envision future arrangements that would likely have harmful unintended consequences, the day-to-day activities of their movements help to create productive and emancipatory forms of voluntary association. The anarchist emphasis on experimentation, direct action, and mutual aid leads to genuinely positive action, regardless of what totalizing visions any given radical may be motivated by.

Conclusion

Regardless of whether the terms I use in the previous section ever catch on within social movements (they likely will not), I hope that this chapter encourages researchers to continue exploring the synergies between mainline economics and radical LGBTQ politics. Analytical anarchism, as well as the related research program of Elinor and Vincent Ostrom regarding polycentric governance, can be quite fruitful for understanding social movements, mutual aid, and anarchist prefigurative politics. Public choice, particularly the analysis of political capitalism, can be fruitfully applied to understand the systems of state violence and economic privilege that radicals rightly critique. Ultimately, mainline economics offers a powerful lens for understanding our world. Through that understanding, radicals can better understand the feasible paths available for emancipatory social change.

Sometimes this means casting cold water on proposed paths towards emancipation. Attempts to remake the world through centralized economic planning will lead not to emancipation, but to calculational chaos and abuses by the wielders of centralized power. Some nominally democratic or decentralized forms of radical social change may be subject to similar pitfalls. Yet the most radical and anti-authoritarian elements of the movement, namely the anarchists and abolitionists, are prefiguring a better world each day. Rather than attempting to impose liberation from the top-down, they are forging new forms of associational life that enable marginalized people to survive, thrive, and govern themselves in the face of hostile power. The insights of mainline economics can help us understand what sets these distinct radical paths towards liberation apart from one another, as well as why imperfect but promising moves towards emancipation have occurred within liberal democracies. The partial liberalism we see around us enables experimentation, entrepreneurship, coordination, and community. Radical critics offer trenchant critiques of violence and inequity in existing institutions. Yet for a radical change to be truly emancipatory, it should preserve and expand this space for experimentation and entrepreneurship, not constrain or crush it.

Notes

1. See Obergefell v. Hodges (2015), and *Lawrence v. Texas* (2003).
2. See Lavoie (1985a) for a thorough overview of the calculation debate.
3. See https://millionexperiments.com.

References

Anderson, G. M., & Boettke, P. J. (1997). Soviet Venality: A Rent-Seeking Model of the Socialist State. *Public Choice, 93*(1–2), 37–53.

Bassichus, M., Lee, A., & Spade, D. (2011). Building an Abolitionist Trans and Queer Movement with Everything We've Got. In E. A. Stanley, & N. Smith (Eds.) *Captive Genders: Trans Embodiment and the Prison Industrial Complex*. AK Press.

Berggren, N., & Nilsson, T. (2013). Does Economic Freedom Foster Tolerance? *Kyklos, 66*(2), 177–207.

Berggren, N., & Nilsson, T. (2016). Tolerance in the United States: Does economic freedom transform racial, religious, political and sexual attitudes? *European Journal of Political Economy*, *45*(Supp.), 53–70.

Berggren, N., & Nilsson, T. (2020). Economic Freedom as a Driver of Trust and Tolerance. In J. Gwartney, R. Lawson, J. Hall & R. Murphy (Eds.), *Economic Freedom of the World: 2020 Edition* (pp. 187–212). Fraser Institute.

Boettke, P. J. [2005] (2018). Anarchism as a Progressive Research Program in Political Economy. In E. Stringham (Ed.), *Anarchy, State, and Public Choice* (pp. 206–220). Mercatus Center at George Mason University.

Boettke, P. J. (2012). *Living Economics: Yesterday, Today, and Tomorrow*. Independent Institute.
Boettke, P. J., & Candela, R. A. (2020). The Positive Political Economy of Analytical Anarchism. In G. Chartier & C. Van Schoelandt (Eds.), *The Routledge Handbook of Anarchy and Anarchist Thought* (pp. 222–234). Routledge.
Boettke, P. J., Haeffele-Balch, S., & Storr, V. H. (2016). *Mainline Economics: Six Nobel Lectures in the Tradition of Adam Smith*. Mercatus Center at George Mason University.
Brown, J. A., & Jenness, V. (2020). LGBT People in Prison: Management Strategies, Human Rights Violations, and Political Mobilization. *Oxford Research Encyclopedias: Criminology and Criminal Justice*. https://doi.org/10.1093/acrefore/9780190264079.013.647
Byas, J. L. (2017, August 30). Radical Liberalism: The Soul of Libertarianism. Center for a Stateless Society. https://c4ss.org/content/49939
Chartier, G., & Johnson, C. W. (2011). *Markets Not Capitalism: Individualist Anarchism Against Bosses, Inequality, Corporate Power, and Structural Poverty*. Automedia.
Chia, J. L. (2019). 'What's Love Got to Do with It?' LGBTQ Rights and Patriotism in Xi's China. *Australasian Journal of Asian Law, 20*(1), 27–37.
Chua, C., Linnemann, T., Spade, D., Syedullah, J., & Maher, G. (2024). Police abolition. *Contemporary Political Theory, 23*(1), 114–145.
Coyne, C. J., & Goodman, N. P. (2020). The Political Economy of the Virtual Wall. *Peace Review: A Journal of Social Justice, 32*(2), 172–180.
Coyne, C. J., & Goodman, N. P. (2022a). The Military-Industrial Complex. George Mason University. Department of Economics Working Paper No. 22–32. https://ssrn.com/abstract=4135811
Coyne, C. J., & Goodman, N. P. (2022b). U.S. Border Militarization and Foreign Policy: A Symbiotic Relationship. *Economics of Peace and Security Journal, 17*(1), 5–16.
Coyne, C. J., & Hall-Blanco, A. R. (2016). Foreign Intervention, Police Militarization, and Minorities. *Peace Review: A Journal of Social Justice, 28*(2), 165–170.
Coyne, C. J., & Hall, A. R. (2018). *Tyranny Comes Home: The Domestic Fate of U.S. Militarism*. Stanford University Press.
Coase, R. H. (1960). The Problem of Social Cost. *Journal of Law and Economics, 3*, 1–44.
Conrad, R. (2014). *Against Equality: Queer Revolution, Not Mere Inclusion*. AK Press.
Craig, A., & Goodman, N. P. (2023). Gender as an Institution: LGBT Identities and Economic Coordination. https://ssrn.com/abstract=4616300

Daring, C. B., Rogue, J., Shannon, D., & Volcano, A. (2012). *Queering Anarchism: Addressing and Undressing Power and Desire*. AK Press.
de Cleyre, V. (1932). *Anarchism and American Traditions*. International Anarchist Publishing Committee of America.
Ghaziani, A. (2024). *Long Live Queer Nightlife: How the Closing of Gay Bars Sparked a Revolution*. Princeton University Press.
Goh, K. (2018). Safe Cities and Queer Spaces: The Urban Politics of Radical LGBT Activism. *Annals of the American Association of Geographers, 108*(2), 463–477.
Goodman, N. P. (2023). Commerce, Spontaneous Order, and Gender Freedom Movements. *Cosmos+Taxis*, *11*(11+12), 24–36.
Goodman, N. P. (2024a). The Military-Industrial Complex and the Militarization of Society. In C. J. Coyne (Ed.), *The Legacy of Robert Higgs* (pp. 221–234). Mercatus Center at George Mason University.
Goodman, N. P. (2024b). Border militarization and domestic institutions. *Constitutional Political Economy*. https://doi.org/10.1007/s10602-024-09440-5
Hayek, F. A. (2021). *Law, Legislation, and Liberty*.Edited by J. Shearmur. University of Chicago Press.
Holcombe, R. G. (2018). *Political Capitalism: How Economic and Political Power is Made and Maintained*. Cambridge University Press.
Feinberg, L. (1999). *Trans Liberation: Beyond Pink and Blue*. Beacon Press.
Feinberg, L. (2009). *Rainbow Solidarity in Defense of Cuba*. World View Forum.
Furton, G., & Martin, A. (2019). Beyond market failure and government failure. *Public Choice, 178*(1), 197–216.
James, S. E., Herman, J. L., Rankin, S., Keisling, M., Mottet, L., & Anafi, M. (2016). *The Report of the 2015 U.S. Transgender Survey*. National Center for Transgender Equality.
Lavoie, D. C. (1977). The Decay of Radical Socialism. *Libertarian Review, 6*(6), 18–24.
Lavoie, D. (1985a). *Rivalry and Central Planning: The Socialist Calculation Debate Reconsidered*. Cambridge University Press.
Lavoie, D. (1985b). *National Economic Planning: What Is Left?* Ballinger Publishing Company.
Lavoie, D. (1993). Democracy, Markets, and the Legal Order: Notes on the Nature of Politics in a Radically Liberal Society. *Social Philosophy and Policy, 10*(2), 103–120.
Lawrence v. Texas, 539 U.S. 558 (2003). https://www.oyez.org/cases/2002/02-102
Long, R. T. (2020). The Anarchist Landscape. In G. Chartier & C. Van Schoelandt (Eds.), *Routledge Handbook of Anarchy and Anarchist Thought* (pp. 28–38). Routledge.

Majied, K. F. (2015). Racism and Homophobia in Cuba: A Historical and Contemporary Overview. *Journal of Human Behavior in the Social Environment, 25*(1), 26–34.

Malamet, A., & Novak, M. (2023). Gender as a Discovery Process: Social Construction, Markets, and Gender. *Cosmos+Taxis, 11*(11+12), 9–23.

Martos, A. J., Wilson, P. A., & Meyer, I. H. (2017). Lesbian, Gay, Bisexual, and Transgender (LGBT) Health Services in the United States: Origins, Evolution, and Contemporary Landscape. *PLOS One, 12*(7), e0180544. https://doi.org/10.1371/journal.pone.0180544

Mises, L. V. (1949). *Human Action: A Treatise on Economics*. Yale University Press.

Mitchell, M. D., & Boettke, P. J. (2017). *Applied Mainline Economics: Bridging the Gap Between Theory and Public Policy*. Mercatus Center at George Mason University.

Obergefell v. Hodges, 576 U.S. 644 (2015). https://supreme.justia.com/cases/federal/us/576/644

Ocasio, R. (2002). Gays and the Cuban Revolution: The Case of Reinaldo Arenas. *Latin American Perspectives, 29*(2), 78–98.

Rothbard, M. N. (1965). Left and Right: The Prospects for Liberty. *Left and Right, 1*(1), 4–22.

Rotondi, N. K., Bauer, G. R., Scanlon, K., Kaay, M., Travers, R., & Travers, A. (2013). Nonprescribed Hormone Use and Self-Performed Surgeries: "Do-It-Yourself" Transitions in Transgender Communities in Ontario, Canada. *American Journal of Public Health, 103*(10), e1-1915.

Shepard, J. M. (2020). The First Amendment and the Roots of LGBT Rights Law: Censorship in the Early Homophile Era, 1958–1962. *William & Mary Journal of Race, Gender, and Social Justice, 26*(3), 599–670.

Spade, D. (2015). *Normal Life: Administrative Violence, Critical Trans Politics, and the Limits of Law*. Duke University Press.

Stanley, E. A., & Smith, N. (2015). *Captive Genders: Trans Embodiment and the Prison-Industrial Complex* (2nd ed.). AK Press.

Storr, V. H. (2008). The Market as a Social Space: On the Meaningful Extraeconomic Conversations that Can Occur in Markets. *Review of Austrian Economics, 21*(2–3), 135–150.

Sylvia Rivera Law Project. (n.d.). SRLP on Hate Crimes Laws. https://srlp.org/action/hate-crimes

Szijarto, S. (2023). Activism and Authority: ACT UP and TAC as Successful Arbiters of HIV Treatment Policy Change. *Aletheia, 3*(1), 36–44.

Tucker, B. (1888, April 28). Should Labor Be Paid or Not? *Liberty*. https://fair-use.org/benjamin-tucker/instead-of-a-book/should-labor-be-paid-or-not#e131p3

Tucker, B. (1890, November 15). Relation of the State to the Individual. *Liberty*. https://fair-use.org/benjamin-tucker/instead-of-a-book/relation-of-the-state-to-the-individual
Tucker, B. (1893). State Socialism and Anarchism: How Far They Agree, And Wherein They Differ. https://fair-use.org/benjamin-tucker/instead-of-a-book/state-socialism-and-anarchism#e1p28
Wagner, R. E. (2016). *Politics as a Peculiar Business: Insights from a Theory of Entangled Political Economy*. Edward Elgar.

CHAPTER 11

Conclusion

Mikayla Novak

The early decades of the twenty-first century have been traumatic. The onset of civil war and interstate conflicts, terrorism, domestic political polarization and civil strife, financial crises and unsustainable public sector indebtedness, and the emergence of matters such as climate change, income and wealth inequalities, and digital technological transformations are among the issues that have dominated public and political attention and discourses. It is not unreasonable to suggest that it is in such domestic and global environments of strain and disaffection that subscription to values, and the sense of commitment toward, liberal commitments have been sorely tested. Following these observations, one could be forgiven for thinking that a predominant school of contemporary thought has emerged to the effect that processes of emancipation guided by liberal principles are either outmoded or irrelevant to the pressing issues of our times.

The proposition of this book is that the value of liberalism is most demonstrable in a period typified by a succession of severe economic, political, and social crises. This is due in non-trivial respects to the

M. Novak (✉)
Mercatus Center at George Mason University, Fairfax, VA, USA
e-mail: mnovak@mercatus.gmu.edu

M. Novak (ed.), *Liberal Emancipation*, Mercatus Studies in Political and Social Economy, https://doi.org/10.1007/978-3-031-94406-2_11

onslaught of illiberal reactions to the (real and imagined) problems at hand. The false hopes of economic autarky, group-based social dynamics, and political populism promise not the liberation of human beings but substantial control regarding the terms and conditions of what individuals and groups can do, be, know, and think. A powerful array of forces conspires to severely limit the ability of individuals to discover their own pathways to fulfillment, and to work collectively not only to resolve social dilemmas but to pursue shared ambitions. This book may well be read in contrarian, and perhaps even radical, terms given its underlying premise that *what the world needs, more than ever, is liberal emancipation* both as an overarching response to our challenging age and as redress for the misguided ideas of economic stagnation, financial repression, social tribalism, the "culture wars," and democratic backsliding that seem to have been proposed as the chief means to deal with contemporary traumas.

This book has been produced with an aim of exploring as well as celebrating the legacies and possibilities of liberal emancipation. Accordingly, it provides a collection of essays produced by renowned scholars specializing in political economy, sociology, and related fields. A common thread that is at least implicitly assumed by the contributors is subscription to the tenets of "mainline" political economy which, as has already been noted, serves as a blend of key insights from the Austrian, Bloomington, and Virginia school traditions which, in turn, can be traced back to the Scottish Enlightenment moral philosophical tradition of Adam Smith. This orientation is unmistakenly liberal, but the contributors argue in turn that the liberal orientation to social scientific inquiry is conspicuously emancipatory both in word and deed. The contributors share a conviction that liberalism is consistent with the objectives of broad-based and emergent development and prosperity. But what is also clear from the chapters is that the ideas and institutions that unleash creative agency not only deliver enrichment but emancipatory effects as more people fairly and reasonably gain access to lucrative economic, political, and social opportunities without fear or favor (Novak, 2022).

As the contributors have indicated, for example in respect of issues of gender, race, and sexual orientation, liberalism features something that its philosophical and ideological rivals do not possess to the same extent: a record of emancipation. In this context, liberal emancipation represents an achievement with concrete historical attributes for it is the case that individuals and groups of individuals, despite considerable odds, successfully orchestrated processes of freeing themselves and others from the bonds of oppression over a long span of time. Whereas liberal adherents can feel justifiably proud of the emancipatory record of liberalism, they cannot afford to rest on their laurels. Changing circumstances and their effects upon the ability of individuals and groups to meaningfully enjoy and apply their hard-won freedoms need to be acknowledged and, if the conditions require it, addressed to ensure that the likes of backlash dynamics or consciously designed illiberal proposals are not to take hold. Understanding the nature of liberalism as a struggle against contrary beliefs and perspectives, and against a variety of threats such as those looming over liberty in the twenty-first century, is essential to ensuring the past achievements of emancipation are consolidated.

It is in the interest of revitalizing the spirit of liberal emancipation for our own period that we propose suggestions for future scholarly investigation. This stance is likewise informed by a sense of humility, in that this book cannot represent the final word on what is the project of liberal emancipation that is hoped and envisaged to persist in the foreseeable future. In what follows, we will suggest potential future research endeavors focused upon liberal emancipation theory which will then be proceeded by questions of application.

There are opportunities to conceptually and analytically refine the theory of liberal emancipation in several ways. Assuming the "micro-meso-macro" framework (Dopfer et al., 2004) for our argumentative purposes, there are three dimensions for potential future research. First, there is a need to further explore the micro-level foundations of emancipation. A promising angle in this regard is the development of theories as to the emancipative function of entrepreneurial activity, a topic that has recently been explored by scholars specializing in entrepreneurship and management studies (e.g., Rindova et al., 2009; Laine & Kibler, 2020; Pergelova et al., 2022; Trivedi & Petkova, 2022; Bacq et al., 2023; Lewis & Crabbe, 2024). Research opportunities are also likely to be uncovered by intersecting liberal emancipation with cognitive and psychological theories focused upon autonomy, aspiration, and the use of imagination to generate mental "images" of freeing oneself (and others) from constraints (Boulding, 1956; Callard, 2018), although as Buchanan (2005) has also indicated there is the potential that certain ideational constraints may induce a lack of emancipation in the form of political and other forms of dependency.

Appraisal of the meso-level, or group, dimensions of economic, political, and social life have increasingly occupied the attention of social scientists (e.g., Dopfer et al., 2004; Turner, 2012; Fine & Hallett, 2014; Wagner, 2020; Flowers & Novak, forthcoming). It is in this context that advances in the study of liberal emancipation is likely to bear considerable fruit, especially in regards to cultural considerations acting as a "lens" defining the feasibility and legitimacy (or otherwise) of efforts by subaltern communities and other marginalized groups in terms of pressing the case for emancipative change (Chamlee-Wright, 1997, 2002; Grube & Storr, 2015; Storr & John, 2020). Consistent with the role of culture in shaping emancipative outcomes in time and place, it is also conceivable that attitudes and norms such as the salience of group stratifications, openness to diversity, receptiveness to change, and so on, will influence the degree to which dominant groups would receive, let alone concede, the case for emancipation in a liberal direction.

A complementary issue for future research consideration is the micro- and meso-level interplaying of internalized oppression, such as beliefs in, and subscriptions to values of, the likes of racism, patriarchy, ableism, and so on, and the nature of efforts undertaken by people to dismantle both the psychological and sociological bases of oppressive attitudes and environments. An array of empirical techniques, including qualitative archival, ethnographic, and field work, have been deployed by social scientists to explore how marginalized and oppressed meso-level groups themselves construct discourses, arguments, and debates surrounding their lack of emancipation, as well as organize to overcome the deprivations of freedom that they experience (e.g., Polletta, 2002). For example, the plethora of social movements now in existence—including those advocating for economic, political, and social forms of emancipation compatible with liberal precepts—seems to provide abundant opportunities for gathering fresh insights regarding the capacities to, and constraints against, achieving emancipation outcomes.

The macro-level analysis of liberal emancipation may complement these perspectives by training attention upon the responsiveness of incumbent institutions and similar structures to emancipative processes which promise broader outcomes such as economic development, defusion of social tensions, and democratization. Any further investigations of liberal emancipation whether through micro, meso, or macro perspectives are likely to facilitate intellectual connections between liberal ideas and non-economic disciplines such as anthropology, sociology, history, law, political science and international relations, psychology, and so on.

The introduction and the chapters that have followed have sought to demonstrate that the principles and practices of emancipation are at the center of liberal thinking. It was also stated that liberalism is a multi-faceted set of ideas and dispositions woven together by ideals of freedom, equality, and justice for all human beings. The differing branches of liberal thought offer opportunities for appraising the opportunities and challenges of emancipation from a variety of intellectual angles. For example, Nathan Goodman's chapter on LGBTQ emancipation is animated by relatively recent efforts to revive the radical spirit and legacies of liberalism in the pre-modern period, a period in which people agitated (at oftentimes at great personal risk) to attain freedom from dominating economic, political, and social powers. In addition to Goodman (2019), intellectual representations of the radical liberal point of view have been espoused by the likes of Lavoie (1993, [1985] 2016) and Byas (2017). Additional explorations of the nature and consequences of liberal emancipation from radical liberalism and the host of alternative liberal sub-branches are likely to aid our broader understanding about the practicalities and limitations of freeing individuals and groups from the strictures of repression.

The trajectories of liberal emancipation both in thought and practice have largely, although not exclusively, proceeded in North America, Europe, and Western colonial outposts in Australasia and elsewhere. The contributions presented in this book reflect the spatialized character of emancipative thought in the liberal tradition and especially its (admittedly imperfect) application. A significant project that lies ahead of social scientists is to explore the extent to which emancipatory processes have achieved gains in terms of liberty in other parts of the world, especially in the "Global South" of Africa, Asia, and South America.

The significance of examining the application and potential implications of liberal emancipation for the Global South transcends the reality that much of the global population live in these locations. Putting aside important exceptions, a study of the Global South is likely to be a study in frustrated desires for freedom. While certain empirical studies have suggested some beneficial emancipatory outcomes, albeit unevenly achieved, outside of the West, or at the very least certain socio-cultural changes that are likely to foster the consolidation of emancipative values (e.g., Welzel, 2013), in certain parts of the world the actualization of liberal emancipative processes have been few and far between. To some extent the emancipatory promises of decolonialization have been frustrated by the replacement of extractive colonial powers with extractive national level kleptocratic or totalitarian administrations (Acemoglu & Robinson, 2012; North et al., 2009; Ostrom, 1999), with an important consequence that individuals and groups have their liberties constrained because of economic, political, or social restrictions. Questions of foreign relations continue to play their role when contemplating the ability of countries outside of the Anglosphere and continental Europe to achieve progress.

Additional research possibilities are imaginable for those interested in examining the applicability and effects of emancipation outside of Western countries. What are the specific contexts that inform the lack of emancipation experienced by minorities and others who suffer from repressive laws and customs? Is it possible to generalize upon local conditions within the Global South to uncover common barriers to emancipation that all humans have confronted? To what extent are emancipation processes in non-Western regions facilitated or constrained by (formal or informal) institutions, and what are potentially suitable remedies to overcome any faltering or nonexistent process of emancipation? Are there any lessons to be learned from the emancipatory experiences of the Western world for the peoples of the Global South? How do attitudes toward the colonial experiences of the past shape local, regional, and national perceptions of the legitimacy of liberal emancipation projects, and the key strategies potentially require for their achievement? It is anticipated that answers to these questions would not only be instrumental in shaping emancipative projects in non-Western countries, but yield better understandings about the process of emancipation for Western scholars.

The liberal ideal of emancipation implies establishment of systems "*absent of all privileges*" (Boettke, 2021: 5; emphasis in original). The radical implication of this statement is that *all* individuals and groups are deserving of freedom to pursue their idiosyncratic projects and strive for their wants and needs (so long as they respect the equal rights and opportunities of others, too, to exercise and enjoy their freedoms). From a research perspective the extension of the benefits of liberal emancipation to each and all provides abundant opportunities to explore how marginalized and oppressed peoples in the present day can realize the fruits of liberty and enhanced rights.

As indicated, the contributors of this book have appraised the historical and contemporary implications of emancipation for blacks, gays, and women, but the underlying concepts and analyses could be applied to additional groups. It is eminently possible to further extend the insights of liberal emancipation to understand the historical circumstances and present day conditions faced by other groups that have endured domination and a lack of equality in respect, such as indigenous groups and people with disabilities (including developmental or intellectual disabilities, and manifestations of neurodivergence). In both of these cases it is anticipated that research will yield fresh perspectives on the character and implications of individual autonomy and its trade-offs with group life, the formation of identity and its functions in galvanizing collective action, and the extent to which socio-cultural configurations and political institutions both enable and constrain the effectuation of emancipative outcomes. Of course, scholars have also indicated that identity and status intersections matter, too, which brings to the fore research opportunities to consider how multiple kinds of marginalization combine to shape liberal emancipative trajectories.

Liberal emancipation has been suggested as bearing normative properties, having concern with how people should bear the presumptive right to be freed from domination, marginalization, oppression, stigmatization, and subjection. It is supposed that the normative dimension of liberal emancipation may be of some use in inspiring critical responses to certain aspects of illiberal thinking sweeping throughout the West and globally in recent years. The recent resurgence of protectionist barriers to trade are considered from the liberal perspective to aggravate price inflation pressures as well as distort domestic structures of production, but the perspective of liberal emancipation also suggests that tariff and non-tariff barriers to global trade could inhibit the very improvement in living standards necessary to deliver economically emancipative outcomes for workers and people in trade-exposed communities. The threat of severe barriers to immigration poses as another important constraint upon emancipation, to the extent that restrictions upon the movement of people both limits the ability of migrants to escape poverty, social discord, and political repression, and the capacity of people in host countries to productively interact with migrants (Kukathas, 2021; Lomasky & Tesón, 2015).

The concept of emancipation has long represented a touchstone issue for classical liberalism. Commonly referred to as a condition in which individuals and groups are liberated from forms of control, domination, or restriction, emancipation normatively corresponds with the humane ethical dimension underpinning liberalism, as well as the liberal political project of progressively extending the principle of equality of dignity and respect to all persons. Liberal emancipation stresses how economic, political, and social freedoms are deeply implicated in promoting upward mobility and individual choice, and countering subjugation and repression, for all human beings, including historically oppressed and marginalized groups.

Emancipation is a core commitment of liberalism, but is also versatile owing to its multi-dimensional analytical implications as well as evaluative and normative and normative properties. Economic interpretations of liberal emancipation stress the achievement of mobility through expanding access to opportunities. The political form of liberal emancipation advocates for principles of legal generality and impartial access to political goods. Meanwhile, liberal emancipation from the socio-moral point of view articulates the desirability of toleration and cosmopolitan attitudes in the face of difference. These dimensions are seen to be commonly underpinned by an ethical spirit favoring emancipative values, including the discovery of new sources of oppression to be overcome. The beauty of liberal emancipation is not only that it inspires people to yearn and organize for freedom, but it provides benchmarks for people to compare different institutions and situations in terms of being freer or less so. When the fundamental principles of liberalism and their applications are being severely challenged by multi-pronged adversaries of individuals and groups being able to act, to choose, to believe, and to think, we argue that a better understanding of the basis and ramifications of emancipation will provide the sound platform necessary for the revival of liberalism in coming years. The future of humanity itself depends upon reinvigorating liberal emancipation for the twenty-first century.

References

Acemoglu, D., & Robinson, J. A. (2012). *Why Nations Fail: The Origins of Power, Prosperity, and Poverty*. Crown Publishers.

Bacq, S., Toubiana, M., Ruebottom, T., Ormiston, J., & Ajunwa, I. (2023). Entrepreneurship Out of Shame: Entrepreneurial Pathways at the Intersection of Necessity, Emancipation, and Social Change. *Organization Theory*. https://doi.org/10.1177/26317877231153185

Boettke, P. J. (2021). *The Struggle for a Better World*. Mercatus Center at George Mason University.

Boulding, K. E. (1956). *The Image: Knowledge and Life in Society*. University of Michigan Press.

Buchanan, J. M. (2005). Afraid To Be Free: Dependency as Desideratum. *Public Choice, 124*(1/2), 19–31.
Byas, J. L. (2017). Radical Liberalism: The Soul of Libertarianism. Center for a Stateless Society. https://c4ss.org/content/49939
Callard, A. (2018). *Aspiration: The Agency of Becoming*. Oxford University Press.
Chamlee-Wright, E. (1997). *The Cultural Foundations of Economic Development: Urban Female Entrepreneurship in Ghana*. Routledge.
Chamlee-Wright, E. (2002). Savings and Accumulation Strategies of Urban Market Women in Harare, Zimbabwe. *Economic Development and Cultural Change, 50*(4), 979–1005.
Dopfer, K., Foster, J., & Potts, J. (2004). Micro-meso-macro. *Journal of Evolutionary Economics, 14*(3), 263–279.
Fine, G. A., & Hallett, T. (2014). Group Cultures and the Everyday Life of Organizations: Interaction Orders and Meso-Analysis. *Organization Studies, 35*(12), 1773–1792.
Flowers, A. C., & Novak, M. (forthcoming). The Hayekian meso-cosmos: Families living in multiple worlds at once. Unpublished mimeo.
Goodman, N. (2019). Don Lavoie's Dialectical Liberalism. In R. E. Bissell, C. M. Sciabarra & E. W. Younkins (Eds.), *The Dialectics of Liberty: Exploring the Context of Human Freedom* (pp. 133–148). Lexington Books.
Grube, L. E., & Storr, V. H. (2015). *Culture and Economic Action*. Edward Elgar.
Kukathas, C. (2021). *Immigration and Freedom*. Princeton University Press.
Laine, L., & Kibler, E. (2020). The Social Imaginary of Emancipation in Entrepreneurship. *Entrepreneurship Theory and Practice, 46*(2), 393–420.
Lavoie, D. C. (1993). Democracy, Markets, and the Legal Order: Notes on the Nature of Politics in a Radically Liberal Society. *Social Philosophy and Policy, 10*(2), 103–120.
Lavoie, D. C. [1985] (2016). *National Economic Planning: What Is Left?* Mercatus Center at George Mason University.
Lewis, A. C., & Crabbe, R. C. (2024). The Entrepreneurship of Marginalized Groups and Compatibility Between the Market and Emancipation. *Journal of Business Venturing, 39*(4), Article 106406.
Lomasky, L. E., & Tesón, F. R. (2015). *Justice at a Distance: Extending Freedom Globally*. Cambridge University Press.
North, D., Wallis, J. J., & Weingast, B. R. (2009). *Violence and Social Orders: A Conceptual Framework for Interpreting Recorded Human History*. Cambridge University Press.
Novak, M. (2022). Review of Peter Boettke's *The Struggle for a Better World*. *Journal of the History of Economic Thought, 44*(2), 313–315.

Ostrom, V. (1999). Cryptoimperialism, Predatory States, and Self-Governance. In M. D. McGinnis (Ed.), *Polycentric Governance and Development: Readings from the Workshop in Political Theory and Policy Analysis* (pp. 166–185). University of Michigan Press.
Pergelova, A., Angulo-Ruiz, F., & Dana, L.-P. (2022). The Entrepreneurial Quest for Emancipation: Trade-Offs, Practices, and Outcomes in an Indigenous Context. *Journal of Business Ethics, 180*(2), 481–503.
Polletta, F. (2002). *Freedom Is an Endless Meeting: Democracy in American Social Movements*. University of Chicago Press.
Rindova, V., Barry, D., & Ketchen, D. J., Jr. (2009). Entrepreneuring as Emancipation. *Academy of Management Review, 34*(3), 477–491.
Storr, V. H., & John, A. (2020). *Cultural Considerations within Austrian Economics*. Cambridge University Press.
Trivedi, S. K., & Petkova, A. P. (2022). Women Entrepreneur Journeys from Poverty to Emancipation. *Journal of Management Inquiry, 31*(4), 358–385.
Turner, J. H. (2012). *Theoretical Principles of Sociology, Volume 3: Mesodynamics*. Springer.
Wagner, R. E. (2020). *Macroeconomics as Systems Theory: Transcending the Micro-Macro Dichotomy*. Palgrave Macmillan.
Welzel, C. (2013). *Freedom Rising: Human Empowerment and the Quest for Emancipation*. Cambridge University Press.

Index

A

African Americans, 6, 22, 34, 46, 116–120, 186, 189, 192, 195
Anarchy, 70, 71, 150
Artifactual man, 23, 59, 60, 62–64, 66–70, 72, 73, 203, 209
Association, 9, 10, 12–14, 28, 107, 111, 114, 115, 118, 119, 121–123, 135, 140, 148, 150, 151, 174, 198, 217, 232–234, 249–251, 253
Astell, Mary, 203, 204, 210, 211, 216, 225
Austrian school, 21, 260

B

Becoming, 4, 18, 58, 59, 73, 204, 209, 214, 222, 223
Bloomington school, 21, 260
Boettke, Peter, 2, 10, 11, 13, 21, 43, 51, 74, 113, 133, 160, 161, 231, 239, 247, 251, 264
Buber, Martin, 65, 66, 75
Buchanan, James, 4, 10, 13, 22–24, 35, 44, 45, 49, 50, 57–75, 104, 107, 139, 141, 148, 158, 203, 205, 209, 210, 214, 223, 224, 261

C

Chicago school of sociology, 25, 159–164, 166, 167, 169, 171–173, 177
Civil Rights, 25, 46, 103, 114, 117–120, 123, 126, 145, 178, 184, 195, 198, 199, 234, 235
Civil society, 9, 12, 70, 83, 109, 125, 150, 212, 232–234, 248, 249
Collective action, 5, 23, 24, 118, 119, 141, 265
Commons, 8, 17, 24, 26, 47, 85, 109, 133–135, 137, 142, 143, 149, 152, 170, 187, 197, 199, 213, 220, 239, 244, 260, 264
Competition, 35, 82, 87, 89, 90, 92–94, 140, 145, 148, 149, 153, 221

M. Novak (ed.), *Liberal Emancipation*, Mercatus Studies in Political and Social Economy, https://doi.org/10.1007/978-3-031-94406-2

Constitutions, 6, 10, 13, 19, 23, 33, 60, 68, 73, 75, 212, 215, 229
Cooperation, 11, 24, 36, 46, 104, 115, 140, 146, 185, 188, 208, 212, 214, 217, 219, 220, 231, 239, 248–251
Cosmopolitanism, 46, 266
Critical race theory, 25, 183, 184, 186, 196, 238
Culture, 26, 59, 69, 87, 108–110, 152, 163, 164, 167, 171, 173, 184, 189, 190, 193, 194, 196, 245, 260, 262

D
Darwinism, 82, 83, 91, 93, 94, 96–98
Discrimination, 6, 7, 12, 14, 20, 26, 35, 47, 48, 51, 116–121, 123, 232, 235
DuBois, W.E.B., 178, 184, 198

E
Education, 47, 49, 116, 117, 120, 121, 137, 140, 145, 187, 194, 196, 204, 205, 207, 209–212, 214, 216–219, 221, 224, 235
Emancipation, 1–8, 10–18, 20–28, 35, 37, 38, 46, 48, 51, 57–60, 64, 66, 68–70, 72–74, 80, 84, 85, 87–98, 103, 104, 115, 116, 118, 120–125, 134, 139, 141, 158–162, 171, 173, 175–178, 184, 205, 206, 223, 231, 233, 234, 243, 249, 251, 253, 254, 259–266
Ethics, 67–70, 138
Evolution, 23, 38, 80, 81, 84–86, 88–96, 98, 120, 144
Exit, 11, 25, 136, 141, 142, 145, 148–151, 153, 242
Experiments, 9, 86, 89, 93, 98, 104, 110, 125, 217, 252

F
Federalism, 107, 108, 117, 133, 134, 139, 141, 144, 145, 152
Federalist Papers, 190
Feminism, 204, 211
Four corners of liberalism, 24, 105–107, 116, 121, 124

G
Gay and lesbian, 121, 122, 124
Gemeinschaft, 16, 163
Generality principle, 266
Generalized increasing returns, 35, 36, 41, 43–51
Gesellschaft, 163

H
Hayek, Friedrich, 9, 12, 13, 24, 33, 35, 79, 80, 83, 87, 91–93, 97, 104, 108, 113, 135, 203, 205–207, 222, 250, 251
Homophobia, 244
Horwitz, Steven, 161

I
Immigration, 21, 151, 153, 235–238, 265
Inequality, 15, 82, 95, 96, 118, 144, 183–185, 187–189, 191, 193, 198, 252, 259
Innovation, 34, 36, 46–48, 83–92, 95, 96, 98, 109, 110, 114, 145, 146, 151, 154
Institutions, 4, 10, 13, 22–24, 26, 34, 37, 39, 40, 42, 44, 51, 52, 59, 70, 73, 80, 83, 84, 89, 91–93,

96–98, 104, 113, 116, 134, 135, 138, 140, 144, 146, 147, 149, 150, 160, 162, 172, 185–191, 193, 194, 196–199, 204, 208–210, 221, 231, 232, 234, 238, 239, 242–244, 246, 254, 260, 262, 264–266

K
Kirzner, Israel, 22, 126
Knight, Frank, 7, 57, 104, 117, 158

L
Lachmann, Ludwig, 206–208
Laissez-faire, 82, 91, 92, 98
Lavoie, Don, 80, 93, 108, 179, 247–249, 263
Learning, 24, 92, 104, 105, 108–112, 114–116, 124, 125, 140, 145, 176, 205, 209–211, 213–219, 223, 241
Leviathan, 71
Levy, David, 37, 117, 141, 158, 170, 171, 176, 188, 197
LGBTQ, 21, 24, 27, 124, 229–238, 243–245, 248, 251, 253, 263
Locke, John, 107, 196, 211

M
Mainline political economy, 112–115
Marx, Karl, 15, 157, 161, 197, 243
McCloskey, Deirdre, 15, 104, 158, 188
Micro-meso-macro, 113, 261
Mill, John Stuart, 8, 19, 37–40, 59, 80, 109, 143, 197, 203, 210, 213, 216, 220–222
Mills, Charles, 196–198
Mises, Ludwig von, 9, 40, 207, 250, 251
Montesquieu, 48, 107

N
New History of Capitalism, 22, 34–38, 40–42, 51
Nozick, Robert, 150, 188

O
Obergefell v. Hodges, 103, 229
Ostrom, Elinor, 24, 104, 133, 134, 136–140, 143, 144, 147, 149, 152, 203, 253
Ostrom, Vincent, 24, 104, 107, 110, 133–136, 138–140, 147, 149, 152, 159, 203, 217, 219, 253, 264

P
Park, Robert, 25, 140, 162–164, 168, 169
Patriarchy, 15, 223, 262
Peart, Sandra, 158, 170, 171
Plato, 108
Pluralism, 9, 26, 110, 160, 172, 185, 186, 189, 190, 234
Polycentricity, 25, 134, 135, 139, 140, 142
Privilege, 2, 14, 15, 17, 19, 33–36, 38–42, 45, 46, 51, 52, 93, 158, 161, 171, 173, 185, 197, 198, 221, 238, 240, 247, 249, 252, 253
Progress, 9, 80, 83, 89, 91, 92, 95, 106, 109, 114, 140, 145, 159, 206, 207, 212, 214, 220, 222, 264
Progressive era, 165
Property rights, 9, 22, 34–36, 40, 42–46, 52, 104, 111, 117, 146, 153, 188, 195, 208, 246–248, 250

R

Racism, 15, 26, 28, 117–119, 184, 193, 194, 198, 262
Radical liberalism, 196, 197, 231, 249, 263
Rawls, John, 143, 144, 197, 198
Responsibility, 59, 68–70, 81, 89, 92, 93, 96, 134, 136, 138, 209, 210, 216, 218
Rule of law, 10, 14, 15, 34, 48, 91, 104, 146

S

Self-governance, 10, 63, 68, 98, 133–139, 141, 142, 145, 147–149, 151, 153
Sexism, 184
Slavery, 2, 4, 17, 19, 20, 22, 26, 34–45, 51, 52, 116, 178, 187, 188
Smith, Adam, 8, 19, 36, 39, 47–49, 80, 91, 92, 104, 106–108, 118, 146, 178, 188, 207, 218, 224, 230, 239, 260
Socialism, 15, 16, 69, 79, 97, 185, 197, 198, 247
Social justice, 14, 80
Social movements, 5, 13, 24, 104, 113, 119, 126, 161, 232, 253, 262
Spencer, Herbert, 8, 80–84, 86, 91, 97
Sumner, William Graham, 80, 91, 97

T

Technology, 88–91, 189
Thomas, William, 25, 37, 162–164, 167, 169–171, 178, 206, 224
Transgender, 20, 21, 120, 121, 124, 229, 235, 236, 242, 244, 252

U

Universal basic income, 23, 94
Utility maximization, 62
Utopia, 79, 80, 150, 243

V

Virginia school, 21, 260

W

Wagner, Richard, 52, 112, 125, 240, 262
Wollstonecraft, Mary, 12, 20, 27, 203–205, 210–221, 224
Women, 12, 16, 18, 20, 26, 27, 71, 121, 142, 150, 152, 158, 159, 168, 177, 178, 184, 203–207, 209–225, 236, 245, 264

Kolibri 360 GmbH
Ferdinand-Jühlke-Straße 7
99095 Erfurt, Deutschland
produktsicherheit@kolibri360.de